RESEARCH IN INTERNATIONAL ECONOMICS BY FEDERAL AGENCIES

———

NUMBER TWO OF THE
INTERNATIONAL ECONOMIC HANDBOOKS
EDITED BY EUGENE STALEY FOR THE
DIVISION OF ECONOMICS AND HISTORY
OF THE CARNEGIE ENDOWMENT FOR
INTERNATIONAL PEACE

RESEARCH IN INTERNATIONAL ECONOMICS BY FEDERAL AGENCIES

By Sanford Schwarz

New York : Morningside Heights

COLUMBIA UNIVERSITY PRESS

1941

FOREWORD

NINETY PER CENT of the economists and other social scientists who pick up this book will be amazed, I feel sure, at the variety and the extent of the research work being done by agencies of the Federal Government on matters connected with international economic relations. Much of this research is of very high quality, too. One competent judge—a man who knows firsthand both the haunts of the bureaucrats and the academic cloisters —remarked recently that in his opinion the economists he meets in the government are at least as competent as those he knows outside, and maybe even more so. Furthermore, they are stimulated by no lack of real and pressing problems. It is a real public service, then, which Mr. Sanford Schwarz has performed in this book by providing information that ought to break down some of the barriers to a free flow of intellectual trade between professional people working on a certain broad range of problems under the auspices of universities or business institutions and their colleagues in government offices.

Everybody knows that the Department of Commerce publishes trade figures, and various kinds of specialists have long counted as part of their stock in trade the financial statistics of the Federal Reserve Board, the commodity studies of the Tariff Commission, and the world-wide crop surveys of the Department of Agriculture. But few realize the full scope of the work of even these agencies, especially where research has been expanded in recent years, or where the emphasis has been shifted. Still fewer have any idea of the wide sweep of government research bearing on international economic problems which appears when the contributions of all the diverse agencies—from Department of State to WPA—are totaled up, as they are in this volume. Frankly, Mr. Schwarz's study was a revelation to me, and I thought I had been following the literature of the field. As soon as a printed copy arrives, I am going through to put check-marks in the margin, and then my expanding shelf of government documents will have a boom, indeed. Doubtless this service as a check-list, both for private libraries and for libraries of educational and business institutions, will be one of the chief uses of the book. It ought also to find a place on collateral reading shelves for college courses in economics, government, and international relations, and it should certainly be called to the attention of every graduate and professional student in these fields.

The labor that has gone into the collection (much of it by personal interview in Washington), organization, and checking of the information in this book is considerable. Mr. Schwarz has done the job not only thoroughly and well, but with a breadth of view, a perspective, that has kept the result from being a mere dry-as-dust compilation.

This is the second in a series of small volumes on international economic relations initiated by the Carnegie Endowment for International Peace, Division of Economics

and History, of which James T. Shotwell is Director. It is
hoped that they may contribute to a rational rethinking and
reshaping of policies in a world where startling changes
force continual readjustment.

EUGENE STALEY

Fletcher School of Law and Diplomacy
Medford, Massachusetts
January, 1941

IN ACKNOWLEDGMENT

THE SCOPE of this book and the basis on which materials have been included in it are discussed in the Introduction. My task would have been much harder without the help in interview and by letter given me by officers of the Federal government in many agencies. Their frequent help in and out of hours deserves particular recital; I am sure they will excuse this collective renewal of thanks spoken personally to each of them. I may add that the faults of the book are mine. My friend Professor Eugene Staley, of the Fletcher School of Law and Diplomacy, has placed me under new obligation to him for his meticulous reading of the manuscript, for saving me from many mistakes, and for his Foreword.

This book is a poor return to Professor James T. Shotwell for the insights into the history of our common humanity and for the great personal kindness he has shown me in more than two years of association at the Carnegie Endowment for International Peace. I hope nevertheless that it will please him.

To Miss Sasha Tushinskaya and Miss Magdelene Faig of the staff of the Carnegie Endowment I am in debt for their helpfulness in preparing the manuscript. The officers and editorial staff of the Columbia University Press have been endlessly patient with my delays and I offer them thanks for this as for other kindnesses. The index was prepared by Mr. Jacob Steinberg.

My wife will know that I have been appreciative of her cheerfulness in the face of constant intrusions upon our leisure.

SANFORD SCHWARZ

New York
January, 1941

CONTENTS

I. Agencies of Research

II. Fields of Research

CONTENTS

INTRODUCTION

IT IS the unfortunate fate of most government publications to be buried in those documentary cemeteries which fill the library stacks of the larger institutions of learning in this country. Despite their importance and frequent scientific merit, most government investigations are neglected by the learned journals so that they neither fertilize nonofficial thought nor are given the critical scrutiny which the products of private scholarship customarily receive. The obscurity in which the output of the government press (and mimeograph) lingers is undeserved, and it is partly with the thought that such a condition requires remedy that the present survey of the international economic relations of the United States as seen from Washington is offered. It is hoped that this volume may help to bridge the gap between public and private research.

Except for a section on national defense added later, this study, which was begun before the outbreak of the present war, had been closed when the conflict changed its character from the slow processes of blockade to decision by the shock of arms in the field and siege by air. The outbreak of total war in May, 1940, gave meaning to the declaration of emergency proclaimed the previous September far beyond any earlier nice calculation of military probabilities and their consequences. The defense of the nation took precedence over all other concerns. As a result, thought has somewhat turned away from the lines of study here described.[1] This account of how the United States had been preparing itself to meet the problems of international economic relations is by no means rendered invalid by these changes. The ends of policy are unaltered; in the achievement of those ends the ways of conducting the public business here described have lost none of their pertinence and they continue.

The increased activity of government in the economic sphere and the consequent growth of economic investigation by government agencies have brought a need for some guide to the research agencies of the government and to their output. Not until 1938, when the National Resources Committee (now the National Resources Planning Board) published its study of the relation of the Federal government to research, was there any major account of official research activity.[2] That study, however, was an attempt to

---

[1] See Leo Pasvolsky, "The United States in the World Economy, 1940," Department of State *Bulletin*, January 11, 1941.

[2] National Resources Committee, *Research—a National Resource*, Part I: "The Relation of the Federal Government to Research" (1938). See also Frederic A. Ogg, *Research in the Humanistic and Social Sciences* (New York, 1928), pp. 301 ff. Descriptions of the research activities of Federal agencies can usually be found in such administrative studies as the Service Monographs of the Institute of Government Research, now part of the Brookings Institution, Washington, D.C. The accounts in the latter are rather meager, and most of them are now quite out of date. Indeed, the recent over-all reorganization of the Government, frequent inter- and intra-departmental changes, and the creation of new agencies, make anachronism hardly to be avoided. As this book is in press word comes that a new Division of Research and Statistics has been set up in the Bureau of Foreign and Domestic Commerce. Some help in following such changes is afforded by the *United States Government Manual*, issued three times a year by the Office of Government Reports.

analyze the administrative conditions making for efficient research by government rather than to present a comprehensive account of the research itself. The need for a guide is only partly supplied in the present work, the scope of which is limited to the international economic relations of the United States, itself part of a much larger field of investigation, only partly described in the following pages.

Examination of the *Directory of Federal Statistical Agencies* (4th edition, January, 1940), issued by the Central Statistical Board, will afford some idea of the multitude of government agencies which now compile and analyze economic data. The volume of routine research activity of departments, bureaus, and other agencies is evidenced by their serial publications, of which there are thousands.[3] Research expenditures of the Federal government are correspondingly large. According to the National Resources Committee, the Federal government spent $124,000,000 for research during the fiscal year ended June 30, 1937, or 2.4 percent of the regular funds of government, plus $20,000,-

---

[3] Of these no systematic account is given here. Concerning them see Laurence F. Schmeckebier, *The Statistical Work of the National Government* (Baltimore, 1925), which is still helpful, though now out of date. Authoritative statements are those in *Statistical Services and Activities of the United States* (Washington, May, 1940), a processed preprint of a chapter of the *Inter American Statistical Compendium*, prepared under the direction of the Central Statistical Board for the Statistical Section of the Eighth American Scientific Congress. See also *Social Science Research Bulletin* 26 (New York, 1937), "Government Statistics," pp. 141 ff. For government publications in general, see Schmeckebier's *Government Publications and Their Use* (Washington, 1940). Most processed publications are now listed regularly in the *Monthly Catalog* of the Superintendent of Documents. *Agricultural Economics Literature*, issued monthly by the Library of the Bureau of Agricultural Economics, is invaluable in tracing processed publications of the Department of Agriculture and, indeed, of other government agencies as well.

ooo of emergency funds. Of the regular funds spent for research, nearly three fourths went to support inquiries in the
natural sciences.[4] In the expenditure of emergency research
funds the scales were tilted the other way by the allotment
of two thirds to the social sciences and statistics. Classified
by field of interest, the principal research expenditures from
regular funds were distributed as follows: one third for
agricultural research, one fifth for the improvement of military and naval equipment and techniques, and one eighth
for aeronautical research. Finally, it is to be noted that $49,-
000,000 of the total expenditure of $124,000,000 was con-
tributed in aid of the researches of non-Federal agencies.

In the fiscal year 1938 the government spent, excluding
grants and contributions to non-Federal agencies, $42,558,-
000 in the natural sciences and $16,809,000 for research in
the social sciences and statistics. Classified by agencies, the
major expenditures in the social sciences in 1938 were as
follows: State Department, $403,000; Treasury Depart-
ment, $1,301,000; Labor Department, $2,030,000; Interior Department, $2,042,000; Agriculture Department,
$2,857,000; Commerce Department, $3,767,000; and independent agencies, $4,306,000.[5]

[4] Expenditures for surveys and mapping and library and other aids to
research have been omitted from the following calculations.
[5] The foregoing statement of research expenditures is based on the National Resources Committee's report, cited above. The report contains
abundant evidence of difficulties encountered in finding an apt definition
of research (pp. 61 ff.). The figures for the Department of Agriculture
are not entirely comparable with those for other departments. Research
expenditures of the Bureau of Agricultural Economics were probably twice
the figure of $2,004,000 shown on p. 74 of the report. The omission of
the Federal Reserve Board from the list of agencies whose research expenditures are reported is presumably to be attributed to the fact that the
Board is supported by assessments on member banks.

It is appropriate here to venture some generalizations concerning the role of research in government, the context of administrative problems and of policy in which it moves, its relation to academic and other private research, and the dissemination of the results of governmental inquiry to the public.

It would be of interest to trace in the broadening lines of governmental inquiry the effects of increased governmental intervention in the social and economic activities of the community and to observe therein the results of changed and changing views of the proper relation of government to the social order. So much is clear: governmental inquiry far exceeds in scope the investigations officially undertaken in earlier periods of our history when the objects of examination were circumscribed by the limited view taken of the functions of government. The official compilation and analysis of economic data were formerly undertaken to serve government needs almost exclusively and were narrow in range because the economic role of government was restricted. Official inquiry has since extended into one economic domain after another as a result of the expansion of governmental activities in the economic sphere.[6] While official research is still carried on primarily in aid of the conduct of government, much of it is in the nature of a governmental service to the public.[7] Moreover, much of the data which

---

[6] See "Government Expansion in the Economic Sphere," *Annals of the American Academy of Political and Social Science* (Philadelphia, November, 1939), Vol. 206, *passim*.

[7] The extension work of the Department of Agriculture and the promotion work of the Department of Commerce are examples of affirmative official endeavor to bring the results of scientific research to the widest possible audience. The extension relations between the Department of Agriculture, the land-grant colleges and state experiment stations, and

forms an administrative by-product is available to the public and is under continual scrutiny by the Division of Statistical Standards of the Bureau of the Budget with a view to improving its utility to others. Of the importance of the data made available by government in innumerable publications or contained in government files accessible to the public, it hardly seems necessary to write. It is a commonplace that without these materials scholarly study of many fundamental problems would be cut short.

Governmental inquiries are not limited to mere compilation; they include, in ever larger proportions, analyses and

the farmers have been utilized in the creation of machinery for the present agricultural program. The activities of the Department of Agriculture merit the closest study for their social inventiveness in dealing with the timeless problem of articulating knowledge and thought with governmental policy and, under conditions of democratic government, all of these with the consent of the governed. The publications of the Department of Agriculture constitute a vast documentation of this riddle and there is a large literature. See Gaus and Wolcott, *Public Administration and the United States Department of Agriculture* (Chicago, 1940); Russell Lord, *The Agrarian Revival* (New York, 1939); Gladys Baker, *The County Agent* (Chicago, 1939); Donald C. Blaisdell, *Government and Agriculture* (New York, 1940); and Milburn L. Wilson, *Democracy Has Roots* (New York, 1939). The Department of Commerce makes extensive use of district offices and local chambers of commerce to spread knowledge of its work. Under the Sheppard-Robinson Bill (76th Congress), coöperative relations between the Department of Commerce and state university schools of business would be established in the interests of small business. Steps have been taken in that direction even without the funds that would have been provided by the bill. On January 28, 1941, announcement was made by the Bureau of Foreign and Domestic Commerce that a Division of Regional Economy (Charles C. Fichtner, Chief) had been established to carry forward such work. The organization of the Bureau is again in flux: a new Division of Research and Statistics (M. Joseph Meehan, Chief) was set up in January, 1941, "charged with the study and analysis of the economic life of the nation as a basis for the general aims and objectives of all Bureau activities . . . In effect this division will establish and maintain the nation's economic books and records."

interpretations of the materials collected.[8] In a volume which it published in 1937, the National Bureau of Economic Research explained the large share of the Federal government in financial research in terms which hold generally for government study of economic problems.[9]

. . . most of the financial data now available [wrote the Exploratory Committee of the National Bureau of Economic Research] have been compiled by public agencies. The larger share of the analytical work current in the field of financial problems also rests in the main on official initiative and support. Research by other agencies into financial problems has been devoted mainly to the analysis of existing data, although occasionally it has taken the form of small sampling surveys. To a certain extent, the preponderance of official activities in the field of financial research reflects simply the fact that public authorities have been in a supervisory relationship to financial institutions and have been required in consequence to compile and publish basic data with respect to the institutions under their jurisdiction. It also reflects the fact that basic exploratory surveys designed to open new areas of financial relationships are costly to conduct and have been dependent, therefore, largely upon public funds for support. In addition to these special factors, however, public authorities have been among the first to recognize the value of research as a tool in the development of operating policies.

Research by policy-making or policy-enforcing organizations is sometimes criticized with particular force. It is asserted that such research must suffer from bias and the sug-

---

[8] See the discussion by Samuel A. Stouffer of the problem of analytical research in the Bureau of the Census, contained in the National Resources Committee's report on research, p. 219.

[9] *A Program of Financial Research* (New York, 1937), pp. 20–21.

gestion is made that government confine itself to compilation and eschew analysis and interpretation. It seems to be perfectly clear that government can hardly be expected to proceed in the dark. Since the conduct of public affairs cannot wait upon the fortuitous coincidence of private research interests with official anxieties, public agencies must seek out their own answers at whatever risk. It is of course true that policy may be and often is mistaken, but policy that is misinformed as well is even worse. Research undertaken without regard to specific aims often proceeds in ignorance of the specific questions which later become important in the reconsideration of policy and therefore must frequently be completely reworked. From analysis of the workings of policy must finally come conviction not only concerning the efficacy of the means chosen to achieve determined ends but concerning the value of the ends themselves. It should not be overlooked that in the social sciences policy occupies a place equivalent to that of hypothesis in the natural sciences. In government research the enforcement of policy frequently serves as the social equivalent of laboratory experiment, and analysis of the results achieved is often productive of better understanding of the problems involved.[10] Whether the analysis will be honest, whether research which is combined with policy-making functions will in fact be impartial, rigorous, and thorough, depends upon the attitudes of the policy-makers and of the researchers. In general, the insistence in government research on application of the canons of scientific method is as rigorous as that characterizing

[10] Compare the studies of the Division of Review of NRA which examined the experience under the National Industrial Recovery Act after that law was held to be unconstitutional. The studies are described below at p. 196.

academic investigations. The best assurance that these standards will be applied unfailingly lies in the training and character of the research personnel and in the publication of the data of research so that it can be scrutinized by outsiders. The tendency to increased coöperation between government and private researchers in the investigation of problems is also helpful in this respect and serves not only to liberalize official thought, but to correct academic myopia as well.[11]

The dissociation of research from policy would in fact run counter to the need, rendered acute after the World War, to make provision "for the organised acquisition of facts and information, and for the systematic application of thought, as preliminary to the settlement of policy and its

[11] Coöperation with government in the social sciences is recent. In the natural sciences it dates from the Civil War. The National Academy of Sciences was established under congressional charter in 1863. In 1916, at the request of President Wilson, the National Academy organized the National Research Council. The British analogue of the latter is the Department of Scientific and Industrial Research which is headed by an advisory committee to the Privy Council under the chairmanship of the Lord President of the Council. There was no confederation of learned societies in the social sciences until 1923, when the Social Science Research Council was organized. The American Statistical Association, founded in 1839, long exercised a benign influence on the scientific standards of the Census and is now represented in the advisory committee to the Census Bureau. In other domains coöperation with government is a matter of the last two decades. Major fields have been agriculture, statistics (together with the American Statistical Association), and social security. In the last-mentioned field the Committee on Social Security of the Social Science Research Council maintains a staff in Washington, some of whom work in the offices of the Social Security Board. Much of the basic data needed by the Board has been prepared by the Committee. See especially the studies by Wladimir Woytinsky: *The Labor Supply in the United States* (Washington, 1937); *Labor in the United States, Basic Statistics for Social Security* (Washington, 1938); and *Seasonal Variations in Employment in the United States* (Washington, 1939).

subsequent administration." [12] The war itself was the forcing house of this problem. In Great Britain it had been marked by the improvisation of an enormous number of state controls of economic life which disrupted the existing allocation of economic functions among the departments of government, and these emergency controls were served by equally as many improvised organizations of investigation and thought. Of this condition of anarchy G. D. H. Cole wrote:

"When in doubt, create a committee," was certainly the first precept of the times; and the second was, "When a committee becomes troublesome, don't dissolve it; for that leads to further trouble. Gradually take away its functions, and let it die of inanition in its own time." The path of war on the home front was strewn with discarded committees painfully dying, and often not quite sure whether they were still alive.[13]

The maintenance of central control over this wilderness of committees was impossible to a government which was bending every effort to free itself of administrative preoccupations and find time to think.

Among the organizations so established were two general committees on reconstruction and a Ministry of Reconstruction to consider the national future. These set up subcommittees to consider particular problems. One such was

---

[12] *Report of the Machinery of Government Committee,* Cd. 9230 (1918), p. 6.
[13] *Trade Unionism and Munitions* (Oxford, 1923), p. xi. The Cabinet did not know how many such committees there were. A typewritten list prepared for its use covered a few pages. The *Dictionary of Official War-Time Organizations* (Oxford, 1928) by N. B. Dearle contains 323 pages. In the United States there was similar improvisation but on a much smaller scale. See Leland and Mereness, *American Official Sources for the Economic and Social History of the World War* (New Haven, 1926).

the Haldane Committee on the Machinery of Government which was instructed "to enquire into the responsibilities of the various Departments of the central executive Government, and to advise in what manner the exercise and distribution by the Government of its functions should be improved." The Committee's report, as one writer has said, "is the key to many post-war developments" and its influence on American thought makes it worth-while to consider it at some length. Underlying the report is the belief that state measures of economic intervention were likely to persist after the war.[14] The Committee recommended that "in the sphere of civil government the duty of investigation and thought, as preliminary to action, might with great advantage be more definitely recognized." In addition to better provision for "enquiry, research, and reflection," provision for the systematic application of thought involved, in the Committee's opinion, reversing the trend toward "Lilliputian administration" and integrating the agencies of government on the basis of function. The report stressed the need to relieve policy-making aides from the pressure of routine business and to associate the administrator and the expert more closely so that the investigations of the latter would have more bearing on the problems facing the former. Finally, more intensive use of advisory committees of persons who represented sections of the community affected

[14] The failure of the government to implement the recommendations of the report was, at least in part, due to the fact that reconstruction was generally conceived in terms of a return to pre-war economics. "The early restoration of unrestricted dealings in the markets of this country and the world at competitive prices is essential to the reëstablishment of British industry and commerce on a sound basis." Balfour Committee on Commercial and Industrial Policy after the War, *Final Report*, Cd. 9035 (1918), p. 26.

by the activities of the departments was recommended.

The Haldane Committee had recommended "that for some purposes the necessary research and enquiry should be carried out or supervised by a Department of Government specially charged with these duties, but working in the closest collaboration with the administrative Departments concerned with its activities." This would have represented the extension to other fields of the device of the Department of Scientific and Industrial Research employed in the natural sciences. The obstacles in the way of such a proposal were well shown three years later in the action taken on a petition presented to the Cabinet by members of the Royal Statistical Society and other distinguished scholars relating to the improvement of official statistics. The committee of departmental statisticians to which the petition was referred for report said that "the responsibility of Government with regard to statistics covering the whole life and activities of the community . . . has never been accepted in this country and no provision is therefore made by the national machinery of administration to discharge such an obligation." The implicit suggestion in the petition for the establishment of a central office of supervision was rejected on the ground that "such an office might consider it desirable for national informative purposes to secure extended or additional statistics, which would impose upon that Minister's officers an additional burden which he might regard as unreasonable or which would, without his agreement, make an addition to the cost of his department which he must defend in Parliament." [15]

---

[15] The need to conciliate departmental susceptibilities is evident. The committee supported an earlier recommendation for the establishment of

In 1925 Lord Haldane, then a member of the MacDonald Cabinet, framed the scheme for the Committee on Civil
Research which the Baldwin government was to put into
effect. "Experience of the Defence Committee had shown
me," Lord Haldane wrote,

how valuable it would be for the purposes of the Prime Minister
if he had a skeleton body to which he could refer questions of a
technical but civil character, as he could refer military questions
to the other existing Committee. I raised the point at the Cabinet and offered to work out a plan. The proposal was approved.

The scheme was drawn up and needed only the Prime Minister's initials. "But this sort of reform did not interest the
Prime Minister, who had never given his mind to administration." The scheme was still merely a scheme when the
MacDonald government went out. In adopting it, Haldane
adds, "the Conservative administration secured much ap-
plause for something the nature of which they appeared to
have barely grasped." [16] When MacDonald returned to
power in 1929 he reconstituted the flexible Committee on
Civil Research in the form of the cumbrous Economic Advisory Council.[17] It has been condemned by Laski as "a large
and fixed body of miscellaneous composition, incapable directly of research, and so composed as to be unlikely to reach

an interdepartmental consultative committee, and this was established with
the title Permanent Consultative Committee on Official Statistics. It has
no administrative responsibilities, no right of access to the Cabinet, and
is not formally accessible to the public. See the *Report on the Collection
and Presentation of Official Statistics* (London, H. M. Stationery Office,
1921). The Permanent Consultative Committee began, in 1922, the issuance of the valuable *Guide to Current Official Statistics*, an annual.

[16] *Richard Burdon Haldane, an Autobiography* (Garden City, 1929),
p. 352.

[17] Treasury Minute, dated January 27th, 1930, Cmd. 3478 (1930).

agreement about its evaluation." [18] Into the abundant discussion of the proposals for an economic general staff made by Sir William Beveridge and others it is impossible here to examine.[19] Laski's exposition of the mistaken political assumptions at the bottom of these idealistic proposals and his analysis of the relation between knowledge and wisdom are in his happiest vein.[20]

The attempt to unify research and administrative organization, hitherto relatively unsuccessful, founders repeatedly on what Walton Hamilton has called the "empirical collectivism" of the state. This manifests itself also in the appropriations of funds for research. Some agencies are granted ample funds for the purpose of tampering with commodity prices in the interest of a factitious stability; others are given fractional allowances to aid the restoration of world trade. The reason for this is not far to seek.

Most official inquiry is designed in the first place to aid in the realization of aims determined by others than the research workers. This signifies that philosophers have by no means become kings. Competing economic and social interests determine and must continue to determine how govern-

[18] Harold J. Laski, *Parliamentary Government in England* (New York, 1938), p. 232. Almost all other writers share this view. W. Ivor Jennings, however, in his *Cabinet Government* (New York, 1936), p. 248, observes with judicious irony that "While it cannot be said that the experiment has failed, it cannot yet be said that it has succeeded." The Council, which has two standing committees, has not met in plenary session for ten years. Its committees apparently met as late as 1935. Compare the situation of the Reichswirtschaftsrat described by Rogers and Dittmar, "The Reichswirtschaftsrat," *Political Science Quarterly*, December, 1935, pp. 489– 490.
[19] See K. B. Smellie, *A Hundred Years of English Government* (New York, 1937), Chapter X, and the citations there given.
[20] *Op. cit.*, pp. 222–234.

ment shall act in those areas of economic and social welfare
in which it is permitted to act at all. Each government department has a clientele which is not always interested in the
existence of other government departments with different
clients. It follows that the purposes for which research inquiries are undertaken are not millennial. While it is true
that, in the conditions of size and tempo of modern society,
human welfare cannot be maintained or improved without
taking thought, it is sometimes forgotten that social principles are many and that the social sciences offer no touchstone
for choosing infallibly between them.[21]

Writing in 1930, Professor J. Anton de Haas of Harvard
University pointed out that in the field of foreign trade,
with which most government services for business were concerned,

The prime objective is the promotion of exports largely through
the provision of elaborate information concerning opportunities
for nationals to sell abroad. Little or no complementary attention is given to the provision of information concerning opportunities for nationals to buy abroad advantageously. Implicitly
underlying this concern for exports is the same philosophy which
defends the protective tariff. With one hand the government
erects tariff barriers to impede importation while with the other
it appropriates vast sums to facilitate exportation. Both hands
are engaged in the promotion of a favorable balance of trade
. . . the prevailing conception of the function of government is
essentially a return to the philosophy of mercantilism. If the business man cannot compete successfully alone in world markets

[21] Professor Viner has drawn an ironic picture of the difficulties in the
way of useful collaboration between the academic theorist and the civil
servant in his presidential address to the American Economic Association,
American Economic Review, Vol. XXX, March, 1940.

it is held that the government should intervene. Such is the accepted doctrine.[22]

The world has witnessed a vast intensification of economic nationalism since the time when Professor de Haas wrote, and the effect of that autarkic growth has been to increase the volume of government research.[23] The effort of investigation itself is neutral and valuable, however unhappy the policy in the shadow of which it occurs. A striking example of this is found in the cost-of-production investigations of the Tariff Commission which laid the foundation for much of the technique of analysis later employed in carrying out the Reciprocal Trade Agreements Program. The cost-of-production formula which the legislature in its wisdom directed the President and the Tariff Commission to apply in the modification of the tariff rate is now happily in abeyance, but the investigations made under it have resulted in the compilation of an important body of material. It is not inappropriate to point out also that the researches of the Commission served to demonstrate the ineptness of the formula itself. Moreover, it is precisely here that there is room for the liberalization of official effort by competent private criticism. As Wylie Kilpatrick has observed,

To energize and suggest the public interpretation of reports, official and private agencies are required to indicate the implications of the information . . . by reporting in turn to the government instead of merely receiving reports [they complete]

[22] *Encyclopaedia of the Social Sciences*, III, 122, *s.v.* "Business, Government Services for."

[23] The volume of statistics compiled in Germany has swelled to such dimensions that a Central Statistical Committee has been set up by the German government so that statistics, like everything else, are now under license. See *The London Economist*, May 25, 1940, p. 934.

the cycle involved in the successive stages of examination, reporting, discussion, and control. Reporting can exercise its function only when agencies either of private associations or of public units assume responsibility for that review and self-examination of operations implicit in democratic government.[24]

Foreign commercial policy reflects the interests and policies which compete at home. The interrelation is well described by the National Resources Committee:

The trade agreements program does not stand alone, however, but dovetails with other programs of the Federal Government. This is particularly true of the farm program, where a healthy restoration of our foreign trade means increased markets, both at home and abroad, for farm products. It is also true of our industrial, social welfare, transportation, and fiscal and monetary policies. Any program which the Government may undertake to stabilize our internal economy bears a very intimate relationship to its program for gearing that economy to international trade.

International commercial agreements are, of course, not solely technical trade agreements but are closely related to the whole development of our national policy, and particularly to any policy dealing with Latin America. Linking up the resources of all the Americas, or more adequately interrelating them, involves raising the general level of productivity and the general standards of living throughout the whole of the Americas. This problem of major strategy in national planning concerns commerce, agriculture, finance, and national defense. Our foreign commercial policy is fundamentally a cross-section of our national policy and planning.[25]

[24] *Encyclopaedia of Social Sciences*, VII, 130 ff., *s.v.* "Government Reporting."

[25] National Resources Committee, *Progress Report* (December, 1938), p. 18.

If the reader of these pages questions whether a guide to the researches of Federal agencies in the field of international economic relations should include so many studies that seem to lie outside the usual limits of that field, the justification therefor will be found in the interaction of domestic and international problems set forth by the National Resources Committee. The tendency to look on international economics narrowly has unfortunate results. One of these is to fortify the primacy of legal postulates over economic reality, so that even tariff-making is held to be a matter of purely domestic concern. We are becoming painfully aware that happenings elsewhere leave their mark on our domestic situation; that the impact of our domestic ups and downs is also keenly felt abroad is not so generally understood. One of the most important single influences on the economic situation of the rest of the world is the violent fluctuation in the American national economy. To deny international bearing to the analysis of the domestic causes of such fluctuation would evidence intellectual myopia. While it may be convenient for pedagogic purposes to mark off international economics from other branches of economic study, the attempt to carry over such distinctions into economic problems themselves soon breaks down.

What appear to be purely domestic questions often involve direct or secondary concomitants of international changes in production, supply, demand, population, and other factors.[26] Many government programs and policies relating to agriculture, industry, relief expenditures on pub-

---

[26] See, e. g., Part II of the *Supplementary Report of the Land Planning Committee to the National Resources Board*, "Agricultural Exports in Relation to Land Policy" (Washington, 1935).

lic works, and the like have their origins in international crisis and depression. The agricultural adjustment program, for example, is an effort at national self-help in meeting difficulties having deep international roots.

In a sense the present war testifies to the folly of attempts to resolve economic difficulties exclusively within national boundaries and constitutes a repudiation of economic nationalism by its principal exponents. But whether economic nationalism be sound or not, it is a philosophy of international relations no less than is economic liberalism. The measures taken in this country to insulate agriculture and industry, labor and the farmer, against outside forces have profound international bearing, precisely because they seek to "adjust" their economic situation on a basis of increased national self-sufficiency. To describe the researches relating to the reciprocal trade agreements program without pointing to economic programs of contrary tendency would be one-sided and something less than candid.

The situation of the migrant worker, the problems of interregional competition which are basic to much of the adjustment work of the Department of Agriculture, land planning and the rational use of the national resources, housing and relief expenditures in their bearing on the stimulation of investment, the economic bottlenecks created by monopoly, the relation of employment and technological change, and many other "domestic" problems represent areas of economic maladjustment conditioned by international factors in many ways. Government researches in these areas exhibit the ramification of such factors in all their detail. Viewed in isolation, many of these researches seem to concern economic minutiae without large significance. Seen in the aggregate, however, they reveal broad patterns of program and policy and it is in that way that they must be looked at.

A prominent mark of contemporary economic nationalism is its subordination of considerations of welfare. Yet the impact on welfare is a measure of the cost of substituting guns for butter and of nationalist economics generally. As Professor Staley has observed,

there is a strong subconscious tendency among many people to react on international economic issues as though the main problem were to find ways of producing less, or of using more labor to produce the same—to defend ourselves against "overproduction" and a "flood of goods." Because such attitudes exist, it is important to see clearly what a great gap there is today between the amounts of various economic goods that people have and the amount that they "need" as judged by modern standards.[27]

Studies of nutrition and dietary standards, income levels and distribution, consumer incomes and expenditures, and related matters afford a means of approach to international economic problems in terms of welfare and free from the ubiquitous obsession with the "favorable balance of trade." Such studies have been made by the League of Nations and the International Labor Organization, which have drawn on the Bureau of Labor Statistics and the Bureau of Home Economics for data. The latter organizations have made similar studies on a national basis, descriptions of which will be found below. In a sense that line of inquiry is paralleled by the resources approach to economic problems taken by the National Resources Planning Board, although the latter un-

[27] Eugene Staley, *World Economy in Transition* (New York, 1939), p. 61.

til recently tended to neglect the international aspects of resources use. The participation of the Board in the Pan American Resources Commission recently established in accordance with the recommendation of the Eighth American Scientific Congress may serve to liberalize its views in this regard. Similarly, the Department of Agriculture is represented on the Pan American Soil Conservation Commission established at the same time.

Unfortunately, the illumination of researches such as those mentioned in the foregoing pages has not yet enlightened American economic foreign policy. The reason for this is its conspicuous want of integration. The record of recent years shows clearly that economic problems cannot be dealt with effectively on the international level until national policy has been integrated. In the absence of integration, policy either is astigmatic or can sometimes not be framed at all. To the integration of policy the coördination of research would make a substantial contribution. There has been some official recognition of this, which is evidenced by the establishment of the Executive Committee on Commercial Policy and the interdepartmental trade agreements organization, and the work of the Central Statistical Board and the National Resources Planning Board. Through the last named, which was represented in the 1938 meeting of the international public works committee of the I.L.O., there has even been some exploration of the possibility of international coördination of public works programs. These are only straws in the wind, however. Basically, the situation continues to be that research is conducted by the various governmental agencies independently of each other. Even agencies at work on opposite sides of the same medal, such as the Tariff Commission and the Bureau of Foreign and Domestic Commerce, fail to coördinate their inquiries except as the trade agreements program draws on both of them. With such methods, it is small wonder that problems are seen out of focus or not perceived at all and that, as K. B. Smellie has said of official British research, the governmental organization of economic inquiry is "a squinting Argus."

Suggestions concerning the reasons for these failures of integration have been offered above. This book is not, however, a study in public administration. It is rather preliminary to such study. Hence, there has been no effort at sustained analysis of the administrative conditions under which research is carried on. The judgments ventured are *ad hoc* impressions rather than conclusions. The integration of research and policy is one of the universal and fundamental problems confronting public administration, and one of the most difficult. That problem the author proposes to treat at another time. But if, as he believes, works on public administration suffer from a tendency to neglect the subject matter with which administrative agencies deal, this volume will perhaps be welcome as a contribution to knowledge of the research activities of administrative agencies concerned with economic problems, and as a preliminary aid in the study of the articulation of administrative structures and workings with economic policy.

For obvious reasons no judgments on the scientific adequacy of the investigations are expressed. Nor is there any discussion of the intensity of official cultivation of the fields of research, since the latter question can hardly be dealt with apart from the problem of quality. Under some heads official research clearly remains an aspiration rather than an accomplishment. Lack of information makes judgment difficult, however. The monetary studies of the Treasury Department, for example, are so closely tied in with confidential questions of policy that there is a natural reluctance to reveal their subject matter. Hence, a basis for judgment is not available. Like difficulties occur in other fields.

The economic inquiries, often of great importance, made by legislative committees are mentioned only in exceptional instances. The research of administrative agencies is in a sense self-contained. That fact, the discontinuous character of legislative inquiries, and the difference in the purposes served by the latter, make it preferable to treat them separately.[28]

[28] See William F. Willoughby, "The Legislative Branch and Research," in the National Resources Committee's report on research, already cited; M. Nelson McGeary, *The Developments of Congressional Investigative Power* (New York, 1940), and the earlier works by Marshall E. Dimock, *Congressional Investigating Committees* (Baltimore, 1929), and Ernest J. Eberling, *Congressional Investigations* (New York, 1928).

RESEARCH IN
INTERNATIONAL ECONOMICS
BY FEDERAL AGENCIES

Explanatory Note

THE ACCOUNT that follows is divided into two parts. In the first ("Agencies of Research"), the research agencies of the Federal Government are described seriatim with reference to their organization, the scope and orientation of their research interests, and the interrelation of their research programs with those of other agencies. The disregard of the alphabet in the arrangement of agencies is deliberate. It seemed better to group together those most active in the field of international economics instead of dispersing them through the following pages in accordance with the surely arbitrary requirements of the alphabet. The Departments are all placed together; following them come the various independent and emergency agencies. The War and Navy Departments and the Advisory Commission to the Council of National Defense are placed together at the end of Part I under the heading "National Defense Organizations."

The second part ("Fields of Research") contains an inventory of official researches, completed and projected, grouped under appropriate economic heads. For the most part the inventory does not go back of 1933 although a few important publications of earlier date are mentioned. The terminal date is October 1, 1940.

I: AGENCIES OF RESEARCH

DEPARTMENT OF STATE

FROM THE standpoint of research, the Department of State has aptly been termed "the stepchild of the government," for it operates on so restricted a budget that it must confine its research activities to the indispensable *ad hoc* routine studies needed for the information of policy-making officers. The principal offices in the Department continuously engaged upon problems of international economic relations are the Office of the Adviser on International Economic Relations (with a total research personnel of six, including the Adviser) and the Division of Commercial Treaties and Agreements, which is an operating agency rather than a research organization.

Charged with the conduct of our foreign relations in an era when politics and trade are almost inseparable, the Department of State must necessarily take the lead in the formulation of American commercial policy. This by no means signifies that the decisions of the other agencies of government in their several fields are subordinate to the policy determinations of the Department of State. But it does mean that a measure of integration is required. The need for integration of commercial policy has resulted in a

considerable development of interdepartmental organizations, and to that extent there has been an enlargement of
the research resources of the Department of State.[1]

EXECUTIVE COMMITTEE ON COMMERCIAL POLICY

The necessity for interdepartmental coöperation under
the leadership of the Department of State in matters affecting the international economic relations of the United States
was recognized even before the establishment of the interdepartmental trade agreements organization. In a letter of
November 11, 1933, to the Departments of State, Treasury, Commerce, and Agriculture and to the Agricultural
Adjustment Administration, the National Recovery Administration, and the Tariff Commission, President Roosevelt
wrote as follows concerning the necessity for the Executive
Committee on Commercial Policy then set up: [2]

(1) Under the Administration's program the numerous recovery departments are assigned powers or duties which directly
touch upon trade relations with other countries. It is plain that
the acts of each of the separate branches of the Government must
be brought into a coherent policy system with the acts of all
the rest.

(2) The changing policies of other governments and the
changing methods of regulating international trade greatly complicate the Government's task of proper direction of American
trade.

I therefore have decided to designate one officer in the Department of State to carry the primary responsibility of supervising the international commercial policy of this Government

---

[1] An excellent account of interdepartmental committees will be found
in Mary Trackett Reynolds' study by that name (1939). It treats the interdepartmental trade agreements organization at pp. 47–70.

[2] *Ibid.*, p. 49.

into a coherent whole. Hereafter may I ask that you give the necessary instructions in your department that before any acts are taken under legislation or otherwise which directly affect the export and import trade in this country, this official should be consulted concerning the action and his approval secured.

It is my idea that this official should be the chairman of an Executive Committee for the coördination of Commercial Policy and the negotiation of commercial treaties and trade agreements, and that in his decisions he would be very largely carrying out the judgment of the Committee. Upon this Committee your Department will be represented.

It is my further expectation that as this committee develops its work, all subordinate interdepartmental committees engaged in the work of negotiating commercial treaties, the elaboration of trade agreements, etc., will report to the responsible official and through him to the government committee.

I also request that you instruct your Department that this official, as chairman of the coördinating committee, should be the regular channel of communication with all foreign governments on all policy matters affecting American export and import trade.

The functions of the Executive Committee on Commercial Policy (Assistant Secretary Dean G. Acheson, chairman) are purely advisory. This Committee at present consists of representatives of the Departments of State, Treasury, Agriculture, Commerce, and Labor, the Tariff Commission, the Agricultural Adjustment Administration, the Export-Import Bank, the Maritime Commission, and the Army and Navy Munitions Board.

COMMITTEE FOR RECIPROCITY INFORMATION

Following the passage of the Trade Agreements Act of June 12, 1934, there was an extensive development of interdepartmental committees under the leadership of the State Department for the implementation of the Reciprocal Trade Agreements program. The principal committees, aside from the Executive Committee on Commercial Policy whose advisory functions extend in somewhat attenuated form to the trade agreements program also, are the Committee for Reciprocity Information and the Trade Agreements Committee. The Committee for Reciprocity Information, the chairman of which has consistently been a member of the Tariff Commission, was established by executive order to carry out the requirement of the Trade Agreements Act that public notice of intention to negotiate an agreement be given, in order that interested persons may have an opportunity to present their views. Since "interested persons" are usually those concerned over the possible effects of tariff reductions on their industries, the work of the Committee for Reciprocity Information falls mainly on the Tariff Commission.[3] In order to immunize the members of the Committee against political pressure it became the practice not to make the names of the Committee's members public, a practice also employed in connection with the Trade Agreements Committee. However, at the recent (1940) hearings on the renewal of the Reciprocal Trade Agreements Act held by the House Ways and Means Committee, the names of the members of the Committee for Reciprocity Informa-

[3] By Executive Order No. 8190, July 5, 1939, the Committee for Reciprocity Information was placed under the jurisdiction and control of the State Department, "its functions to be exercised under the direction and supervision of the Secretary of State, who is to designate its Chairman." The Executive Committee on Commercial Policy continues to select certain members.

tion were made public, and the effort to keep them secret was abandoned.[4]

TRADE AGREEMENTS COMMITTEE

The Trade Agreements Committee, of which the chairman is Harry C. Hawkins, Chief of the Division of Commercial Treaties and Agreements of the Department of State, is also an interdepartmental committee and was established by the Executive Committee on Commercial Policy on June 22, 1934, in response to the provision in the Trade Agreements Act that in the negotiation of trade agreements the President should seek advice and information from the Departments of State, Agriculture, and Commerce, the Tariff Commission, and other appropriate sources. The major part of the burden of preparing for the negotiation of trade agreements rests on this committee, which advises in respect to the organization and execution of the work connected with trade agreements, arranges for the necessary general economic studies, and coördinates the work of the participating agencies.

The division of functions between the Executive Committee on Commercial Policy and the Trade Agreements Committee is described by Mrs. Reynolds as follows:

The Committee on Trade Agreements and the Executive Committee on Commercial Policy often cover the same ground.

---

[4] They are listed in the latest issue of the Committee's *Rules of Procedure* (1940). On the question of the democratic character of the trade agreements procedure, see Larkin, *Trade Agreements* (1940), *passim*, with which compare Carl Kreider, "Democratic Processes in the Trade Agreements Program," *American Political Science Review*, April, 1940, p. 317.

However, the vote taken by the Executive Committee on each trade agreement is merely a formality, while the scrutiny given to trade agreements by the Committee on Trade Agreements is detailed and complete, and the decisions of the latter group are decisive as to what concessions shall be included in the draft agreement. The members of the Committee on Trade Agreements are technical or professional people, permanent career men rather than political officials. Members of this group customarily devote their full time to the preparation of trade agreements, while many of the members of the Executive Committee on Commercial Policy consider the trade agreements program only one part of their activity in the national administration. In practice, the distinction between administrative problems and political problems as the concern respectively of the Committee on Trade Agreements and the Executive Committee largely disappears. The Committee on Trade Agreements does not attempt to frame a commercial policy for the country, and refers to the Executive Committee matters which are broadly political in nature. But the discussions of the Executive Committee are almost always based on facts supplied by the Committee on Trade Agreements or its subcommittees. Moreover, there is a good deal of interrelation of personnel between these two policy-framing committees. For example, when the Executive Committee on Commercial Policy created a subcommittee to study our trade relations with Japan, officials of the Committee on Trade Agreements served as members of the subcommittee.

The Division of Commercial Treaties and Agreements, created on July 1, 1940, to replace the Trade Agreements Division of the Department of State which had been established in 1935, is the Central Secretariat for the program. In it are centralized the Department's functions of leadership in the execution of the program. Rather an operating agency than a research organization, the Division of Commercial Treaties and Agreements initiates the appointment of subcommittees, assigns research, and watches the development of the interdepartmental work. It issues a large volume of material, principally in the form of press releases, concerning trade agreements. The newly organized division will handle not only trade agreements but commercial agreements of all kinds.

The Committee on Trade Agreements from time to time sets up *ad hoc* "country committees," "commodity committees," and special committees to study special questions in connection with such matters as quotas, exchange control, discrimination, branch factories, transportation, and so forth. The operation of the country committees, so called because they do the spade work on the agreements to be concluded with a particular country, was described as follows by former Assistant Secretary of State Sayre:

The Department of Commerce member is responsible for having prepared in that Department statistical tables showing the quantity and value of, and the trends in, the trade between the two countries over a considerable period of years. He is also responsible for the preparation of detailed studies of each of the products we *export* to the designated country, indicating with respect to each product the proportion of American production which is exported, the proportion of imports to the country involved supplied by the United States, and the relative value of the particular market to American exporters. Each study also contains information relative to foreign tariff rates and other import restrictions affecting the product, the extent to which a reduction of trade barriers might be expected to result in increased importations from the United States, and the prospects of obtaining such a reduction in the light of economic and other conditions in the foreign country. In each case the study concludes with a tentative recommendation as to the desirability of attempting to obtain a concession.

Similarly the Tariff Commission member of the country committee is responsible for having prepared in the Tariff Commission tables and studies analyzing and digesting in the same fine detail all pertinent information relative to our *imports* from the country under consideration. These studies show with respect to each import item the proportion of American imports originating in that country and in other supplying countries. They deal *in extenso* with conditions in competing American industries, particularly as they are or may be affected by foreign competition. Each study concludes with a tentative recommendation as to the possibility of granting a concession on the product in question if, in the event actual negotiations ensue, such action should appear necessary to secure more favorable treatment for our export trade.

In the meantime, agricultural experts are preparing studies of agricultural products which enter into the trade between the two countries, and Treasury experts are considering questions relating to tariff classifications and customs administration. The State Department member of the country committee studies the commercial policies of the other country, and is responsible for the formulation of the general provisions of the proposed trade agreement. He also assumes responsibility for the coördination and general progress of the work.

After sufficient progress has been made on these studies and reports, the country committee begins a series of meetings for the purpose of formulating tentative recommendations as to the items which might be considered in a trade agreement . . . if the problem with regard to a particular product is unusually complex, or if its ramifications extend to questions referred for intensive study and report to a permanent or *ad hoc* commodity or technical committee.

. . . Using as a basis the carefully worked out statistics and digests prepared by the Tariff Commission,[5] the country committee launches into an even more intensive study, commodity by commodity, of each item of our imports from the country in question . . . it is painstakingly examined in the light of our past tariff treatment of the commodity, of the proportion of imports to domestic production, of the status and conditions of the domestic production of the commodity, of the probable effects upon domestic production of greater competition from the country under consideration and from all other countries, and of possible effects upon allied or competing domestic industries . . . partisan or purely political considerations play no part throughout this long study. . . .

From this expert study and many-sided consideration of each commodity involved comes a profound understanding of the entire trade between the United States and the country in question with all its hindrances, its possibilities for improvement, and its limitations. The Belgian Country Committee, to cite a concrete example, put forth 10 or 11 massive volumes in Belgian-American trade; and other country committees in like proportion.[6]

Mr. Sayre's account may be supplemented by a brief description of what follows up to the moment that the Trade Agreement is concluded. The recommendations of the country committee are submitted to the Committee on Trade Agreements which goes over them and the supporting data in detail. After the Trade Agreements Committee has approved the report, the Executive Committee on Commercial Policy votes on it although its action is largely a formality.

[5] For a detailed description of the Tariff Commission's work in this connection, see the statement of Commissioner Fox before the House Ways and Means Committee, January 15, 1940, *Hearings* on H.J. Resolution 407, on Extension of Reciprocal Trade Agreements Act, pp. 492ff.

[6] Sayre, "How Trade Agreements Are Made," State Department, *Commercial Policy Series* 47 (1938).

Following scrutiny by the Secretary of State, the proposals are submitted to the President. When his approval has been obtained, the recommendations serve to guide the American representatives in the negotiation of the trade agreement for which all this work of preliminary study has been done.

The studies made in connection with trade agreement negotiations, the exploratory studies of the possibility of other agreements, the studies of the effects of agreements which have come into force, and related studies touching the gearing of our foreign trade to our domestic economy, all taken together, constitute, in the opinion of the Adviser on International Economic Affairs, one of the best existing surveys of the American industrial structure. Because of their confidential nature, such studies are not available in their entirety to the public, although parts of them are made public from time to time by the government agencies primarily responsible, notably by the Tariff Commission in its trade agreement digests and commodity surveys.[7]

OFFICE OF THE ADVISER ON INTERNATIONAL ECONOMIC AFFAIRS

Limitations of funds and personnel restrict the activities of the office of the Adviser on International Economic Affairs (Herbert Feis, Adviser) to "production for the kitchen" (Mr. Feis's phrase). That "production" which is primarily in aid of policy-making and policy-enforcing functions of the Department of State, is of wide range and variety and, indeed, covers the entire field of international economic relations. None of this material is published except as members of the staff may, in their private capacities, publish occasional

[7] Concerning these, see *infra*, p. 96.

articles based on such studies. Over a period of time the areas explored have included international investment; international raw material controls, touching sugar, rubber, tin, wheat, and other commodities; trade controls, such as tariffs, quotas, exchange restrictions; particular forms and types of competition encountered abroad; the bearing of armament activity here and abroad on international trade; and analyses of the factors accounting for year-to-year shifts in our international trade by commodities and by countries. Analyses are made of the economic position of particular foreign countries and of the problems presented by the monetary and exchange policies of other countries. On the domestic side examination is made of the bearing upon our international economic relations of domestic policies, legislation, or proposed legislation.

Much of the research activity of the Office of the Adviser on International Economic Affairs involves coöperation with other agencies. In all its activity it draws upon the research and statistical services of other related departments or agencies. It helps to suggest problems for investigation and to direct a vast amount of reporting by the Department's officers in the field. Moreover, its members participate in the work of many interdepartmental committees engaged in preparing reports on particular policy problems. In addition there is much informal contact with other agencies. The Adviser on International Economic Affairs was, for a time, a trustee of the Export-Import Bank of Washington.

FOREIGN SERVICE

Under the President's Reorganization Plan No. II, effective July 1, 1939, the Foreign Commerce Service, formerly in the Bureau of Foreign and Domestic Commerce, and the Foreign Agricultural Service, formerly in the Department of Agriculture, were transferred to the Department of State to be consolidated with and administered as a part of the Foreign Service of the United States under the direction and supervision of the Secretary of State. They have therefore ceased to exist as independent services. All the functions of the Secretaries of Commerce and Agriculture in respect to the services formerly under their jurisdiction were transferred to the Secretary of State, who is, however, directed to make

(1) Such investigations relating to commerce and industrial conditions and activities in foreign countries and such other specific investigations relating to foreign commerce as the Secretary of Commerce shall determine to be in the public interest; and (2) Such investigations relating to world competition and demand for agricultural products, to production, marketing, and disposition of such products in foreign countries, and to farm management and other phases of agricultural industry in foreign countries, and shall conduct abroad such activities (including the administration of standards for cotton, wheat, and other American agricultural products), as the Secretary of Agriculture shall determine to be in the public interest.

Activities in the United States based on the work of these services—such as the compilation, publication, and dissemination of information—remain with the Secretaries of Commerce and Agriculture.

The part played by the Foreign Service in the actual conduct of research in international economic relations or in the compilation of data on which analysis is based is of the first importance. The transfer of the foreign commerce service and the foreign agricultural service to the State Department seems to mark recognition of the fact that trade has become a matter of political arrangement to such an extent that non-diplomatic aids to private endeavor are no longer adequate to promote it.[8]

The combined services will be administered by the newly created Division of Commercial Affairs (Raymond H. Geist, Chief).

ADVISORY COMMITTEE ON PROBLEMS OF FOREIGN RELATIONS

On January 8, 1940, it was announced by the Department of State that, as a consequence of the war and the measures and policies adopted by belligerents and neutrals which affect the United States immediately, and may have enduring consequences on its foreign relations once peace is established, an Advisory Committee on Foreign Relations to study the problems presented had been set up. Sumner Welles is Chairman and Hugh Wilson Vice-Chairman of this Committee. The announcement states that

[8] See address by former Assistant Secretary of State George S. Messersmith before the Twenty-Sixth National Foreign Trade Convention, New York City, October 11, 1939, on "The Assistance Rendered by Government in the Promotion and Protection of American Foreign Trade," Department of State *Commercial Policy Series* 62 (1939). See also Department of State *Bulletin*, August 3, 1940, p. 87, and Willoughby, *The Reorganization of the Administrative Branch of the National Government* (1923), pp. 170 ff.; *Investigation of Executive Agencies of the Government* (75th Cong., 1st Sess., Sen. Report No. 1275), pp. 696 ff.; and, for the handling of the same problem in Great Britain, *Memorandum by the Board of Trade and the Foreign Office with Respect to the Future Organization of Commercial Intelligence*, Cd. 8715 (1917); and *Report of the Committee to Examine the Question of Government Machinery for Dealing with Trade and Commerce*, Cmd. 319 (1919).

Some of the most important and immediate of these measures and policies are in the field of economic activity and relations. The war has absorbed the labor and production of much of the world in armament and military activity. When the war ends, problems of readjustment to peace-time production will be presented, which may gravely affect the United States.

Accordingly, the Secretary of State has set up in the Department a Committee which will gather data on and study both the immediate and long-range results of over-seas war measures and the manner in which the problems arising from them may best be handled so as to avoid shock and to prevent undesirable enduring results.

Three sub-committees have been set up. The first, directed by Mr. Welles, is studying general political problems of post-war reconstruction in the light of past policies and current happenings. The late R. Walton Moore led the second group in examining the record of accomplishment and failure in disarmament. His successor has not yet been named. The third group (of which Leo Pasvolsky, Special Assistant to the Secretary of State, is in charge) is studying current developments in their bearing on post-war economic problems. This group has now become interdepartmental in composition and it coöperates with the Interdepartmental Committee on Inter-American Affairs, of which the Coördinator of Commercial and Cultural Relations between the American Republics (Nelson A. Rockefeller), whose office was established on August 16, 1940, is chairman.

Department of Commerce

BUREAU OF FOREIGN AND DOMESTIC COMMERCE

The Bureau of Foreign and Domestic Commerce of the Department of Commerce was established in 1912 by merger of the Bureau of Manufactures with the Bureau of Statistics; the latter had previously (1903) taken over the Bureau of Foreign Commerce from the Department of State. In addition to continuing the established tasks, including the issuance of statistics of foreign commerce and navigation of the United States, the furnishing of information on foreign tariffs, and the publication of consular and trade reports, the new Bureau was charged in general to "promote and develop the foreign and domestic commerce of the United States." In the expansion of its work a number of specialized or related functions within that general field have been added.

From 1921 to 1939 the Bureau consisted of twelve commodity or industrial divisions, and of ten technical divisions. In 1939 the Bureau was reorganized, and it is now divided into five principal units: the International Service, the Basic Problems Service, the Industrial Service, the Commercial Information Service, and the Field Office Service. The Foreign Commerce Service, formerly a unit of the Bureau of Foreign and Domestic Commerce, was transferred on July 1, 1939 to the Department of State.[9]

The principal periodical publications of the Bureau are *Commerce Reports* and the *Survey of Current Business*, the former devoted to foreign trade and the latter, principally, to domestic business. It was announced in September, 1940, that with the issue of October 5, 1940, *Commerce Reports* will be replaced by *Foreign Commerce Weekly*, which

will contain data on foreign business news, broken down by country and by commodity and including one or more leading

---

[9] The Bureau was further streamlined for defense in January, 1941. See *Foreign Commerce Weekly*, February 8, 1941.

articles in each issue by Bureau specialists. The new publication averages 48 pages and incorporates data previously carried in 33 separately processed bulletins. News items are broken down by countries under the following subtitles: General conditions, foreign exchange and finance, tariffs and trade regulations, commercial law notes, and transportation and communications. Twenty pages of each issue will contain commodity news classified alphabetically under the following subtitles: Aeronautical products, air conditioning, beverages, ceramics and clay products, etc. In addition, a regular feature will be foreign exchange rate tables, available trade lists, trade-mark applications, foreign trade opportunities, and new books and reports. On the front cover of each issue will be a detailed index for countries, commodities, and special subjects.

The publications of the Bureau have increased in number of recent years in a rather haphazard way. Each division has issued many processed periodical statements (usually on a subscription basis) and it became evident that coördination of the Bureau's publication program was desirable at least so far as concerned the multitude of divisional publications. In October, 1940, it was announced that most of these subscription services would be consolidated in four series, namely, *Foreign Commerce Weekly*, Industrial Service (divided into 14 sections which may be subscribed for individually), International Reference Service (foreign data), and Economic Reference Service (confined to the domestic field).

International Service

The Division of Foreign Tariffs (Henry Chalmers, Chief) is concerned with both the general economic problems and the special technical questions involved in the application to American trade of foreign governmental controls of imports and exports, such as tariffs, quotas, license restrictions, documentary requirements and customs regulations. Functionally viewed, the Division is primarily a service rather than a research organization. It is predominantly engaged in furnishing information and assistance on the particular situations or problems presented to it by American business men engaged in foreign trade. Secondarily, it follows the moving current of developments in foreign commercial policy so it may be able to serve as adviser on those matters to other branches of the government, and to handle general inquiries from the public. The day-to-day demands made upon the time of the Division's personnel are so heavy as to preclude the frequent publication of long-range studies on the problems of commercial policy.

Current changes and developments in the import tariffs of foreign countries, their quotas, license restrictions, commercial agreements, and other forms of trade restriction, are regularly announced by the Division in *Commerce Reports*, the Bureau's news weekly. Brief but valuable annual reviews of the trends in foreign tariffs and commercial policies and semi-annual analyses of the effects of the reciprocal trade agreements program [10] have for some years been prepared by the Chief of the Division, and also published in *Commerce Reports*. As time allowed, a series of tariff handbooks or pamphlets on special subjects or on selected groups of products has been issued; the principal

[10] The preparation of this analysis of results has recently been transferred to the Trade Agreements unit of the Bureau, which now coördinates all studies by the Bureau bearing on the trade agreements, and is the general representative of the Department of Commerce in the interdepartmental committee on the subject.

titles of economic interest are given in Part II of this book under the heading "Governmental Controls."

The Division of Regional Information (Louis Domeratzky, Chief) is the foreign economic survey office of the Bureau. It is charged with the study of international economic movements, American branch factories abroad, cartels, problems of international trade, and so forth. An exacting part of its work is furnishing information to American business men. In connection with the negotiation of trade agreements, the Division compiles statistical data, market analyses, and general economic information regarding foreign countries for the interdepartmental committees. Its chief represented the Department of Commerce on the Interdepartmental Philippine Committee, the Joint Preparatory Committee on Philippine Affairs, and the Committee on Japanese Trade Relations. The *Foreign Commerce Yearbook* and the annual *Economic Review of Foreign Countries* [11] are prepared in the Division. It also issues monthly economic and trade reports on China, Japan, southeastern Asia, the Philippines, Canada, and France. *Russian Economic Notes*, issued by the Division, contains abstracts of articles from official Russian publications. A section of *Commerce Reports* entitled "The Business Situation Abroad," summarizing latest economic developments reported by government representatives abroad, was prepared by this Division but has now been discontinued as have the monthly periodicals.

The Finance Division (Amos E. Taylor, Chief) is the chief official source of information on foreign public finance and budgetary practices, United States investments in for-

[11] This was formerly the *World Economic Review* and included a domestic section which is now published separately.

eign countries, foreign investments in the United States, foreign trade financing, foreign exchange restrictions, clearing agreements, and so forth. The Bureau's annual report on the balance of international payments of the United States, and its periodic studies on international insurance transactions, international tourist travel and international investments are prepared in this Division. The Division issued semi-monthly *European, Far Eastern and Latin American Financial Notes* and occasional circulars on selected subjects supplementary to the *Notes* until October, 1940.

The Division of Commercial Laws (Guerra Everett, Chief) reports on changes in foreign laws affecting commerce, published the monthly *Comparative Law Series,* and issues occasional studies of trading problems under the laws of foreign countries. An important part of its work relates to copyright and industrial property protection abroad; another part relates to the insurance business abroad.

Basic Problems Service

The Division of Foreign Trade Statistics (Bernard Barton, Chief) compiles statistics relating to the foreign trade of the United States, prepares the annual report on *Foreign Commerce and Navigation of the United States* and issues two hundred monthly statements of trade statistics broken down by countries and by key commodities. This Division also prepares the Bureau's monthly report on foreign trade statistics, a monthly statement of the trend of the United States foreign trade, and the *Annual Review of United States Foreign Trade.* It also issues weekly reports on exports and imports of gold and silver.

The unit most recently established is the special Research

and Analysis Section (Walter F. Crowder, Chief), which has no routine responsibilities. It will be concerned with research in business practices as they affect the volume of business, employment, and income.

The Division of Business Review (M. Joseph Meehan, Chief) has as its major function the continuing study of economic trends and developments in the United States. For this purpose it gathers together for publication the available monthly economic statistics, and prepares indexes for particular areas of the national economy, mostly related to the trade field. Its principal publication, the *Survey of Current Business*, is a well-known and widely-used source of information as to the current state of domestic business.

The work of the Construction and Real Property Section (Samuel J. Dennis, Chief) which prepared quarterly and annual estimates of construction activity and studied the factors which affect the volume of outlay on various kinds of construction projects has been distributed among other divisions. Mr. Dennis has become Assistant Chief of the National Income Division.

The National Income Division (Robert R. Nathan, Chief) engages in the compilation and analysis of data in the fields of national income, income by states, long-term debts, consumer income, and related subjects.

The Division of Marketing Research (Nelson A. Miller, Acting Chief) formulates specific recommendations in respect to marketing based on its research into cost of operation, methods of distribution, and trade practices. Studies are also made of market indexes, consumer markets, and advertising and trade associations.[12]

[12] See "Marketing in Our American Economy," *Annals of the American Academy of Political and Social Science*, CCIX (May, 1940),183 ff.

Industrial Service

Through its Industrial Divisions, the Bureau establishes direct contact with American businessmen who seek enlarged markets or increased efficiency of operation. Specific trade opportunities for the sale of particular American commodities to individual foreign firms are examined, evaluated, and made public by these divisions.

Exigencies of space prevent separate treatment of the Industrial Divisions which are as follows: Automotive-Aeronautics Trade (Paul R. Mattix, Chief), Chemical (Charles C. Concannon, Chief), Electrical (John H. Payne, Chief), Foodstuffs (Fletcher H. Rawls, Chief), Forest Products (Phillips A. Hayward, Chief), Leather and Rubber (Everett G. Holt, Chief), Machinery (Lewis M. Lind, Chief), Metals and Minerals (Walter A. Janssen, Chief), Motion Picture (Nathan D. Golden, Chief), Specialties (Horace N. McCoy, Chief), Textile (Edward T. Pickard, Chief), and Tobacco (Benjamin D. Hill, Chief). The Transportation Division (Thomas E. Lyons, Chief) collects data on ocean shipping, foreign railway and highway transportation, trade and cable routes, rates, charters, port and harbor conditions, on all forms of communications in relation to commerce, on packing and potential traffic, inland waterways, and on ship and railway operating costs. The Division administers the Foreign Trade Zones Act under the Foreign Trade Zone Board.

The principal function of these divisions, as already indicated, is trade promotion which up to 1932, at any rate, proceeded primarily on a theory of salesmanship.[13] That

[13] ". . . the spirit of the Bureau follows the spirit of American busi-

view of their functions persists in varying degree in the industrial divisions.[14] Such activities also have characterized the work of some of the technical divisions. The emphasis on promotion has in recent years, however, given place in good measure to emphasis on service. The industrial divisions are now service agencies for manufacturers, exporters, importers, for other government agencies, for research, advertising, and educational institutions, and for individuals. In recent years there has been an increasing output of processed periodical bulletins issued by the industrial divisions, which in the aggregate deserve special mention. Correspondence involves much research, in widely separated subjects, and the use of scientific techniques in the analysis of data drawn from numerous sources.

The recent reorganization of the Bureau represents a slight shift in emphasis from the foreign to the domestic aspects of industry and to that extent is a modification of the export promotion effort which has been so prominent in the past. The industrial divisions now endeavor to provide business men and other government agencies with information upon the economic conditions in their various industries

---

ness, which is to make sales in spite of difficulties, or to find ways of doing seemingly impossible things. As officials we should be encouraging whenever possible and discouraging only in the last extremity. We are builders, promoters—even propagandists, although never to such an extent that we fail to recognize and point out difficulties." From a letter of instructions of May 20, 1927, sent by Thomas R. Taylor, then Assistant Director of the Bureau to the commercial attaché at Lima, Peru, quoted by Barnes, *Government Promotion of Foreign Trade in the United States* (1933), p. 12. Cf. Stouffer, in the National Resources Committee's report on research, p. 208, Note 19.

[14] The Leather and Rubber Division is perhaps the most marked exception—principally because we are on an import basis for leather and rubber materials and the principal problems confronting the industries served have been those of access to supplies of raw materials.

within the United States as well as information upon foreign markets. The research activities of these divisions (Lowell J. Chawner, Chief Economist, Industrial Service) [15] are directed particularly toward the development and analysis of information upon the economic organization, the current operations (production, sales, inventories, and shipments), the rate of additions to plant and equipment in specific industries, and the influence of economic and other conditions in foreign countries upon these industries. Monthly analyses of general and specific industrial problems, primarily for official use, are now prepared.

The difficulties of the small businessman have been taken up by the Bureau of Foreign and Domestic Commerce, which has undertaken a rapidly growing program of research relating thereto. Related to that program was the Sheppard-Robinson Bill (76th Congress, 1st Session, H.R. 3395, June 13, 1939) sponsored by the Department of Commerce, which would establish coöperative research relationships in the interests of small business between the Department of Commerce and state university schools of business, much like those between the Department of Agriculture and the land-grant colleges. The proposed measure would grant to the Secretary of Commerce authority to disburse funds appropriated by Congress in aid of state university business research projects approved by him.

The Department of Commerce has not waited for the enactment of the Sheppard-Robinson Bill to initiate voluntary coöperative research relationships with the state uni-

---

[15] Mr. Chawner was, before the reorganization of the Bureau of Foreign and Domestic Commerce, Chief of the Division of Economic Research in which were centered the researches on income, debt, urban real property, construction, and analysis of industries.

versity business schools and with trade associations. Steps are being taken to clear their researches through the Department of Commerce, and a survey of business research throughout the country is being made by the Bureau of Foreign and Domestic Commerce. Some thirty-six schools are now acting as business research stations, and several hundred research projects have been filed with the Bureau which has classified them by type. The parallel with the set-up in the Department of Agriculture is most marked in the proposal to tie in research with action programs. Several experiments in that direction are now being made in collaboration with local business institutions, such as banks and trade associations, and even with a municipality. Eventually, it is proposed to establish regional offices with an economic analyst in charge to report on the economic problems of the several regions of the country. To that end efforts are being made to strengthen the Bureau's district offices. The object of these new activities is to extend to small business through government services some of the advantages of overhead reduction which large units possess because of their ability to obtain and analyze for themselves the necessary data. Emphasis is laid on the distribution rather than the production of information. Efforts at such distribution are being made through open forums and through local institutions. The problem of developing reservoirs of personnel for the Bureau itself is also being considered, and it is felt that one useful result of coöperative research relations with state universities will be to develop such research resources.

Commercial Information and Field Office Services

The Correspondence Division supplies general information requested by businessmen and other interested persons.

This division also compiles a Business Information Service file on a wide range of business subjects. This file is furnished free to libraries, trade associations, universities, and chambers of commerce, and is available for reference in all field offices of the Bureau.

The Division of Commercial Intelligence (E. E. Schnellbacher, Chief), which functions primarily in the fields of foreign sales analysis, foreign trade practice, and development of new foreign business, furnishes business leads and data on foreign importers and exporters to American business men.

The following is an official description of the work of that Division: [16]

On the basis of data received from the agencies of the American Government abroad, this Division has set up and periodically revises lists (by countries, and classified by commodities or lines of business) of foreign buyers or sellers. There are 32,000 such lists now available to American business. The Division maintains, from information received from official sources, sales-information reports, known as "World Trade Directory" reports, on approximately 650,000 foreign buyers or sellers. This number is being constantly augmented as requests for such dependable information are received from American firms or individuals desiring to enter into business relations with firms abroad, and these reports are made readily available to American importers or exporters. The Commercial Intelligence Division also contributes to the verification and the expeditious handling of the numerous notifications of specific opportunities for American firms to buy or sell abroad; these notifications, known as "Trade Opportunities," are also reviewed by the appropriate Industrial Divisions; and, through various Bureau mediums, their avail-

[16] Department of Commerce, *Promotion of American Commerce at Home and Abroad* (1937), p. 7.

ability is promptly made known to the business community at large. There is made regularly available by this Division current information on credit payment terms in foreign countries, through the "Credit Situation Abroad" service.

The Bureau maintains thirty-five district and coöperative offices (connected with the local chambers of commerce) in various cities. Through these field offices, the Bureau transmits trade information useful to exporters; renders special services to localized industries in the vicinity of these offices; assists in the development of a program of coöperative research with the universities in the various states; [17] and assists in making available the services of the Washington office in the current reporting of business statistics in local areas. District offices located in Federal Reserve centers are to be converted into regional offices to "enable the Bureau to obtain at first hand reliable reports regarding the business conditions and business interests of various regions or geographical areas at any given time."

BUREAU OF THE CENSUS

This statistical office (William L. Austin, Director) established on a permanent basis in 1902, is a striking example of the growth of governmental inquiry to serve the need for comprehensive economic and social information. The decennial census of population conducted by this Bureau, originally prescribed in the Constitution as the basis for apportioning membership in the House of Representatives

---

[17] In this connection see *Hearing* before subcommittee of the House Committee on Interstate and Foreign Commerce, 76th Cong., 1st Sess., on H.R. 3395 (Sheppard-Robinson Bill) to promote business and economic research by establishment of research stations in the state university schools of business.

among the several states, has by the extension of its scope become one of the principal sources of knowledge of the economic and social facts concerning the United States. In addition to the decennial census of population, the Bureau makes a quinquennial census of agriculture, a biennial census of manufactures, and censuses of business at irregular intervals. After a lapse of six years, financial statistics of cities and state governments are again being compiled annually. A decennial canvass of state and local government finance is also made. There are weekly, monthly, and annual reports on births and deaths, and special studies of cause of death, and so forth. Periodic statistics are compiled relative to religious bodies, industry, crime, prisoners, mental defectives, electric light and power stations, telephones, telegraphs, electric railways, occupations, unemployment, irrigation, drainage, mines, and cotton.

Special tabulations are made for other governmental agencies and for outside organizations. The sampling and estimating procedures of many government agencies, such as the Bureau of Labor Statistics and the Crop and Livestock Reporting Service of the Department of Agriculture, are based on the periodic enumerations of the Bureau of the Census without which they would necessarily be much less accurate.[18] The annual *Statistical Abstract of the United States* which, through 1937, was prepared by the Bureau of Foreign and Domestic Commerce, has since that date been prepared by the Bureau of the Census. Under a reallocation of work between the Bureau of the Census and the Bureau of Foreign and Domestic Commerce several current report-

[18] Cf. M. R. Benedict in *Journal of Farm Economics* (November, 1939), Vol. XXI, p. 739.

ing services have been taken over by the Bureau of the Census. The Bureau is aided in its work by a general census advisory committee appointed by the American Statistical Association. In addition special committees are invited to serve by the Secretary of Commerce upon the recommendation of the Director of the Census. The latest decennial census of the United States was taken in April, 1940.[19]

DEPARTMENT OF AGRICULTURE

A brief account of the development of the Department of Agriculture will serve to clarify its present set-up.[20] The Department was established in 1862, the year of the first Homestead Act and of the first Congressional grant of lands for the endowment of the state agricultural colleges which have since come to play a major role in the Department's work.

In 1863 was established a Division of Statistics—the name of which was changed in 1914 to the Bureau of Crop Estimates. In the interval there had been added a Section (later Division) of Foreign Markets. In 1906 an Office of Farm

[19] Stouffer's study of the Bureau of the Census in the National Resources Committee report on *Relation of the Federal Government to Research* illuminates the peculiar conditions in which the Bureau has developed, and the reasons why it has not become the central statistical agency of the government. It sets forth vividly the dependence of other governmental agencies and of the public on the data provided by the Bureau, and the development of the activities of the Bureau in response to the growing specialized needs of public and private agencies for the compilation of data classified to afford such agencies the maximum service in dealing with their problems. Appendix B to Mr. Stouffer's report, which was prepared by Dr. Joseph A. Hill of the Bureau, lists the analytical publications of the Bureau of the Census since 1900.

[20] The present organization of the Department is most fully described in its publication, *The United States Department of Agriculture, Its Structure and Functions*, revised to May, 1940 (1940).

Management was established in the Bureau of Plant Industry. In 1913 an Office of Markets was established and in 1915 an independent Office of Farm Management. Further changes ensued until in 1922 a Bureau of Agricultural Economics was organized by merger of the Office of Farm Management and Farm Economics with the Bureau of Markets and Crop Estimates.

In 1930, subsequent to the passing of the Act of June 5, 1930, which created the Foreign Agricultural Service, a Foreign Agricultural Service Division was set up as part of the Bureau of Agricultural Economics. In the beginning, the staff of this Division consisted of the previous Foreign Section of the Division of Statistical and Historical Research and the foreign field representatives of the Bureau. The Bureau of Agricultural Economics came eventually to consist of twenty-three divisions, concerned primarily with the economics of farm production and marketing and with economic policies in the fields of land utilization, credit, taxation and so forth, as they affected agriculture and the farmer. Until its reorganization in 1938, the Bureau had three main functions: research, service, and regulatory work. Analyses and interpretations were made of current crop and market news. Periodical reviews of world conditions and prospects with respect to specific commodities, including visible supplies, production estimates, exports, imports, market demands and prices, were prepared.

In 1933 the Agricultural Adjustment Administration was set up in the Department of Agriculture to carry out the provisions of the Agricultural Adjustment Act of 1933, later voided. Subsequently, it was charged with the enforcement of the Soil Conservation Act of 1936, the Marketing Agreement Act of 1937, the Sugar Act of 1937, and the Agricultural Adjustment Act of 1938. These involved the establishment of nation-wide action programs. Each of the five regional divisions of AAA included a research and economics section. The Program Planning Division, however, was the nerve center of the Administration. The Program Planning Division contained a production planning section, an agricultural-industrial relations section, and an import-export section, and was charged with economic research and "outlook work" on land policy, import-export relations, and replacement crops. Coöperative research relations with the Bureau of Agricultural Economics were maintained. It was evident, however, that there was much overlapping and that a major reconstruction would have to occur in the interests of integration and efficiency.

Moreover, there had taken place a remarkable reorientation of the extension work of the Department, and a basic change in the role of the land-grant colleges and agricultural experiment stations in the agricultural program of the country, so that closer relations between program planning and research became necessary. The latest expression of these changes is found in the Mount Weather Agreement of July 8, 1938, between the Association of Land-Grant Colleges and Universities and the Department of Agriculture, which outlined the role of the former in the building of land-use programs.

On October 6, 1938, the research, planning, and program functions of the Agricultural Adjustment Administration were transferred to the Bureau of Agricultural Economics, the former becoming an operating agency, while the marketing and regulatory work formerly performed by the latter organization was transferred to several newly established divisions outside the Bureau.

BUREAU OF AGRICULTURAL ECONOMICS

The Bureau of Agricultural Economics (H. R. Tolley, Chief) correlates all planning and program development work of the Department, and provides machinery for encouraging farmer participation in agricultural program-making.[21] There are now about 200,000 farmer committeemen and Federal and state agricultural workers in the field.

In the development, coördination, and integration of the work of the Bureau, the Chief of the Bureau is assisted by six counselors, each of whom is in charge of a general field, such as general planning, rural welfare, conservation and land-use adjustment, market planning, the agricultural outlook, and program relations. These six counselors and the heads of the Bureau's twelve divisions are members of the Inter-Bureau Coördinating Committee, of which the Chief of the Bureau is chairman. This Committee synthesizes the plans coming from the county and state planning committees, technical offices, and administrators, and prepares the recommendations thereon which are submitted to the Agricultural Program Board [22] and the Secretary of Agriculture for action.

The divisions of the Bureau of Agricultural Economics are as follows:

[21] This description of the Bureau of Agricultural Economics is drawn from the *BAE Handbook*, December, 1939.

[22] The Agricultural Program Board consists of the Land-Use Coördinator (Chairman), the Chief of the Bureau of Agricultural Economics, the heads of the action agencies (such as AAA), the Director of Extension and others. The Board reviews all plans and programs submitted by the

Agricultural Finance (Norman J. Wall, Head)

Economic Information (Russell Smith, Acting Head)

Farm Management and Costs (Sherman E. Johnson, Head)

Farm Population and Rural Welfare (Carl C. Taylor, Head)

Land Economics (Maurice M. Kelso, Head)

Marketing Programs and Coördination (not yet set up)

Marketing and Transportation Research (F. V. Waugh, Head)

Program Development and Coördination (O. V. Wells, Head)

Program Study and Discussion (Carl F. Taeusch, Head)

Program Surveys (Rensis Likert, Head)

State and Local Planning (Bushrod W. Allin, Head)

Statistical and Historical Research (O. C. Stine, Head)

The Division of Agricultural Finance is concerned with problems of agricultural credit, farm insurance and taxation, and local government.

The Division of Economic Information prepares and disseminates economic information. Its editorial functions extend beyond questions of style to clearing editorial matter for agreement on disputed points between subject matter divisions and with other bureaus in the Department and for Bureau and departmental policy.

The Division of Farm Management and Costs deals with the internal economy of farms in relation to local, regional, and national agricultural policies and programs.

The Division of Farm Population and Rural Welfare

_____

Chief of the Bureau of Agricultural Economics before they are approved by the Secretary.

studies social and cultural factors affecting the conditions of life of rural families.

The Division of Land Economics conducts research looking to such policies and programs of land utilization as will best promote human welfare.

The Division of Marketing and Transportation Research deals with the transportation aspects of agricultural problems, development of more accurate and complete market news services, economic factors governing the flow of commodities into given markets, location of markets, problems involving large-scale processors and distributors of agricultural products, internal trade barriers to agricultural products, price spreads between farmer and consumer, and methods of handling farm surpluses.

The Division of Statistical and Historical Research applies statistical and historical methods in analysis of the economic problems of agriculture and keeps records of statistical and historical data relating to agriculture. It is primarily concerned with explaining agricultural commodity prices, incidental consideration being given to factors affecting price levels in general, such as national and international financial policies. Estimating farm income is another major task. Research in agricultural history is carried on and statistical and non-statistical data relating to agriculture are compiled. The Statistics Service of this Division operates a central file for all statistical data relating to agriculture. Requests for statistical data relating to agriculture are now handled in this central unit and not by the special subject units as formerly. A complete index of all statistical series relating to agriculture is proposed for early preparation.

The four divisions of the Bureau of Agricultural Economics listed above and not described here serve various administrative liaison and extension purposes. The program divisions, which were formerly the Program Planning Division of the Agricultural Adjustment Administration, are, of course, of the first importance in the work of the Department.

Finally, the Bureau of Agricultural Economics maintains an Economic Library (Mary G. Lacy, Librarian) which is housed separately from the Department library, although it is a branch of the latter. The Economic Library employs a large staff of trained librarians and bibliographers and is an important adjunct in the research activity of the Bureau. Since 1922 the Economic Library has compiled more than one hundred extensive annotated bibliographies in the field of agricultural economics. It also issues a processed monthly, *Agricultural Economics Literature*, which is of importance as a bibliographical aid, not merely in the field indicated by its title, but to economists generally.

The Bureau of Agricultural Economics issues several important periodicals. Among them are: *Agricultural Finance Review* (issued in May and November in processed form), *Crops and Markets* (printed monthly), *Farm Population and Rural Life Activities* (multigraphed quarterly), *Agricultural Situation* (printed monthly), *Demand and Price Situation* (mimeographed monthly), and *The Land Policy Review* (printed monthly). Individual commodity situation reports are issued at regular intervals and annually there is an omnibus *Agricultural Outlook Report*, in the preparation of which the other bureaus of the Department of Agriculture and the land grant colleges assist.

AGRICULTURAL MARKETING SERVICE

The Agricultural Marketing Service (C. W. Kitchen, Chief), which was set up as a result of the Secretary's reorganization order of October 6, 1938, and established on a statutory basis by the Agricultural Appropriation Act of 1940, consolidated and coördinated the marketing work formerly lodged in seven different agencies of the Department of Agriculture. The new unit is one of four responsible to the Secretary of Agriculture through an official known as the Director of Marketing and Regulatory Work. Its principal activities are marketing research; service and regulatory work in connection with cotton, dairy and poultry products, fruits and vegetables, grain, livestock, meats and wool, hay, feed and seed, warehousing, and tobacco; the conduct of a market news service, and the preparation of crop and livestock estimates. In addition it administers the Packers and Stockyards Act, the Federal Seed Act, and the Dairy Exports Act. Its staff numbers about 2,750 of whom nearly 2,000 are located in the field. There are six commodity divisions and four functional divisions. The division of greatest general interest is the Division of Agricultural Statistics (W. F. Callander, in charge), although all the other divisions conduct research and issue important current statistical compilations.

The Division of Agricultural Statistics under other names has existed continuously since the establishment of the Department of Agriculture in 1862. Agricultural statistics had been collected as early as 1839 in a more or less desultory fashion and the first Census of Agriculture was taken in

1840, but the continuous collection of information on acreage, and the condition and production of crops which eventually developed into the present remarkable Crop and Livestock Reporting Service of the United States began only in 1862.

The information gathered today is officially described as follows:

(1) Estimates of acreage, yield, production, and value of practically all crops grown in the United States; monthly forecasts of yield and production for many of these crops during the growing season; stocks estimates for a number of crops and sales and utilization estimates for individual crops. One or more reports a year are issued on each of more than 100 crops, including cotton, 11 grain crops, 10 hay crops, 6 legumes, 17 clover and grass seeds, 4 sugar or sirup crops, 21 fruits, 4 nut crops, 26 vegetables and truck crops, tobacco (23 types), and 6 miscellaneous crops.

(2) Estimates of the numbers of all classes of livestock (horses, mules, cattle, sheep, swine and goats) on farms; meat-animal production, sales, disposition and value; wool and mohair production; also forecasts and estimates of numbers of hogs, sheep, and cattle on feed or available for market.

(3) Estimates of milk production, utilization, sales, and value.

(4) Estimates of numbers of poultry on farms, and poultry and egg production, sales, utilization and value.

(5) Monthly reports of commodities in cold storage warehouses.

(6) Periodic reports on production, stocks, manufacture, or other commercial pre-market handling of dairy and poultry products, i. e., monthly manufacture of dairy

products, butter and cheese production estimates, evaporated and condensed milk production and stocks, commercial hatching of chicks and turkey poults.

(7) Reports on railroad, boat, and truck movements of agricultural commodities.

(8) Reports on farm labor supply and demand, wage rates, and estimated farm employment.

(9) Reports on prices farmers receive for their products and prices they pay for the things they buy, including monthly price indexes and ratios of prices received to prices paid, interest, and taxes.

(10) Crop and weather research to develop improved methods of forecasting the yield of various crops during the growing season.

(11) Collection from primary sources of special economic information relative to farm income and expenditures, taxes, land values, and rents.[23]

The quinquennial Census of Agriculture constitutes a periodic check on the Division's crop and livestock estimates.

The work of gathering the data is done by voluntary reporters of whom there are more than 200,000 in all the counties of the United States. Their reports are collected in the 41 state field offices. Summaries of the reports prepared by the field offices are reviewed by the Crop Reporting Board of the Department of Agriculture at Washington where they are held in strictest confidence until the day appointed for their release to the public.[24]

[23] *Agricultural Marketing Service: Organization and Functions* (July, 1939), pp. 18–19. The November, 1939, number of the *Journal of Farm Economics* is devoted to a review of one hundred years' progress of agricultural statistics, principally in the United States, since the Census of Agriculture of 1840.

[24] See Department of Agriculture, *The Crop and Livestock Reporting Service of the United States* (Miscellaneous Publication No. 171, Novem-

Complementary to the crop and livestock reporting system just described are daily reports on supply and demand for more than one hundred agricultural products at important markets. The nature, need for, and advantages of this service are officially explained as follows:

The information is obtained at terminal markets and shipping points, and from producing sections. It covers movement, market supplies, quality, and prices of livestock, meats, wool, fruits, vegetables, dairy and poultry products, grains, hay, seeds, feedstuffs, cotton and cottonseed, tobacco, rice, honey, and miscellaneous products.

For nearly 25 years this information has been made available each market day to the general public. Though the service is now usually taken for granted, it has become an indispensable factor in the American system of marketing. Reliable market news is now practically a necessity in the operations and plans of everyone who produces, buys or sells.

The basic information is collected in numerous ways—by interviews with buyers and sellers in the markets during the trading hours, by telegraphic reports from railroads on shipments to and arrivals at important markets, by reports on truck arrivals at major markets, by warehousemen who report stocks in storage, by inspecting records made available by individuals and agencies engaged in buying and selling, and by numerous contacts with other groups.

To distribute the information in time to be of practical use, the Agricultural Marketing Service maintains an extensive leased wire system. More than 7,500 miles (airline) of leased telegraph wires make it possible to send the material promptly from one market to another. Information received at any one market is quickly made available to the public by means of radio, tele-

ber, 1933); and *Seventy-Fifth Anniversary of the United States Crop Reporting Service, 1863-1938* (May, 1938).

phone, press and mail, and by posting on bulletin boards. It is further distributed widely through trade and farm publications, commercial and financial institutions, and other agencies.

Approximately 350 radio stations are regularly broadcasting current market news as compiled by the commodity reporters. A number of the stations supply remote control facilities which enable the reporter to broadcast direct from the market. Some of the stations provide 3 to 5 scheduled reports daily in order that producers in the territory they serve may be kept fully informed on the changes and trends in the market.

Such blanketing of the entire country has decreased the disadvantage of the individual producer and the small shipper who are in competition with the stronger commercial organizations better capable of obtaining information for themselves through far-flung trade connections. It helps to promote orderly marketing. It facilitates and equalizes distribution, discourages the dissemination of fictitious and misleading market information by unscrupulous persons, and aids economic research looking toward improved marketing methods. The recording of the day-to-day happenings in permanent form provides a continuous story for use by marketing specialists and economists in making studies and analyses of production, demand, prices, and distribution.

The Federal Government is the only agency in a position to furnish such a service impartially to all concerned on commodities in which there is a Nation-wide interest.[25]

Apart from its numerous releases, reports, and printed bulletins, the Agricultural Marketing Service issues two periodicals: *Crops and Markets* (a printed monthly publication) and *Marketing Activities* (a processed monthly).

Other activities of the Agricultural Marketing Service have to do with standardization and inspection, research in

[25] *Agricultural Marketing Service: Organization and Functions* (July, 1939), pp. 5–6.

standards of quality and marketing practices, and the administration of various statutory prescriptions concerning agricultural marketing.

OFFICE OF FOREIGN AGRICULTURAL RELATIONS

Now attached to the office of the Secretary of Agriculture, this agency (Leslie A. Wheeler, Director) was formerly the Foreign Agricultural Service Division of the Bureau of Agricultural Economics, from which it was separated as of December 1, 1938. Under the President's Reorganization Plan No. II, effective July 1, 1939, the field officers were transferred to the Department of State. As now constituted, the Office of Foreign Agricultural Relations is charged with the "collection, through the Foreign Service of the United States, the International Institute of Agriculture at Rome and other sources, of information on foreign agricultural production, foreign markets, foreign trade and related matters of significance to American agriculture and the dissemination of this information to all branches of the Department interested and to the public." It maintains liaison between the Department of Agriculture and the Department of State. One of the primary functions of the office is the direct conduct of specialized research in the field of foreign competition and demand for American agricultural products. In general, the studies are along two lines: (1) studies of situations affecting particular commodities, for example, cotton production in the various parts of the world; the market situation in the principal importing countries for particular commodities, such as fruit and tobacco; and (2) general agricultural studies (tenancy, coöperative marketing, and so forth) and analyses of agricultural policies in particular countries affecting agricultural production and consumption.

The Office of Foreign Agricultural Relations directs and coördinates the participation of the Department of Agriculture in the reciprocal trade agreements program and in the general program of coöperation between the United States and the other American republics. It also coördinates the relations of the Department of Agriculture in respect to foreign trade and related matters with the Department of State and other departments and agencies of the government and with foreign governments and private agencies. It is the liaison agency between the Department of Agriculture and the International Institute of Agriculture. A Department Committee on Foreign Relations considers questions involving foreign trade. The agricultural experts in the field now number seven; of these two are in Europe, one in the Far East, and four in Latin America.

While the researches of the office of Foreign Agricultural Relations are occasionally published in full dress as separate bulletins, printed or processed, most of them appear—in somewhat abbreviated form—in its monthly, *Foreign Agriculture,* publication of which was begun in January, 1937. Current information on crop and market conditions is published in the weekly, *Foreign Crops and Markets.*[26]

SURPLUS MARKETING ADMINISTRATION

This unit of the Department of Agriculture (Milo Perkins, Administrator) was created as a result of the President's Reorganization Plan No. III, effective June 1, 1940,

---

[26] Under the sponsorship of the Tariff Commission a WPA staff has prepared a cumulative index to *Foreign Crops and Markets.*

which consolidated the Division of Marketing and Marketing Agreements and the Federal Surplus Commodities Corporation in one organization because of the close relationship of their aims and work. The functions of the new unit are the same as those of the organizations which it succeeds.

This organization administers the marketing agreement program under the Agricultural Marketing Agreement Act of 1937 and the surplus diversion programs authorized by Section 32 of Public No. 320 of August 24, 1935.[27] The marketing agreement program is designed to promote more orderly marketing of agricultural products and to assure farmers of returns for their products at a level "more nearly approaching the level of the prices of things farmers buy."

The surplus diversion programs are designed to encourage

the exportation and domestic consumption of agricultural commodities by diverting burdensome surpluses of farm products from normal commercial channels to foreign markets, to relief, to by-products and to new uses.

On the basis of economic analyses of the current market situation purchase and distribution plans are developed and, after approval by the Secretary, executed by the Administration. Departing from the direct distribution of commodities for relief, there has been considerable study of the so-called food stamp plan for the diversion of agricultural surpluses in the elaboration of which the Department of Commerce has assisted, and the plan is being carried out in about one hundred cities. The Administration has the assistance of WPA and the Social Security Board in obtain-

[27] See *Report of the Associate Administrator of the Agricultural Adjustment Administration, in Charge of the Division of Marketing and Marketing Agreements*, 1939.

ing relief data needed for the administration of the stamp plan. The subsidized agricultural export programs for wheat, flour, and cotton also have been carried out by means of this organization and have already necessitated measures to stop imports of these commodities into the United States.[28]

MISCELLANEOUS

Many other units in the Department of Agriculture conduct research pertinent to this discussion. Such units are the Farm Security Administration and the Bureau of Home Economics, the first of which makes important research contributions in the fields of rural sociology and welfare, while the second has made important income studies. In view of their fundamental importance in agricultural research, what will appear as the merest mention must suffice for the studies made by the land-grant colleges and experiment stations with which the Department of Agriculture has the closest statutory relationships. The magnitude of the researches of these organizations can be appreciated from an examination of the index of names in the latest list of workers in subjects pertaining to agriculture in land-grant colleges and experiment stations (issued by the Office of Experiment Stations of the Department of Agriculture) which contains sixty-seven double-column printed pages. The July, 1939 issue of the *Experiment Station Record* (published monthly by the Department of Agriculture) which abstracts briefly the results of researches in all branches of agricultural study contains one hundred and sixty printed pages. As was pointed out above, the land-grant colleges have now been drawn

[28] See U.S. Tariff Commission, *Cotton and Cotton Waste* (1939). A wheat investigation is under way.

into the agricultural action programs of the Government. No attempt is made here to tell the story of the development of the land-grant colleges and experiment stations, and of their connection with the Federal Government, or to recount the related history of the Agricultural Extension Service and of the growth in the field of agriculture of the conception of research, planning, and action programming as an integrated process. It is enough to suggest here that these would repay study for the purpose of discovering how the results of scientific inquiry can be made effective by being fed in a steady stream into the habits of the community.

DEPARTMENT OF THE INTERIOR

BUREAU OF MINES

The functions of the Bureau of Mines of the Department of the Interior, established in 1910, were at first technological, with particular emphasis on the safety of miners and the improvement of conditions under which mining operations are carried on. By Act of February 25, 1913, they were expanded to include the study of economic conditions affecting the mining industry, and the conservation of mineral resources, although up to 1925 the principal studies in this field were conducted by the United States Geological Survey. In 1925 the work of collecting and publishing statistics relating to the operations of the mineral industry was transferred from the Geological Survey of the Department of the Interior, to the Bureau of Mines, and the latter was transferred to the Department of Commerce. In 1926 most of the work on mineral economics of other units of the Bureau of Foreign and Domestic Commerce, Department of Commerce, was transferred to the Bureau of Mines, where all mineral economics study was consolidated in a new Economics Branch. In 1935 the Bureau of Mines was returned to the Department of the Interior, and there was a transfer to the Bureau of those activities of the Mineral Division of the Bureau of Foreign and Domestic Commerce concerned with economic and statistical analyses of mineral commodities, domestic and foreign. The Bureau of Foreign and Domestic Commerce retained a small unit to collect non-technical foreign information on minerals and to act as a liaison agency with the Bureau of Mines.

The Economics and Statistics Branch of the Bureau of Mines (E. W. Pehrson, Chief) studies the economic problems of the mineral industries, compiles statistics on the production and movement of mineral commodities, and investigates domestic and foreign trade conditions. A specialist on foreign minerals is detailed to the Foreign Service, Department of State, and serves in an advisory capacity to consular officers abroad. Formerly stationed in Europe, he was assigned last year to South America in furtherance of the program for establishing closer relations with the Latin American Republics. The following periodicals dealing with the economics of foreign minerals are issued: *International Coal Trade, Mineral Trade Notes, International Petroleum Trade,* each appearing monthly; and *Foreign Minerals Quarterly* and *World Retail Prices and Taxes on Gasoline, Kerosene, and Motor Lubricating Oils,* issued quarterly. The *Minerals Yearbook,* successor to the annual volume entitled *Mineral Resources of the United States,* provides a comprehensive economic and statistical survey of developments in the mineral industries, including data on production of minerals in foreign countries. While lack of funds has prevented the Bureau from making extensive economic investigations, which it deems vital, it collaborates most fruitfully and generously with other government agencies and with numerous private organizations and individual researchers in important mineral economic studies.[29]

DEPARTMENT OF LABOR

BUREAU OF LABOR STATISTICS

The Bureau of Labor Statistics of the Department of Labor (Isador Lubin, Commissioner of Labor Statistics) is the leading statistical agency concerned with non-agricultural industry from the labor side. There are eleven divisions grouped in three branches: Employment and Occupational Outlook (Donald H. Davenport, Chief) Working Conditions and Industrial Relations (N. A. Tolles, Chief) and Prices and Cost of Living (Aryness Joy, Chief).

[29] Under the act of Congress of June 7, 1939, the Bureau is authorized to conduct an investigation of the country's resources of strategic minerals. Money was appropriated for that purpose by the Deficiency Appropriation Act of August 9, 1939. While they are not part of the Bureau of Mines, the Bituminous Coal Division (formerly the National Bituminous Coal Commission), the Geological Survey, and the Petroleum Conservation Division, all of the Department of Interior, may appropriately be mentioned here because of their importance as agencies of mineral economics investigation. The Geological Survey participates with the Bureau of Mines in the strategic minerals studies authorized by the legislation mentioned above. The statistical labors of the Bituminous Coal Division are particularly great since the 13,500 coal code members are required by statute to file with the Division copies of all invoices, contracts for the sale of coal, and credit memoranda.

On June 17, 1940, a special defense resources committee was named by Secretary Ickes to coördinate the Department's control over strategic minerals, hydro-electric power, coal, oil, and other national defense essentials.

A. F. Hinrichs, formerly Chief Economist, is Assistant Commissioner. The Bureau is concerned with construction, private and public employment and pay rolls, labor turnover, cost of living, retail and wholesale prices, wages, hours and working conditions, food and diets from the cost side, industrial relations, industrial injuries, labor law, labor productivity, prison labor, and foreign labor legislation and working conditions. It compiles and publishes numerous indexes of economic trends, including the widely used wholesale price index and employment index. The Bureau's principal publications are the *Monthly Labor Review* and the *Labor Information Bulletin*. Some technical studies appear as bulletins, but as printing funds are limited, many of the surveys are summarized in the *Monthly Labor Review*, and some are available only in mimeographed form.

The Bureau also serves as an information clearing house on statistical matters for state departments of labor and industrial commissions, and maintains coöperative relationships with the states in matters affecting labor. It has collaborated with many other Federal agencies in important research projects.

A word is in place here concerning the relations between the Department of Labor and the Department of State in matters relating to the International Labor Organization. The Government representative of the United States on the Governing Body of the International Labor Office is appointed by the President on the recommendation of the Secretary of Labor which is transmitted through the Department of State. The government representative so appointed also serves, in his capacity as United States Labor Commissioner in Geneva, as head of the liaison office main-

tained in that city by the Department of Labor to deal with
I.L.O. matters. On matters of fundamental policy he seeks
instructions directly from the Department of Labor (and, on
political questions, also from the Department of State) to
which he also reports directly on all matters arising in the
I.L.O. which might affect or interest the Government of
the United States. On the Commissioner of Labor Statistics
in Washington rests the responsibility for seeing that requests for instructions are placed before the appropriate governmental officials and before other persons best qualified to
give advice or most competent to make final decisions. He
has also the task of discussing the requests for instructions
with officials of the agencies or departments concerned, or
with United States members of the I.L.O. Governing Body
representing employers and workers. His Bureau also prepares the reports required for the I.L.O.

The Department of State, for its part, designates an official
in Washington to handle I.L.O. matters of interest to it,
such as questions relating to the annual budgets of the
I.L.O. and political questions as distinct from technical
problems of labor. At Geneva one of the officers of the
American consulate is charged with the handling of I.L.O.
matters for the Department of State.

Between the Department of Labor and the Department
of State the most intimate coöperation exists; the Commissioner of Labor Statistics consults his State Department
colleague and the head of the liaison office consults his consular colleague at Geneva on any major problem arising in
connection with the I.L.O., whether strictly within the
sphere of the State Department or not. It is the practice for
the consular officer at Geneva to accompany the government

representative at Governing Body meetings and to serve as a government adviser at the International Labor Conferences.

The Geneva liaison office has important European labor research functions. Indeed, these preceded its duties of liaison with the I.L.O. in point of time. The office serves as an observation post for the study of European labor matters and many of the studies of that subject described in the second part of this book stem from it. With the transfer of the I.L.O. office to Montreal late last year the Geneva liaison office was temporarily closed.

In the *Annual Report of the Secretary of Labor* for 1939, Mr. Lubin observes that the lack of funds, the expansion of the frontiers of inquiry at a more rapid rate than the resources of the Bureau, the need for more intensive as well as extensive information, and the lag in the interest of the public have prevented the Bureau of Labor Statistics from carrying out fully the Congressional direction in its organic act "to acquire and diffuse among the people of the United States useful information on subjects connected with labor, in the most general and comprehensive sense of the word, and especially upon its relation to capital, the hours of labor, the earnings of laboring men and women and the means of promoting their material, social, intellectual and moral prosperity." He adds that the demand today is not only for the facts but also for an explanation of "why these facts are as they are." This may be supplemented by Mr. Lubin's statement in the *Annual Report of the Secretary of Labor* for 1938 that "Labor Statistics, as now usually defined, are only a part of a larger picture embracing one whole economic structure. The problem of the future is to integrate and correlate these statistics so that they may serve their most useful purpose."

The researches of the Department of Labor are not confined to the Bureau of Labor Statistics. Other units engaging in important research are the Division of Labor Standards, the Children's Bureau, and the Women's Bureau. The work of these agencies sometimes bears on international economic relations, particularly as proposals for international labor conventions and proposals affecting their fields of interest come before the International Labor Organization and before the League of Nations.

DEPARTMENT OF THE TREASURY

There are three research divisions in the Office of the Secretary—the Division of Research and Statistics, the Division of Monetary Research, and the Division of Tax Research. These divisions carry on analyses and research in their respective fields, as described below, for the use of Treasury officials in determining policy and dealing with specific problems of administration and operation. The work of these divisions thus involves the analysis and interpretation of data for specific purposes, and is frequently of a confidential nature, at least at the time the studies are made. Their work does not include the assembling of primary data except on occasion when this is necessary for special requirements which cannot be met otherwise.

In addition, there are in various other offices and bureaus of the Department statistical units engaged in the compilation, largely for administrative purposes, of primary data available in connection with Treasury operations. Such units are to be found, for example, in the Bureau of Internal Revenue, the Bureau of Customs, and the Office of the Comptroller of the Currency. Statistics on receipts, expenditures, and the public debt are compiled as a necessary part of their operations by the respective offices concerned, although not by separate statistical units so designated. The Coast Guard, the Bureau of the Mint, and the various enforcement agencies likewise maintain statistical information relating to their administrative and operating functions. Certain of this information which is of more or less general interest and which is not of a confidential nature is made available to the public in response to requests.

In January, 1939, the Treasury Department began the publication of the *Bulletin of the Treasury Department*, a monthly publication compiled in the Office of the Secretary from material available in various Treasury divisions. The *Bulletin* contains statistical data on Federal receipts and expenditures, the Treasury's General Fund, the public debt, governmental corporations and credit agencies, international capital movements between the United States and foreign countries, gold, silver, and foreign exchange movements, and on other miscellaneous subjects. Special data such as the balance sheet of the exchange stabilization account and the security holdings of government trust funds are published from time to time. The *Bulletin* was designed as a convenient compilation of scattered statistical material which it was desirable to make easily and compactly available to the various divisions of the Treasury Department. In addition to its distribution within the Department, it has been sent to private individuals and organizations requesting it.

The Division of Research and Statistics (George C. Haas, Director) was established in the Office of the Secretary by Treasury Order No. 8, September 17, 1934, to supersede the Section of Financial and Economic Research. This Division serves as a research staff for the Secretary and other Treasury officials on matters relating to fiscal operations and policies, the estimated volume and source of future revenues, actuarial considerations involved in certain Treasury functions, and various general economic problems arising in connection with Treasury activities.

Current and prospective conditions in the money and capital markets are studied in relation to both longer-term programs of Federal financing and to the types of securities, the coupon rates, and the maturities to be employed in particular financing operations. The effects of actual and proposed fiscal operations on the credit structure and general economy of the country are analyzed and long-range trends are appraised. Studies are made of existing laws and of legislative proposals in their relation to Treasury financing and Federal fiscal policies.

Estimates of Federal receipts from internal revenue taxes and from customs duties under existing laws are prepared for the Bureau of the Budget for use in all regular and interim budget reports, and for such other purposes as may be required. Special revenue estimates are prepared for Treasury officials and for Congressional committees working on tax legislation.

Reports are prepared on the actuarial status of pension and trust funds for which the Treasury is responsible. In connection with retirement legislation, estimates are made of probable cost of existing and proposed plans. Other actuarial analyses are made as required. The Government Actuary, who is on the staff of the Division, is a member of the Board of Actuaries, established under the Civil Service Retirement Act, and is the Treasury Department's representative on the Actuarial Advisory Committee of the Railroad Retirement Board. He serves in a consulting capacity on actuarial matters for governmental agencies outside the Treasury Department.

In addition to the preparation of memoranda and reports for the confidential use of Treasury officials, the Division performs research services of a general nature, including the preparation of replies to inquiries from outside the Treasury for information of a more or less technical nature, the preparation of publications within the field of its activities, the partial preparation and the editing of the Annual Report of the Secretary, and the review of other Treasury publications of an economic or statistical nature.

DIVISION OF MONETARY RESEARCH

The Division of Monetary Research (Harry D. White, Director) was established in the Office of the Secretary on March 25, 1938, by Treasury Order No. 18. This Division provides information, economic analysis, and recommendations for the use of the Secretary of the Treasury and other Treasury officials to assist in the formulation and execution of the monetary policies of the Department in connection with the stabilization fund and other operations under the Gold Reserve and the Silver Purchase Acts.[30] Analyses are

[30] See *Hearings* (1939) before sub-committee of the Senate Committee

made pertaining to gold and silver, the flow of capital funds into and out of the United States, the position of the dollar in relation to foreign currencies, monetary, banking, and fiscal policies of foreign countries, exchange and trade restrictions abroad, and similar problems. Analyses are also prepared relating to the customs activities of the Department and to the duties of the Secretary of the Treasury under the Tariff Act and on other matters pertaining to international trade, including the trade agreement program.

DIVISION OF TAX RESEARCH

The Division of Tax Research (Roy Blough, Director) was established in the Office of the Secretary on June 1, 1938, by Treasury Order No. 18. This Division analyzes taxes and tax systems and prepares studies on the economic aspects of tax matters for the use of the Secretary, the Under-Secretary, and other Treasury officials, and upon request, for the Congressional Joint Committee on Internal Revenue Taxation.

Surveys of the Federal tax structure are made in the light of immediate and contemplated revenue needs and deal with the effectiveness, equitableness, and economic effects of the existing Federal tax system, and of proposed changes in it. Studies are made of the distribution of the tax burden, both for specific taxes and for the tax system as a whole.

---

on Banking and Currency, 76th Cong., 1st Sess., on S. 910 relating to devaluation of the dollar and to the stabilization fund, March and May, 1939. The Senate Committee on Banking and Currency began a comprehensive study of the country's monetary and banking systems with the issuance in May, 1940, of an eighty-three page questionnaire sent to governmental agencies, banking supervisors, and bankers.

The operation of certain state and local taxes is studied in connection with related problems of Federal taxation. As a further basis for the study of the Federal tax structure comparative analyses are made of selected taxes in foreign countries and of foreign tax systems as a whole.

The Division also is responsible for the assembly and publication of all statistical information pertaining to Federal taxation, and in this connection exercises general supervision over the work of the Statistical Section of the Income Tax Unit in the Bureau of Internal Revenue.

Estimates of the extent and nature of the Federal, state, and local tax-exempt debt are furnished annually to the Secretary. Replies to correspondence dealing with taxation are prepared and other functions of similar nature are performed.

EXECUTIVE OFFICE OF THE PRESIDENT

The President's Reorganization Plan No. I, effective July 1, 1939, transferred to the Executive Office of the President, the Bureau of the Budget, the Central Statistical Board (as part of the Bureau of the Budget), and the National Resources Committee (renamed the National Resources Planning Board). This was the first step taken under the Reorganization Act of April 3, 1939 (Public No. 19, 76th Congress, 1st Session) to improve the administrative management of the Executive establishment in accordance with the legislative direction that reorganization should be undertaken when necessary to accomplish any of five purposes: (1) reduction of expenditures; (2) increase of efficiency; (3) consolidation of agencies according to major purposes; (4) reduction by consolidation of agencies with similar functions and abolition of unnecessary ones; (5) elimination of overlapping and duplication of effort. Because of statutory exemption, the Civil Service Commission could not be so transferred; therefore, one of the President's administrative assistants serves as liaison agent with the Civil Service Committee on personnel management.

The effect of the Reorganization Plan is to give the President direct access to the agencies dealing with over-all problems of executive management, namely, (1) budget, and efficiency research, (2) planning, and (3) personnel. The inclusion of the Central Statistical Board in the Bureau of the Budget makes the latter a powerful instrument of research coördination in the statistical field and the association of the Central Statistical Board with the National Resources Planning Board makes for coördination of planning.

DIVISION OF STATISTICAL STANDARDS

The Central Statistical Board, now the Division of Statistical Standards of the Bureau of the Budget (Stuart A. Rice, Assistant Director) was originally established by Executive order in July, 1933. By Act of Congress, July 25, 1935 (Public No. 219, 74th Congress), it was reorganized and set up for a term of five years as an independent agency, with a chairman appointed by the President, six members designated by the heads of government agencies from within those agencies, and seven elected members, not more than three of whom are to come from outside the government service.[31] While its statutory life as the Central Statistical Board terminated on July 25, 1940, its functions are con-

[31] In fact, there was only one such member among the seven elected members.

tinued in the Division of Statistical Standards which continues to be headed by Mr. Rice, former Chairman of the Board, as Assistant Director of the Bureau. In general, the description of the work of the Central Statistical Board which follows holds for its successor, except that the legal authority of the latter is not as precisely defined. The members of the Board now serve as members of a Statistical Advisory Committee of which Mr. Rice is Chairman. Its purpose is

. . . to plan and promote the improvement, development, and coördination of, and the elimination of duplication in, statistical services carried on by or subject to the supervision of the Federal government, and, so far as may be practicable, of other statistical services in the United States . . . plan and promote the economical operation of agencies engaged in statistical work and the elimination of unnecessary work both on the part of such agencies and on the part of persons called on by such agencies to furnish information.

The Board is empowered (1) to investigate and make recommendations with respect to existing or proposed statistical work by Federal agencies or agencies supervised by the Federal government and (2) to require from any such agency information, papers, reports, and original records concerning statistical work. It is empowered, with the consent of the agency concerned, to make like investigations and recommendations concerning the statistical work of non-Federal agencies. The recommendations of the Board are entirely advisory; it has no power to enforce them. Its consolidation with the Bureau of the Budget under the reorganization plan, however, involves a significant addition of strength to the force of its recommendations. As the Board itself has indicated in its annual reports, there is not, nor in general is there likely in future to be any suggestion of compulsion in the relations of the Board to the statistical agencies with which it deals. Some account of the aims and methods of the Board will clarify its relations with such agencies.

Except for preparing a weekly summary of the business situation for the use of government officers,[32] the Central Statistical Board has acted throughout as a coördinating agency and has not itself engaged in the regular collection and publication of statistics. In the coördination of the statistical services, its aim, as stated in its first annual report, has been to fill major gaps in information; to integrate piecemeal contributions; to make data comparable; to maintain adequate standards; to effect greater interchange of information between agencies; to improve efficiency and economy of operation; and, finally, to eliminate duplication. The principal problems of coördination arise from (1) the "variations in degree and quality of cultivation of the several fields of statistical information," and (2) the necessary decentralization of the statistical services in many fields because of the diverse administrative functions of the agencies to which such statistical services are attached. For the solution of the first class of problems, the Board has recommended the use of focal agencies through which data would be channeled to the related statistical services and which would undertake to fill in gaps in information and round out the statistical picture. For the solution of the second class of problems the Board has recommended the establishment of specialized coördination machinery run by committees of the agencies

---

[32] Now consolidated with the summary prepared by the Department of Commerce.

involved. The Board has stated emphatically that analytical work and research should be highly decentralized and that concentration of statistical services should not proceed beyond the limits of the major field. Thus "for each major phase of our economic and social system there should be a single statistical and research organization that will constitute a focal or concentration point for all the information pertinent to the field in which it is operating." This would involve, in some cases, a prior consolidation of administrative responsibility.[33]

The Board's principal contact with the other government agencies is through recurrent review of questionnaires, forms, and other plans for, and operations of, statistical studies. This review is handled by the permanent expert staff under the supervision of standing committees of the Board and is a coöperative procedure involving clearance with other Federal agencies and with non-governmental organizations. Review, however, while important, is rather a means for disclosing the various aspects of the larger problems of coordination, development, and improvement of the statistical services, for the treatment of which the Board's general staff functions exist. These larger problems are handled by temporary special subjects committees for which the permanent staff serves as secretariat. The special subjects committees consist of representatives designated by the agencies directly interested and, often, of specialists in the problem. The com-

---

[33] On the whole subject, in addition to the annual reports of the Board, see the study prepared by the Committee on Government Statistics and Information Services of the American Statistical Association and the Social Science Research Council, "Government Statistics," *Social Science Research Council Bulletin* 26 (1937). See also Rice, "The Role and Management of the Federal Statistical System," *American Political Science Review*, XXXIV (June, 1940), p. 48.

mittees are, however, not collective agencies, but they act as representatives of the Board. Informal liaison and advisory relations are also maintained.

Among the many activities of the Board, the following may be noted: It has assisted in the development of informal agreements for the efficient division of statistical labor between the Bureau of the Census and various other organizations, such as the Bureau of Foreign and Domestic Commerce, the Federal Power Commission, the Interstate Commerce Commission, and the Federal Communications Commission. It has inventoried the statistics in various fields, and has collaborated with private organizations, as in the inventory of banking and credit research made in collaboration with the National Bureau of Economic Research.[34] It acts as a clearing house of information for executive departments and agencies, Congress, and the public on the availability, uses, limitations, and interrelationships of statistical data.[35] It has made a report to the President on decreasing burdens on respondents to official statistical inquiries (76th Congress, 1st Session, House Document No. 27). An outstanding example of the Board's statistical administrative management has been its work through committees of interested official agencies on standard industrial and foreign

[34] Published as Vol. 2 of the *Inventory of Financial Research* (1937).

[35] A fourth edition of its *Directory of Federal Statistical Agencies* (processed) was issued in January, 1940. The Board prepared, in collaboration with the National Resources Committee, the *Federal Chart Book* (rotoprint, January, 1938) in which each chart is accompanied by a brief description of the series shown, by citations to facilitate the location of current data, and comments on use. The charts cover national income, production, population and occupations; employment, wages and hours; prices and cost of living; foreign exchange; international payments and foreign trade; public finance; currency and banking; and many others.

trade classifications.[36] In order to eliminate the multiplicity of bases now used, adoption of a 1935–39 base for all general purpose index numbers prepared by Federal agencies has been recommended. With a view to the establishment of current reporting systems, it has inventoried all the regular and special forms in use during the fiscal year 1939 and maintains files of report forms used by Federal agencies for obtaining information from the public. It has advised the Civil Service Commission on the development of an adequate personnel program for the Federal government in the social sciences, particularly in respect to classification, recruitment, and examination. It has made surveys, on request, of the organization of statistical work within various Federal agencies (notably the Census Bureau), and has submitted detailed recommendations for reorganization. It has ex-

[36] "For years it has been recognized that the antiquated industrial classification of the census of manufactures and inconsistencies from census to census in allocating particular plants to given categories prevented realistic research. The situation was made all the worse because the industrial classifications of the Bureau of Labor Statistics and of other agencies also left much to be desired and were not comparable with each other or with the Census of Manufactures. A sub-committee of the Central Statistical Board, comprising representatives of six Federal agencies including the Bureau of the Census and of one State agency, is now preparing a standard industrial classification. The hope is to secure an agreement not to change the classification oftener than once in 5 years and to refer any questions in the interim to an inter-agency 'supreme court,' where rulings will be final." Stouffer, in National Resources Committee, *Relation of Federal Government to Research*, p. 207. A uniform industry classification was adopted on June 1, 1939. It provides for twenty major groups of industries and about 430 separate industry classifications. The Biennial Census of Manufactures, 1939, employs the new classification. With the aid of WPA, a standard classified list of leading enterprises, arranged in accordance with the standard industrial classification, is being prepared as an aid in obtaining the uniform presentation of collected data. Occupational classifications are also being standardized.

plored, with the Canadian Dominion Bureau of Statistics and with the League of Nations Committee of Statistical Experts, various problems of uniform classification. It has made a canvass (at the request of the Bureau of Research and Statistics of the National Defense Advisory Commission) of all new governmental statistical activities and plans connected with defense.

One activity of the Executive Secretary of the Board (Morris Copeland) deserves particular mention because it points the way to that coördination and clearing of analytical study by governmental agencies which is sorely needed—if in different measure from the coördination of their statistical plans. This is the making of reports to the Board on "Significant developments in the statistical, economic and research work, and in the organization of the Federal agencies." These reports were made irregularly until January, 1939, when they were placed on a bi-monthly basis. Beginning June 15, 1940, the bimonthly reports were supplemented by fortnightly supplements containing material of the same character. With the issue of July 31, 1940, the report became the *Report to Federal Statistical Agencies* by the Division of Statistical Standards, was fused with the supplement, and is now issued twice a month. The report is circulated to a limited number of Federal officials and is not public. Its publication would appear to have a distinct value in effecting greater intimacy of contact between private and public research interests.[37]

What may perhaps prove to be a defect in the Board's constitution is the absence of provision for the participation by

[37] Some information concerning current research activities of government agencies can be obtained from *Domestic Commerce Weekly*, issued by the Bureau of Foreign and Domestic Commerce.

members of its staff in the research of the agencies on whose statistical procedures they pass. One result may be to deaden perception of new needs and to routinize attitudes to new statistical plans, a prospect which is more to be feared in view of the increased influence acquired by the Board in its new character as part of the Bureau of the Budget. If members of the staff could be detailed for periods of a year or more to participate in the research activities of other agencies the narrowing influences to which excessive exemption from research duties exposes them might be avoided.

NATIONAL RESOURCES PLANNING BOARD

The National Resources Planning Board succeeds the National Resources Committee, which was established June 15, 1935.[38] The latter organization continued the work of two earlier organizations—the National Planning Board of the Federal Emergency Administration of Public Works, and its successor, the National Resources Board—which had derived their powers from the National Industrial Recovery Act. Since the lapse of that Act their successors have been without permanent statutory authority.

[38] There are three members, Frederic A. Delano (Chairman), Charles E. Merriam, and George F. Yantis. They serve on a per diem basis. Its predecessor, the National Resources Committee, had six ex-officio members, the Secretaries of Interior, War, Agriculture, Commerce, and Labor, the Works Progress Administrator, and two former members of the National Planning Board—Mr. Delano and Mr. Merriam. It was, however, the advisory committee, consisting of Mr. Delano, Mr. Merriam, Henry S. Dennison, and Beardsley Ruml, which gave the organization executive direction. It is to the advisory committee that the present Board may be said to have succeeded. Mr. Dennison and Mr. Ruml continue to serve as Advisers to the Board. Charles W. Eliot, 2d, continues as Director. The President's Reorganization Plan No. I also transferred the functions of the Federal Employment Stabilization Office of the Department of Commerce to the present Board.

The function of the National Planning Board had been to advise and assist the Public Works Administrator "through the preparation, development, and maintenance of comprehensive plans . . . through surveys and research . . . and through the analysis of projects for coördination and correlation of effort among the agencies of the Federal, State, and local Governments." [39] The second organization, the National Resources Board, was "to prepare and present to the President a program and plan of procedure dealing with the physical, social, governmental, and economic aspects of public policies for the development and use of land, water, and other national resources and such related subjects as may from time to time be referred to the Board by the President." This was a continuation in expanded form of the work of President Hoover's Research Committee on Social Trends. The two agencies just described were followed by the National Resources Committee (now renamed and transferred to the Executive Office of the President), one of whose principal continuing tasks was the encouragement of advance planning of public works and the outlining of a public-works policy which would fit the public construction program to cycles of business depression and boom, in order to assure the wisest use of the huge sums spent on public works each year.[40]

In accordance with the policy of urging the decentraliza-

[39] See the *Final Report* of the National Planning Board, August 1, 1934 (1935), for a useful discussion of planning in the United States and abroad.

[40] In this connection, it is of interest to note that the Committee's State Planning Consultant, Robert H. Randall, was the official American delegate to the preparatory conference of the International Public Works Committee of the I.L.O., held at Geneva in June, 1938.

tion of planning, the creation of state planning boards has been encouraged, and these now operate in forty-two states. Regional planning agencies have been established and the National Resources Planning Board maintains in the field nine regional planning offices, under the direction of regional chairmen and counselors.

The foregoing functions have made necessary, in a number of specific areas, research on water conservation and development, land-use and conservation, submarginal areas, resettlement policies, drainage and irrigation, soil erosion, farm tenancy, mineral policy, and other subjects. In performing its functions the Board seeks, in so far as possible, to proceed by liaison and by coördination of the activities of other agencies, and by suggestion to other agencies of researches to be undertaken, as when it mobilized the resources of the Department of Agriculture for the report of the President's Committee on Farm Tenancy. Where this has not been possible it has utilized its own resources in the task of research.

The Board operates through *ad hoc* mixed technical committees and a panel of consultants on part time service, both of which are served by a permanent technical staff which is an expert research and planning secretariat. The technical committees are usually composed of persons drawn from outside and inside the government; in the case of the Advisory Science Committee the members are designated by private scientific organizations. The technical committees are thus the means of establishing and maintaining liaison between government and private agencies, as well as providing coördination within the government itself. The Public

Works Committee and the State Planning Consultant, Robert H. Randall, perform the same office in respect to WPA and other works program agencies.

The technical committees are the following: land, water resources, energy resources,[41] public works, industrial (composed altogether of government officials),[42] and local planning. There has also been an Urbanism Committee. The committees organize and supervise the research projects of the Board, some of which are carried out by the Board's technical staff. The members of the Board and of its staff likewise maintain important liaison relationships between the Board and other government agencies. Mr. Delano serves on the Fiscal and Monetary Advisory Board which was established by the President in November, 1938, to advise with him in the development of a fiscal and monetary policy which will permit, among other things, the most effective use of public works expenditures and other governmental expenditures for the purpose of raising the national income to the capacity which our resources can sustain. The

[41] The successor to the Planning Committee on Mineral Policy of the National Resources Board. That committee was set up in connection with the work of the Science Advisory Board of the National Research Council of the National Academy of Sciences. See *Second Report of the Science Advisory Board* (1935), pp. 58 ff., 357 ff.

[42] The Board, in its *Progress Report for 1939*, p. 21, observes of the Industrial Committee that "it has provided a central point for the coördination of economic policies and actions of the various government departments whose economists are represented on it. Its activity has been particularly important to the work of the National Resources Committee in dealing with emerging economic problems . . . such as the size and timing of Government expenditures, the relationships between Government activity and private industrial activity, the methods of Government accounting and budgeting, size of relief needs, social security taxes and payments, the possibilities of self-liquidating public works, and the relationship between Government taxing policy, expenditure policy, and monetary policy."

National Resources Planning Board is also represented by Mr. Delano, who serves as observer, on the National Power Policy Committee. All of these activities culminate in, and contribute to making more effective, the Board's advisory functions.

For its work in correlating and encouraging planning activities of the Federal Government the National Resources Committee has developed technical committees and special investigating staffs. In order to understand public policies, it brings together the men in different departments of the Government and in the world of science and engineering, to collect into one place the facts that underlie each kind of public activity . . . All these different lines of information need to be laid out on the table . . . to see where they fit into the picture and affect one another . . .

Each Government office is not only provided with its own line of factual material; it is also entrusted by congressional authority with an administrative program . . . The operations of one department often develop those of another to some extent; sometimes their policies are in apparent conflict. Only by bringing the different programs into a single picture is it possible to find out where the duplications and conflicts are.[43]

. . . the Committee does not expect to be able to burst forth at any time with a perfected program for all governmental services, even for the Federal Government alone. It hopes only to be able to provide a background of coördinated knowledge that will make it easier for the President and Congress to judge the various proposed programs of action with which they have to deal.

Moreover, public policies are not made up entirely of scientific

[43] On one aspect of interagency coöperation, see Fesler's *The Loan of Expert Personnel Among Federal Agencies,* a report prepared for the National Resources Committee, September 9, 1935.

facts. Facts are only the background; they determine what lines of action are possible. The policies that will actually be adopted depend upon the desires of the people, modified by their understanding of the facts. The function of a National Resources Committee is therefore purely advisory . . . to present alternative lines of procedure from which the elected authorities of State or Nation can select the course they wish to follow.[44]

On June 24, 1940, the Board announced a reorientation of its activities to carry out the provisions of the Federal Employment Stabilization Act.[45] The statute requires the Board to aid in the preparation of six-year programs of public works and "to advise the President from time to time of the trend in employment and business activity and of the existence or approach of business depression and unemployment in the United States or in any substantial portion thereof." Executive Order No. 8455, relating to construction activities of Federal agencies, provides for advance planning of public works by the various construction agencies and the coördination of their plans by the Bureau of the Budget and the National Resources Planning Board. Class I agencies, which are those agencies concerned with actual Federal construction, must prepare and keep up to date six-year advance plans and programs of public works construction and submit such plans and programs annually to the Bureau of the Budget and the National Resources Planning Board. Class II agencies, which are those agencies concerned with Federal financial assistance, guarantees, and other aids

[44] National Resources Committee, *Planning Our Resources*, pp. 12–13.
[45] This was made necessary by the fact that the Independent Offices Appropriation Act, 1941, which provides $710,000 for the Board, stipulates that the money shall not be used for other purposes than those authorized by the Federal Employment Stabilization Act of February 10, 1931.

for construction by private agencies, must submit such reports as are requested by the National Resources Planning Board. The latter and the Bureau of the Budget will, each year when the budget is being prepared, develop an overall six-year public works program. To aid in the fulfillment of these duties, the Board will maintain a review staff to work in close collaboration with the Director of the Budget on the principal aspects of the public works program, related to land, water, transportation, and other public works. In fulfillment of its duty to advise the President of the trend in employment, and so forth, the Board will develop staff and coöperative arrangements with other governmental units concerned with problems in that field. The Board's Committee on Work Relief and Relief Policies has been at work in this field for some time.

The Board has not been conspicuous for its appreciation of the international setting of the problems with which it deals. While its annual reports indicate awareness of the relation between foreign and domestic problems, its researches have treated economic problems almost entirely without regard to international influences. So important a study as that on *Technological Trends and National Policy* offered little light on the international aspects of technological change and the profound effects of technological change on our international relations, and treated the subject, except for a few random references, as if it derived entirely from forces at work within our borders. The same deficiency appears in the work of many of the other committees, conspicuous exceptions being the work of the Land Planning Committee [46] and the Energy Resources Committee.

[46] See Part II of the *Supplementary Report of the Land Planning Committee to the National Resources Board.*

The researches of the Board are presented in two forms: full-length reports and popular summaries—a procedure which other agencies might well adopt.

BOARD OF GOVERNORS OF THE FEDERAL RESERVE SYSTEM

DIVISION OF RESEARCH AND STATISTICS

The research interests of the Division of Research and Statistics (E. A. Goldenweiser, Director) are closely integrated with the Board's functions of exercising control over rediscount rates, reserve ratios, open market operations, reserve and member bank examination, relations with foreign central banks, foreign branch banking, interlocking bank directorates, collateral lending, margin requirements and interest on time and savings deposits. Other research interests arise out of the relations of the Federal Reserve System with other fiscal agencies of government, in respect to the currency, the administration of the stabilization fund, the government depository functions of the Reserve Banks, and the financing of government bond issues.

The major units of the Division of Research and Statistics are Domestic Finance and Business, Monetary Problems, International Finance and Business, Open Market Operations and Capital Markets. The Domestic Finance Unit (Woodlief Thomas, Assistant Director, in charge) is divided into the following sections: (1) Federal Reserve Banks, (2) Bank Credit, (3) Banking Structure and Earnings, (4) Corporation Finance and Treasury Operations, and (5) Industry, Agriculture and Statistical Work of Federal Reserve Banks. The Domestic Business Unit (Frank

Garfield, Senior Economist, in charge) is concerned with industrial production. The Monetary Problems Unit (Emile Despres, Senior Economist, in charge) is concerned with special problems of research in money and credit and related economic developments, with governmental recovery measures, with taxation, with durable goods production, and with industrial price and labor policies. The International Finance Unit (W. R. Gardner, Senior Economist, in charge) studies central bank developments, money markets, foreign exchange, balance of payments, gold and silver, capital movements, world trade, commodity prices, international business conditions, and prepares the *Weekly Review of Periodicals*. The Open Market Operations Unit (L. M. Piser, Senior Economist, in charge) also studies treasury financing, questions arising in connection with the Federal Reserve System portfolio, and government security markets. The Capital Markets Unit (Miss Sue Burr, Senior Economist, in charge) studies problems of the private security markets.

The principal publication of the Division is the *Federal Reserve Bulletin,* a monthly, which, in addition to a regular review of business and credit developments, runs special articles embodying the results of the Division's studies and contains also the numerous indexes and statistical series maintained by the Board. The *Annual Report* of the Board contains important statistical and analytical material prepared by the Division of Research and Statistics. A mimeographed *Weekly Review of Periodicals* digests articles of importance drawn principally from various foreign journals.

While it is hardly possible to popularize the researches of the Division, a manual, *The Federal Reserve System—Its*

Purposes and Functions, published by the Board in 1939, endeavors to convey in non-technical language some understanding of the role of the Federal Reserve System. What is more important, with the January, 1940 issue of the *Bulletin,* a policy of publishing signed articles by members of the research staff was initiated. These interpret various aspects of the data in the Bulletin and analyze problems with which the Board is currently concerned.

United States Maritime Commission

The United States Maritime Commission was created by Act of Congress on June 29, 1936, as an independent promotional and regulatory agency to carry out the merchant marine policy laid down by Congress. The Commission took the place of the Shipping Board Bureau of the Department of Commerce and succeeded to all properties, including vessels, of the Bureau.

The Merchant Marine Act, 1936, makes the following declaration of national policy:

It is necessary for the national defense and development of its foreign and domestic commerce that the United States shall have a merchant marine (a) sufficient to carry its domestic waterborne commerce and a substantial portion of the water-borne export and import commerce of the United States and to provide shipping service on all routes essential for maintaining the flow of such domestic and foreign water-borne commerce at all times, (b) capable of serving as a naval and military auxiliary in time of war or national emergency, (c) owned and operated under the United States flag by citizens of the United States in-so-far as may be practicable, and (d) composed of the best-equipped, safest and most suitable types of vessels, constructed in the United States and manned with a trained and efficient citizen personnel. It is hereby declared to be the policy of the United States to foster the development and encourage the maintenance of such a merchant marine.

In order to give effect to the policy so declared, the Commission is empowered to grant so-called differential subsidies in aid of the construction and operation of American vessels.[47] If the differential subsidy method of encouraging the building of a merchant marine is found by the Commission to be inadequate, it may, with the President's approval, construct ships itself and charter them to a private operator under an operating subsidy.[48]

The Commission, which also possesses all the powers conferred by the Shipping Act of 1916, by the Merchant Marine Acts of 1920 and 1928, and by the Intercoastal Shipping Act of 1933, has extensive regulatory functions which concern rates, competitive practices, financial organization and operation of subsidized earners, employment and wage conditions, public safety, health and convenience, and standards of efficiency and performance.

It also has the broadest duties of investigation and research. The Merchant Marine Act of 1936 is quite excep-

[47] Construction subsidies may be granted only for the building of ships to be used in foreign commerce. The ocean mail contract method of subsidy was discontinued by the Act which required that existing contracts be terminated by June 30, 1937. The adjustment of claims of contract-holders was the Commission's principal preoccupation in its first year of existence. In all, 33 contracts were cancelled at a net cost to the government of approximately $1,000,000.

[48] The Commission has so found; its findings received Presidential approval on April 29, 1938.

tional in the specific character of its wide direction to the Commission concerning the investigations to be made by it as an aid in performing the functions described above.

The act directs the Maritime Commission "to make a survey of the American merchant marine, as it now exists, to determine what addition and replacements are required to carry forward the national policy" laid down in the statute. The Commission is "to study, perfect, and adopt a long-range program for replacements and additions to the American Merchant Marine."

Section 211 (a) of the act requires the Commission to determine "the ocean services, routes, and lines from . . . the United States . . . to foreign markets . . . essential for the promotion, development and maintenance of the foreign commerce of the United States."

In reaching its determination the Commission is instructed to

> . . . consider and give due weight to the cost of maintaining each of such steamship lines, the probability that any such line cannot be maintained except at a heavy loss disproportionate to the benefit accruing to foreign trade, the number of sailings and types of vessels that should be employed in such lines, and any other facts and conditions that a prudent businessman would consider when dealing with his own business, with the added consideration, however, of the intangible benefit the maintenance of any such line may afford to the foreign commerce of the United States and to the national defense.

If, in addition to the last instruction of the passage, Congress had directed the Commission to weigh the imponderable, its directions could hardly have made the Commission's task more difficult.

Other problems which the Commission is directed by the Act to study are:

1. The planning of better and safer vessels than now exist
2. American and foreign construction costs
3. American and foreign operating costs, broken down by items
4. The extent and character of foreign governmental aid and subsidies granted to other merchant marines and the effects on American services
5. American shipyards
6. Aircraft in overseas trade
7. Possible emergency aid to farmers and producers of coal, lumber and cement, through provision of vessel tonnage, rate reductions, etc.
8. New designs, new methods of construction, and new types of vessel equipment
9. The possibilities of promoting the carriage of American foreign trade in American vessels
10. Intercoastal and inland water transportation and their relation to transportation by land and air
11. Discriminatory rates, classifications, and practices
12. Recommendations for new legislation
13. Scrapping or removal from service of old or obsolete tonnage
14. Tramp shipping and the advisability of American citizens' participating in such service with American vessels
15. Relative ship construction or reconditioning costs in various sections of the United States, with a view to recommending how shipyards may "compete on an equalized basis"
16. Vessel and cargo movements in foreign and intercoastal trade

The Commission's Division of Research has rather piled Ossa on Pelion, when it lists, in an inter-office memorandum, the following factors among those "to be fully covered" in reports to the Commission in aid of its trade route determinations: [49]

1. World trade regions; trade routes in such world trade regions from various sections of the United States
2. Steamship services in each trade route (a) from the United States (b) from foreign countries; types of cargo and passenger vessels employed, foreign and American; proposed new vessel additions, American and foreign; service competition; projected services; unusual competition, fighting ships, rate wars, rebates; indirect competition; indirect routes to common foreign markets; trans-shipment services
3. Data necessary as to ports served
4. Commercial geography of countries of each region; enumeration by areas of commodities produced, mineral deposits, forests, agricultural areas, manufacturing, livestock and dairy areas; state of development of natural resources, by areas, potential future development, sources of imports of manufactures used in the development of resources, future import prospects, replacements of materials and equipment; ports to be used to serve various areas of development; productions of various countries for domestic use and for export; effect of development upon interchange of commodities with U.S.
5. Communications within foreign regions; coastwise by land and water; from ports to interior areas; railways, highways, airways; telephone, telegraph, radio, cables
6. Methods of handling foreign trade; free exchange, tariffs customs, barter and trade agreements; governmental participation in trade agreements; quotas and restrictions—

---

[49] United States Maritime Commission Division of Research: *Memorandum Outline of Factors for Consideration in Trade Route, Commerce and Economics Studies.* This list is somewhat abbreviated.

exports and imports; cartels; subsidies for exporters and importers; reciprocal trade agreements; laws, rules and regulations, of foreign countries and of United States affecting commerce

7. Banking facilities and credits—monetary systems; established banks and control—government or private, government and private; United States bank representatives and banking control of countries other than local; currency and exchange value; free markets; governmental control—decrees in effect; financing of external loans, cities, state, national; financing commercial transactions; relation of public debt to commercial credits; exports as basis of credits; credit practices of United States business vs. other foreign countries; effect of state governments upon credits and finance; documents used in financing commercial transactions; remittances, exchange permits, taxes on business

8. Passenger travel requirements between United States and various foreign regions

9. Shipping activities of various governments whose nationals operate in competitive foreign regions; shipping activities of government of regions served; aid to own nationals; aid to foreign shipping, subsidies, concessions, allowances for immigrant travel, preferential berthing arrangements; government-owned merchant marine services

10. Methods of controlling traffic, promotional publicity activities of foreign competitors; practice of agents and brokers; steamship conference activities in foreign regions

11. Volume of trade

12. Value of trade

13. Passenger statistics

14. Trends of commodity movements, changes in principal commodities; unusual commodity movements; seasonal and special contract movements of commodities. The cost of maintaining American flag vessels and the trend of revenues

and expenses of American and foreign vessels in such trade routes

DIVISION OF RESEARCH

The Division of Research (Alfred H. Haag, Director) is the chief research agency of the Commission. It compiles statistical information on the water-borne commerce of the United States and makes analytical studies of:

1. Construction and operating cost differentials existing between the United States and other world maritime powers
2. United States foreign trade routes, including studies leading to the determination of the essentiality of each route, prevailing economic and competitive conditions, and the evaluation of all other factors necessary to the complete study of trade routes
3. Government aids and subsidies granted or provided by foreign governments to their own shipping or that of other countries
4. Port surveys (published jointly with the Board of Engineers for Rivers and Harbors)
5. Coördination of shipping and aeronautic activities, with comparisons of the relative effects trans-oceanic aircraft may have on steamship services, and the possibility of substitution of heavier-than-air craft for superliner service
6. Maritime labor
7. Special studies of foreign shipping companies, and shipping policies

In view of the foregoing it is difficult to resist the conclusion that the Research Division's budget of $300,000 and its personnel of ninety-eight, large as they are, are not adequate to enable it to perform the duties of research imposed by the statute.

The other divisions of the Commission are also investigating agencies. The Divisions and their field of interest are: the Legal Division and the Division of Regulation (rates and services); Division of Operations and Traffic (operation of American vessels in foreign trade, assignment of vessels to various services, promotion of carriage in American ships, subsidy agreements, pools, conferences, and relationships between lines); Division of Insurance (insurance and reinsurance of hulls and cargoes in the American market); Technical Division (ship design and propulsion).

The Commission is represented in the Executive Committee on Commercial Policy and has many statutory and informal liaison relationships with other agencies.

United States Tariff Commission

The present Tariff Commission, established in 1916, is the first of its kind that has been relatively permanent. Previously, there had been six unsuccessful efforts to establish enduring fact-finding tariff machinery.[50] The career of the present Commission has also been attended by difficulties, for the administration that came to power in 1921 found the presence of Wilson appointees on the Commission embarrassing, especially after the introduction of the flexible rate provision of the 1922 Act (section 315).[51] A reorganization took place in 1930; and proposals to alter the functions of the Commission in relation to the tariff persist.[52]

[50] These efforts were made in 1865, 1866–1870, 1882, 1888–1889, 1909–1912, and 1912.

[51] See Larkin, *The President's Control of the Tariff* (1936), chap. I.

[52] On February 1, 1940, Senator Vandenberg introduced a bill (S. 3238, 76th Cong., 3d Sess.) to abolish the Tariff Commission and create instead a Foreign Trade Board with wide regulatory as well as advisory

Although the Commission has certain important administrative duties, it is primarily a fact-finding body. Research is its method of work as becomes clear when its statutory instructions are examined.

Section 332 (a) of the Tariff Act of 1930 makes it the duty of the Commission

. . . to investigate the administration and fiscal and industrial effects of the customs laws of this country now in force or which may be hereafter enacted, the relations between the rates of duty on raw materials and finished or partly finished products, the effects of ad valorem and specific duties and of compound specific and ad valorem duties, all questions relative to the arrangement of schedules and classification of articles in the several schedules of the customs law, and, in general, to investigate the operation of customs laws, including their relation to the Federal revenues, their effect upon the industries and labor of the country, and to submit reports of its investigations as hereafter provided.

Paragraph (d) of the same section makes it the duty of the Commission, in order that the President and Congress may secure information and assistance, to

1. Ascertain conversion costs and costs of production in the principal growing, producing, or manufacturing centers of the United States of articles of the United States, whenever in the opinion of the commission it is practicable
2. Ascertain conversion costs and costs of production in the principal growing, producing, or manufacturing centers of foreign countries of articles imported into the United States, whenever in the opinion of the commission such conversion costs or costs of production are necessary for comparison with

powers in the control of foreign trade and in which would be centralized all the government's foreign trade functions and services.

conversion costs or costs of production in the United States and can be reasonably ascertained

3. Select and describe articles which are representative of the classes or kinds of articles imported into the United States and which are similar to or comparable with articles of the United States; select and describe articles of the United States similar to or comparable with such imported articles; and obtain and file samples of articles so selected, whenever the commission deems it advisable

4. Ascertain import costs of such representative articles so selected

5. Ascertain the grower's, producer's, or manufacturer's selling prices in the principal growing, producing, or manufacturing centers of the United States of the articles of the United States so selected and

6. Ascertain all other facts which will show the differences in or which affect competition between articles of the United States and imported articles in the principal markets of the United States

Paragraphs (b) and (c) of the same section empower the Commission

. . . to investigate the tariff relations between the United States and foreign countries, commercial treaties, preferential provisions, economic alliances, the effect of export bounties and preferential transportation rates, the volume of importations compared with domestic production and consumption, and conditions, causes, and effects relating to competition of foreign industries with those of the United States, including dumping and cost of production.

The flexible tariff provision (Section 336) of the Act directs that at the request of the President, of either or both Houses of Congress, upon its own motion, or for "good and sufficient reason" shown upon application of any interested party, the Tariff Commission

. . . shall investigate the differences in the costs of production of any domestic article and of any like or similar foreign article. . . . If the Commission finds . . . that the duties expressly fixed by statute do not equalize the differences in the costs of production of the domestic . . . and the . . . foreign article when produced in the principal competing country, the commission shall specify . . . such increases or decreases in rates of duty . . . (including any necessary changes in classification) as it finds shown by the investigation to be necessary to equalize such differences. In no case shall the total increase or decrease of such rates of duty exceed 50 per centum of the rates expressly fixed by statute.

When differences can not be equalized by the foregoing method the Commission is to specify the ad valorem rates of duty based upon the American selling price (defined in section 402 [g]) of the domestic article, shown by the investigation to be necessary to equalize such differences. No decrease based on American selling price may exceed 50 percent of the statutory rates and no increase may be made. By proclamation the President is to approve the rates of duty and changes in classification and in basis of value [53] specified in any report of the Commission, "if in his judgment such rates of duty and changes are shown by such investigation of the Commission to be necessary to equalize such differences in costs of production." [54]

[53] A change in the basis of value permits an alteration in the *duty* collected far in excess of 50 percent. Cf. Larkin, *op. cit.*, pp. 78–88, where will also be found a discussion of the custom appraiser's discretion to take "United States value" as the basis for the assessment of duty.

[54] Section 336, (h) (4) reads: "The term 'cost of production,' when applied with respect to either a domestic article or a foreign article, in-

Section 337 empowers the Commission to investigate violations of the statutory prohibition against unfair practices in import trade, "the effect or tendency of which is to destroy or substantially injure an industry, efficiently and economically operated, in the United States, or to prevent the establishment of such an industry, or to restrain or monopolize trade and commerce in the United States . . ." [55] Section 338 directs the Commission "to ascertain and at all times to be informed" whether discriminations against American commerce are being practiced by foreign countries.[56]

---

cludes, for a period which is representative of conditions in production of the article: (A) The price or cost of materials, labor costs, and other direct charges incurred in the production of the article and in the processes or methods employed in its production; (B) the usual general expenses, including charges for depreciation or depletion which are representative of the equipment and property employed in the production of the article and charges for rent or interest which are representative of the cost of obtaining capital or instruments of production; and (C) the cost of containers and coverings of whatever nature, and other costs, charges, and expenses incident to placing the article in condition packed ready for delivery." Under par. 336 (e) (2), relating to production cost of foreign articles, if the cost of production "is not readily ascertainable, the Commission may accept as evidence thereof, or as supplemental thereto, the weighted average of the invoice, prices or values for a representative period and/or the average wholesale selling price for a representative period (which price shall be that at which the article is freely offered for sale to all purchases in the principal market or markets of the principal competing country or countries in the ordinary course of trade and in the usual wholesale quantities in such market or markets)." In ascertaining differences in costs of production the Commission is also to consider transportation costs and other costs of delivery and other relevant factors that constitute an advantage or disadvantage in competition. Cf. the definition of cost of production in section 402 (f) of the Tariff Act of 1930.

[55] When the existence of such unfair practices is established to the President's satisfaction, he "shall direct that the articles concerned . . . shall be excluded from entry"; Section 337 (e).

[56] The President is empowered by proclamation to impose new or additional duties not to exceed 50 percent on imports from the discriminating country and if, after such proclamation, the discrimination is persisted in, to exclude such imports altogether.

The so-called flexible tariff based on cost of production investigations was hailed in 1922 as introducing scientific tariff making. Since it is the President, however, who raises or lowers the rates, and since he is not bound by the conclusions of the Commission, changes in the tariff are still politically determined. The legislative history of the flexible tariff makes clear that it was introduced as part of a high tariff policy. The provision was a compromise with the House proposal to change the basis of valuation from foreign value to the American selling price—a proposal that would practically have prohibited imports. Professor Taussig has written that

. . . "Cost of production" is a slippery phrase. Costs differ in different establishments, and cannot be figured out accurately in any one establishment without an elaborate system of special accounts, such as few establishments keep. None the less, approximate figures are to be had. If the principle is sound, it will be of great service to have careful preparation for its application, and to reach the nearest approach to accuracy that the complexities of industry permit. To repeat—how far is it all worth while? . . .

Consider for a moment what equalization of cost of production means. The higher the expenses of an American producer, and the greater the excess of the expenses incurred by him over those incurred by a foreign competitor, the higher the duty. Applied unflinchingly, this means that the production of any and every thing is to be encouraged—not only encouraged but enabled to hold its own. If the difference in expenses, or cost, is great, the duty is to be high; if the difference is small, the duty is to be low. Automatically, the duty goes up in proportion as the American cost is large. If the article is tea in South Carolina, for example, ascertain how much more expensive it is to grow the trees and prepare the leaves than it is in Ceylon, and put on a duty high enough to offset. If it is hemp in Kentucky, ascertain how much more expensive it is to grow it than in Russia or in Yucatan (for the competing sisal), and equalize conditions with a high duty.

It was on this ground—though, to be sure, with gross exaggeration as to the facts—that the duties on lemons and prunes were raised in the Payne-Aldrich tariff: equalize conditions for the California lemon-growers! If lemons in California, why not grapes in Maine? They can be grown, if only the duties be made high enough. Obviously, the more unfavorable the conditions, the higher the duties must be. The climate of Maine is not favorable for grapes; they would have to be grown in hot-houses. But make the duty high enough, handicap the foreign producer up to the point of complete equalization, and the grapes can be grown. So as to Kentucky hemp, or Massachusetts pig-iron. Make your duty high enough—and on this principle you *must* make your duty high enough—and anything in the world can be produced. The inevitable consequence is, however, that the more unsuited the conditions are for efficient and economical production, the greater will be your effort to bring about protection. Under this equalizing principle, the worse the natural conditions, the more extreme will be the height of protection.[57]

But even if "cost of production" be taken as merely a convenient designation for the method of tariff fixing prescribed in the statute, it is proper to inquire what the effect of equalizing costs of production will be. Clearly, it will stop international trade since "the difference in money costs of production is the main cause of such trade."[58] Moreover, even if the statutory formula were sound, its application would

[57] Taussig, *Free Trade, The Tariff and Reciprocity* (1920), pp. 135–136.
[58] Larkin, *op. cit.*, p. 113.

be difficult because it leaves many things undetermined: which market shall be chosen as the chief competitive market in the United States; within what radius shall transportation costs be determined, what are representative costs, how shall joint costs be dealt with, and others. Finally, one problem is overlooked altogether: that costs determined as of one date may have no application to the situation that obtains when the investigation has been completed.[59]

The Tariff Commission's difficulties in ascertaining and comparing domestic and foreign costs were increased during the crisis years.[60] The Commission observed in its 1934 report that

. . . the rapid changes in the basic elements of costs, such as material, labor, and especially overhead expenses, which vary greatly with the volume of production, make it almost impossible to determine significant and representative costs in either domestic or foreign industries . . . the instability of international exchanges made comparison between domestic and foreign costs peculiarly difficult. The depreciation of the American dollar, in terms of the currencies of other countries, in the latter

---

[59] *Ibid.*, p. 115. For an excellent summary account of the difficulties encountered by the Commission in attempting to apply the vague and illusory standard of the Act, see pp. 117–31. I am indebted to Mr. George D. Watrous, Jr., of the Commission's staff, for the information that under the 1922 Act the average elapsed time between the date of institution of a rate investigation and the date when the Commission's report was transmitted to the President was 27 months. Under the 1930 Act it was one year. Under the 1930 Act it also took a little over a month more before the Presidential proclamation was issued.

[60] See Coulter, "The Tariff Commission and the Flexible Clause," *Proceedings of the Academy of Political Science*, June, 1933 (note that Mr. Coulter was formerly a Republican member of the Tariff Commission); see also memorandum on "Some Difficulties Encountered in Applying the Cost-of-Production Formula in Section 336 Investigations," *Hearings before the Senate Finance Committee on H.R. 8687*, 73d Cong., 2d Sess., p. 149; and Larkin, chap. VI.

part of the calendar year 1933 only added to the difficulties of international cost comparison.

The cost-of-production formula, even in its improved statement in the Tariff Act of 1930, does not permit of exact application, and its many uncertainties leave much room for the entrance of political judgment. In short, it is at best an imperfect and partial aid in the determination of one kind of tariff—a prohibitively high one. To be sure, the statute permits the formula to be used to lower tariffs, but its logic requires revision upward of all rates except those that are already higher than they need be to stop imports.

From 1922 to 1929, there were 83 investigations and 37 changes of duty by Presidential proclamation, 32 upward and 5 downward.[61] The value of the imports affected by increases was far greater than the value of the imports on which duties were reduced. The fluidity of this "scientific" mode of fixing the tariff was further illustrated by its subsequent history. Following the reorganization of the Commission by President Hoover under the 1930 Act, ninety-five investigations were ordered. Under the Roosevelt administration, nineteen more investigations were ordered from 1933 to 1937, and there has been none since.[62] This

[61] Two of the decreases affected live bob-white quail and paint brush handles.

[62] Of the 114 investigations ordered, 75 were completed, 54 before the end of President Hoover's term. The number of Hoover duty increases was 16, and of decreases, 20. The number of duty increases in the Roosevelt administration was 10 and the number of decreases was the same. There have been no changes under Section 336 since 1937. Cf. the nine investigations completed under Section 3 (e) of the National Industrial Recovery Act, which required the President, after investigation by the Commission, to limit by fee, quota, or other appropriate action, imports which endangered the National Industrial Recovery Program. The President's discretion extended only to the determination whether he should

result was to be expected since the formula is without value to an administration which seeks an increase of trade.

Under the Reciprocal Trade Agreements Act the operation of the flexible tariff provisions was suspended with respect to articles on which the United States concluded a foreign trade agreement. The enactment of the Reciprocal Trade Agreements Act may be said to mark the resumption by the Tariff Commission of the duties of scientific investigation from which it had been diverted by the cost equalization provisions of the 1922 and 1930 Tariff Acts.

The initiation of the Trade Agreements Program resulted in the practical cessation of rate investigations under section 336, because the Administration's plan of tariff bargaining looked to broader and more important factors than mere arbitrarily established differences in costs of production. Nevertheless, in view of prevalent emphasis on the principle that trade should be based upon the underlying

---

order an investigation. Once ordered, he was bound to act on the Commission's recommendations. In only one case, that of cotton rugs, was an import fee imposed. For the action taken in the other cases see *Nineteenth Annual Report of the United States Tariff Commission* (1935), pp. 16–17. Under sec. 22 of the Agricultural Adjustment Act, as amended, similar provision, limited to the imposition of import quotas, was made to safeguard the agricultural program. On January 15, 1940, sec. 22 was amended to permit the imposition of fees. The first investigation under this section was ordered in July, 1939, in connection with the cotton export subsidy plan. The Commission recommended the imposition of quotas on certain types of cotton and cotton wastes, and the quotas were proclaimed, effective September 20, 1939. A second investigation relating to wheat was ordered in December, 1939, and is now in progress. By Act of Congress (Public 698, 76th Congress, July 1, 1940), the Commission was directed to determine whether, in 1939, red cedar shingles imported for consumption or withdrawn from warehouse for consumption exceeded 30 percent of combined imports and domestic shipments. On approval of its report by the President a duty of 25 cents per square was to be imposed on the excess. Red cedar shingles have repeatedly been the subject of investigation by the Commission. Crabmeat imports are being studied.

physical and industrial structure of the national economy, the cost studies remained of considerable importance in the industrial surveys subsequently undertaken by the Commission in aid of the new method of tariff making. Thus, the experience gained from the enormous effort put forth in attempts to apply the pseudo-scientific cost equalization formula was used to great advantage.

It is surely no injustice to those charged with the conduct of the Trade Agreements Program to say that to date their major achievement has been not in the restoration of international trade but in the establishment of a new method of tariff making free from the defects that attended the periodic legislative revisions of the tariff. The transfer of tariff revision by Congress to the Executive does not of itself assure a "scientific" tariff, as experience with Section 336 well shows. But when the context of that transfer, as in the case of the Reciprocal Trade Agreements Act, is the restoration of international trade rather than the single-minded protection of special producer interests, the first step toward tariff-making based on relatively sound economic principles and framed in the national interest has been taken.

The role of the Tariff Commission has been changed since 1933 from one of technical commodity research, commodity by commodity, to one of economic research into the problems of industry. It is no longer exclusively concerned with producer interest as such, but studies the relation of that interest to the national welfare as focused in the problem of dealing with the competitive impact between imports and domestic products. Thus the view taken is a larger one which includes the general competitive situation of entire industries and permits the weighing of such questions as whether an industry is on an export or import basis, whether the level of production is increasing or decreasing, how wage levels are related to the competitive situation of the industry, and what is the cost to the community of carrying the industry along by means of tariff protection.

The Tariff Commission's work in connection with the trade agreements program concerns principally the import side of that program, and its functions are much the same as they were when it prepared the *Summaries of Tariff Information* for Congress to use in its tariff revisions in 1922 and 1930. The *Summaries of Tariff Information*, which are no longer published as such, but are kept in manuscript form in order that they may be more easily revised and drawn on in current foreign trade work, are described by the Commission as follows: [63]

In general, each summary covers a commodity, or a group of related commodities, specifically mentioned in the tariff act, whether dutiable or free. The tariff paragraph of the act of 1930 is quoted in substantial detail and a comparison is made with the rates of duty under the acts of 1922 and 1913, with any interim changes under section 336 or other provisions of law. After the rates of duty come a description of the article and a statement of its uses; these are brief when the facts are generally known but necessarily more extended and carefully worded for less well-known products. Then follows a condensed summary of statistics of production, imports, and exports of the article. After this is a detailed section on domestic production in which the available information for a number of years is reviewed, special grades and types are segregated, and the geographical location of the producing units is discussed with special reference to the tariff.

---

[63] *Nineteenth Annual Report of Tariff Commission* (1935), pp. 4–5.

The size of the producing units and the degree of competition among them often become important in the production analysis. Closely related to the description of domestic production is the section on foreign production, with a statement as to grades and types actually exported to the United States and the degree of competition of these grades with similar American products, as well as of grades and types which might be exported to this country under a lower rate of duty.

Next comes a detailed analysis of imports covering a number of years; first in totals by quantity, value, unit value, with rates of duty, then by countries of origin, and sometimes by ports of entry in the United States. This must often be followed by a breakdown of the import statistics by grades and by seasons and months if these are significant. In the case of fresh vegetables, for example, the monthly or seasonal imports from the various countries of origin are of decisive importance.

Exports are similarly analyzed with special reference to principal countries of destination and the geographical origin of the exported products within the United States.

After the production, import, and export data are sections covering special problems concerning the commodity, such as the effect of depreciated exchange on the trade with certain countries, problems of transportation or marketing when these are important, and when available cost-of-production data, both foreign and domestic.

Toward the end of each summary is a section on competitive conditions, in which are set forth clearly but briefly the peculiar competitive problems affecting the particular commodity. In cotton textiles, for example, it is shown that certain types of products meet little direct competition from abroad, that other types meet it in a small way from a number of countries, and that for some competition may be severe. For example, in recent months imports of some cotton fabrics well within the competitive range of domestic products have been increasing from Japan, whereas from other countries, notably England, imports of cotton fabrics have been declining. In this important section of the summaries, use is made not only of the statistics set forth in earlier sections but of all information obtained by direct contact of the Commission and its staff with the producing and importing interests.

The summaries conclude with a résumé of important legal decisions which are pertinent to the particular product under consideration.

The *Summaries* provide the basic information needed in the analysis of the recurring import problems involved in trade agreements work. These are

1. The economic and technical history of important industries possibly to be affected by tariff concessions on imports; this economic and financial situation with particular reference to the members employed in the industry, the wages paid, capital and profits

2. Commodity import trends in relation to domestic production

3. Production trends and competitive position of domestic commodities likely to be affected by imports

4. Present tariff treatment

5. Producer interests likely to be affected by tariff changes

6. Consumer interests likely to be affected by tariff changes

7. Sources of imports with a view to calculating the benefits of generalization of any concessions that may be made [64]

The relation of the cost investigations of the Commission to its current work is analyzed as follows by the Commission: [65]

---

[64] Tasca, *The Reciprocal Trade Policy of the United States* (1938), pp. 57–58. With these standards compare those prescribed by the Board of Trade for the inquiries to be made in connection with duties proposed for the safeguarding of industries, memorandum of February, 1925 (Cmd. 2327).

[65] *Twentieth Annual Report of Tariff Commission* (1936), pp. 5–6.

. . . The work under the "flexible" provision may be looked upon as a special phase of the Tariff Commission's duties. Its significance lies not only in its being an experiment in tariff administration under a rule prescribed by the Congress but in the effect which the thorough-going cost investigations have in broadening the Commission's comprehension of the essential problems involved in the competition between domestic and foreign products and in the adjustment of tariff rates.

Regardless of the success or failure of the "flexible" provision as a method of adjusting tariff rates, the experience of thoroughly investigating industries affected by tariffs and their cost situations has been invaluable to the Commission. Through these investigations, the Commission and its staff have come in direct contact with the fundamental problems of tariff making and have gained a comprehension of their ramifications. In consequence, much has been learned about the character and the range and variety of information needed for the intelligent formulation of tariff policies and the adjustment of tariff rates.

More and more the commodity study of the Commission has become a means to larger economic analysis. Costs of production studies have become studies of the trend of production costs by industries. Regional cost variations in the United States are analyzed and comparisons are made between costs trends in the United States and abroad on the basis of data supplied by American producers having foreign plants.

Two important developments in the Commission's work have been its industry surveys and its commercial policy studies.[66]

[66] Much of the Commission's work in the years from 1916 to 1921 was devoted to studies of foreign tariffs and tariff policies, such as most-favored-nation agreements, tariff bargaining, and discriminatory preferential tariffs. Some of the reports then made have become classic in the

Of the industry surveys the Commission observes: [67]

The character of information developed incidental to the revision of the summaries of tariff information for trade negotiations has drawn the attention of the Commission to an aspect of its primary function hitherto only slightly developed, namely, a study of the relationships of tariff rates on raw materials to those on finished products and of tariff rates on articles otherwise closely related. In consequence a new program of preparing more comprehensive industry surveys is being initiated as intensively as present resources and pressure from more direct demands will permit. In the new series special emphasis is being laid upon the interrelations of related or competing commodities and of the industries which produce them, and the needs for coördinating the tariff treatment applied to them. While it is believed that the structure of compensatory tariffs for most of the obvious cases of interdependent industries, such as basic raw materials and their manufactures, is reasonably well adjusted, there are unquestionably a number of instances wherein the relationships have been altered by modernization of production methods and the like. Also there are many relationships growing out of industrial and marketing integrations and the substitution of one product for another which are not so obvious but which may require coördination no less.

Concerning the commercial policies studies the Commission observes:

---

literature. Among these are the studies of *Colonial Tariff Policies* (1922) and *Reciprocity and Commercial Treaties* (1919). To judge by the influence of the latter report in bringing about the adoption of the unconditional most-favored-nation policy in 1923, the course of commercial history might have been far happier had the Commission been permitted to continue its work along that line instead of being diverted to rate investigations.

[67] *Twentieth Annual Report of Tariff Commission* (1936), p. 7.

In the wake of the many changes that have occurred during the depression in the commercial policies of foreign countries, new methods of controlling imports have developed. Chief among these are exchange controls, quotas, and clearing agreements. These new methods have, of course, had repercussions upon the policy of most-favored-nation treatment—a situation that has led the Commission to give increased attention to questions of foreign trade policy.

The circumstances requiring renewed attention to problems of commercial policy described by the Commission lend added weight to its statement concerning the need for objective methods of tariff making.[68]

Today's need for an authoritative source of impartial yet comprehensive information for tariff purposes is probably greater than ever before. Tariff making under conditions prevailing throughout the world at the present time has become a complex matter even for experts of long experience. Under present conditions changes in rates not only affect the flow of trade in the specified commodities but are likely to draw more remote reprisals in the form of trade restrictions affecting other products or in fact the whole trade with particular countries. The tendency is for the repercussions and reverberations of any national action for trade control to become promptly world-wide.

Tariff making has benefited too greatly from the application of objective methods of approach based on comprehensive summaries of facts for such methods to be abandoned. They are not only practical and expedient, they are essential. Twenty years of specialization in this field by the Tariff Commission have provided it not only with an accumulation of resources but with an organization flexible enough to meet or anticipate the demands of changing times and to offer solutions based on experience and

---

[68] *Ibid.*, p. 8.

on authentic knowledge. All of these resources the Tariff Commission makes available to those interested in tariff problems.

The foregoing needs merely to be underlined. Tariff-making is less than ever a matter of mere domestic concern; it is a part of commercial policy, that is to say, of our foreign policy, and, consequently, produces effects outside our borders which react on us. However much the lawyers may say that the tariff falls within the sphere of domestic jurisdiction, it is yet inescapable that the exercise of such an instrument for the direction and control of trade, if effected with little regard to the influence of that instrument on the fortunes of other nations, has inevitable repercussions in economic distress at home and abroad, and may help bring political disaster as well. In the contracting and increasingly interdependent modern world, tariff action requires such study as no legislature can give it. Tariff making is a matter of policy, but if that policy is one of good will, it requires the aid of such an instrument for the examination of the problems involved as the Tariff Commission and, indeed, the whole trade agreements organization provide.[69]

The annual appropriation of the Commission is in the neighborhood of $900,000, practically all of which is spent for research. The research of the Commission is planned

[69] Unhappily, as is shown by the recent testimony of members of the Administration before the House Ways and Means Committee on the extension of the reciprocal trade agreements act, it is still necessary to defend the trade agreements program on mercantilistic lines. The actual work of the trade agreements organization shows a full understanding of the requirements of our international net creditor position, but there can be no doubt that its efforts have been much limited by the need to propitiate traditional attitudes and opinions concerning the tariff.

and reviewed by a Planning and Reviewing Committee composed of a chairman, Mark A. Smith, and three permanent members, namely, the Chief of the Technical Service (Eben M. Whitcomb), the Chief of the Economics Division (Howard S. Piquet), and the Assistant Chief (Loyle A. Morrison) of that Division. When their services are required, others participate in the work of the Planning and Reviewing Committee. There is also a Special Adviser on International Trade Policies (Benjamin B. Wallace).

The research of the Commission is carried on principally in the Economics Division and the Technical Service. The former is divided into an international relations section and an editorial section. The latter embraces seven commodity divisions: Agricultural (O. A. Juve, Chief), Ceramics (Frederick L. Koch, Chief), Lumber and Paper (Franklin H. Smith, Chief), Metals (F. Morton Leonard, Chief), Textiles (W. A. Graham Clark, Chief), Sundries (Louis S. Ballif, Chief). The Accounting Division (Howard F. Barker, Chief), Distribution and Markets Division (Robert C. King, Chief), and Statistical Division (Arthur E. Woody, Chief) are directed by the chairman of the Planning and Reviewing Committee, who also supervises the investigational work of the field office maintained by the Commission in New York. Continuing WPA project staffs are also maintained in Richmond, Washington, and New York.

As of October 31, 1939, the professional members of the staff numbered 139. There were 22 accountants, 1 marine and foreign transportation specialist, 1 distribution and traffic analyst, 47 commodity specialists, 33 economists, 10 commercial policy analysts. The rest are supervisory officers in one division or another. As in other branches of the government, the library (Cornelia Notz, Librarian) is an active research adjunct.

Non-commodity research assignments, such as commercial policy studies, are usually carried out by members of the economics division working in pairs under a senior economist or division chief or a survey committee. Commodity surveys are usually conducted by a commodity specialist and an economist in collaboration. For most of these the survey committee acts as adviser. This method of work is also used in the preparation of the Commission's reports for the trade agreements country committees. Thus a commodity specialist will write an analysis of the import situation relating to steel bars, and a member of the economics division will review the analysis with him. The result is that the industrial and broader economic points of view are blended in these studies.

The Tariff Commission is represented on the following interdepartmental committees: the Executive Committee on Commercial Policy, the Executive Committee on Trade Agreements and its country sub-committees, the Committee for Reciprocity Information (the Chairman and Vice-Chairman of which are members of the Tariff Commission) and its sub-committees, interdepartmental committees on coöperation with American Republics,[70] sub-committees of the Army and Navy Munitions Board, interdepartmental committees on Philippine affairs, and others.

Section 334 of the Tariff Act requires the Commission in appropriate matters to act in conjunction and coöperation with other agencies of government, and this is the statutory

[70] Public, No. 545, May 25, 1938; Public, No. 63, May 3, 1939.

basis for a large volume of interchange of services between the Commission and other government agencies. In the past year, one of the Commissioners and two members of the staff of the Commission have been detailed to various economic missions in South America under the government's program of coöperation with the American Republics. The Commission's staff is now giving considerable assistance to the new Defense Advisory Commission. The Chief of the Economics Division is on temporary part-time detail with the Defense Advisory Commission's Bureau of Research and Statistics as is one of the Tariff Commission's senior economists. Others serve from time to time on special jobs.

FEDERAL TRADE COMMISSION

The Federal Trade Commission is the authority having the most general control over business and industry. Its jurisdiction is defined in five statutes: (1) the Federal Trade Commission Act, (2) the Sherman Act as amended by the Miller-Tydings Act, (3) the Clayton Act, (4) the Export Trade (Webb-Pomerene) Act, and (5) the Robinson-Patman Act. The Commission is directed to prevent unfair competition and unfair or deceptive acts or practices in commerce. It is also empowered to gather information concerning, and to investigate the organization, business, conduct, practices, and management of, corporations engaged in commerce, their relations to other business enterprises, and trade conditions in and with foreign countries "when associations, combinations, or practices of manufacturers, merchants, or traders, or other conditions, may affect the foreign trade of the United States."

The Webb-Pomerene law was passed in 1918 to promote

foreign trade by exempting associations organized to engage exclusively in foreign trade from the anti-trust laws. The Commission's functions in relation to the Webb law groups are regulatory rather than promotional. The export associations are required to file with the Commission various papers at the time of their formation and annually thereafter. They must also furnish such information as the Commission may require concerning their organization, business, conduct, practices, management, and relation to other associations, corporations, partnerships, and individuals. The Commission's supervisory powers in respect of Webb law groups relate to acts done by them within the United States or elsewhere which are in "restraint of trade within the United States or in restraint of the export trade of any domestic competitor or . . . which artificially or intentionally enhances or depresses prices within the United States of commodities of the class exported by such association, or . . . substantially lessens competition within the United States or otherwise restrains trade therein . . ." If the Commission concludes that the law has been violated by the doing of any of these forbidden acts, it "may make to the association recommendation for the readjustment of its business, in order that it may thereafter maintain its organization and management and conduct its business in accordance with law." [71] On the failure of the association to comply with such recommendations the matter is referred to the Attorney General for action.

[71] Advice and recommendations have been made without formal complaint or public hearings. The first formal "recommendations for readjustment" appear to have been those issued on January 27, 1940, in the case of *Pacific Forest Industries*, an export trade association engaged in export sales of Douglas fir plywood.

EXPORT TRADE SECTION

The export trade activities are carried on by the Export Trade Section (Miss Ellen L. Love, Chief) which is part of the office of the Chief Counsel (William I. Kelley). The export trade work was, from 1919 to 1927, carried on by an Export Trade Division of which William F. Notz was in charge. A reduction in the Commission's appropriation in the latter year resulted in the abolition of that Division. The work formerly conducted by it was then turned over to the present Export Trade Section under the direction of the Chief Counsel.

As of June 30, 1939, 43 export associations were registered with the Commission. These associations represented 425 enterprises. Total exports of these groups in 1938 were $161,244,820. In 1929 they exceeded $700,000,000.

While the Federal Trade Commission is thus charged with the regulation of the export trade associations, the promotion of the organization of such associations has been assumed by the Department of Commerce and, particularly, by the Division of Commercial Laws of the Bureau of Foreign and Domestic Commerce. It is worthy of note that there has never been a comprehensive inquiry by the Federal Trade Commission or by the Department of Commerce into the experience of the export trade associations.[72]

[72] Such an inquiry has now been made by the Department of Commerce for the Temporary National Economic Committee as part of its study of trade associations. There has been some reluctance on the part of the associations to coöperate. See Temporary National Economic Committee Release No. C. 4, May 3, 1939. The Federal Trade Commission contributed a historical statement to the study. See also Barnes, *Government Promotion of Foreign Trade in the United States* (1933), pp. 20 ff.

ECONOMIC DIVISION

It is the Economic Division (William H. England, Chief Economist) which carries the major part of the Commission's work of economic investigation. The Economic Division has been little concerned with problems of international trade. Its function has been to implement the Commission's duty of maintaining competition by investigating the conduct of business and by giving "pitiless publicity" to the results of such investigation.

Prior to the Federal Trade Commission Act, competitive conditions could be maintained only by the use of common law remedies against restraint of trade or through institution by the Department of Justice of proceedings under the Sherman Act against combinations in restraint of trade. The object of the Sherman Act was to prevent monopoly. Since, however, monopoly came about not only through such combinations but also through unfair methods of competition it was necessary to make provision against these. The Federal Trade Commission was given two weapons against them: (1) the power to issue cease and desist orders against various acts prohibited by the Federal Trade Commission Act and the Clayton Act; and (2) the power to investigate the conduct of business and publish its findings.[73] The theory underlying the grant to the Commission of the power to investigate was that by investigation of the circumstances impeding competition and by giving publicity to the findings

[73] Blaisdell, *The Federal Trade Commission* (1932), chaps. V–VII. These chapters constitute a valuable case study in the relationship between economic investigation and policy enforcement. The description of the Commission's functions of economic investigation is based on Blaisdell's work.

the public would know what was needed to make conditions in the market more nearly approximate the ideal of free competition. Moreover, investigation and publicity would contribute to the restoration of conditions of free competition by making available current data concerning prices, profits, output, stocks, orders, shipments, and general business conditions.[74] In addition to data concerning market conditions the Commission has sought information concerning the industrial conditions in which competition is carried on, for example: forms of business organization, trading customs, business methods, indications of industrial concentration (such as percentages of control, ownership of patents, relation of size and efficiency, vertical integration, trade associations, and the relation of financial management and control to operations). The Commission has had to investigate every phase of the industrial process—sources and nature of raw materials; technology; financing, investment, and profits; organization, ownership, size, and capacity; costs of production; market organization and distribution processes; price quotations and trends; forms of contract;

[74] "Under present conditions sellers are apt to be more adequately informed in such matters than buyers. Some trade associations already provide their members with such information. Trade and business journals contain valuable data. Many large businesses have special employees to collect information from a wide range of sources. But data made public by private organizations are open to suspicion. Too often materials purporting to be honest statements of facts have been 'inspired.' Informed persons are apt to view all such material skeptically. Uninformed persons, who have the greatest need for the information, are most apt to be misled. The dissemination of accurate information may well be regarded as a governmental function. The Bureau of the Census, the Federal Reserve Board, the Departments of Commerce and Agriculture, as well as other governmental boards and commissions already issue masses of data. The Federal Trade Commission has conceived that it also should add to this information." Blaisdell, *op. cit.*, pp. 113-14.

and wages and working conditions. The Commission's investigations have furnished the seed for many activities now undertaken by other agencies. It pioneered in the field of cost accounting, now so important a part of the regulatory work of such an agency as the Securities and Exchange Commission,[75] and in the educational work undertaken lately by the Department of Commerce among small businessmen. The Commission's cost of production data were basic in the price determinations of government agencies during the war. Its investigation of the grain trade was responsible for the legislation placing the trading in grain futures under the supervision of the Department of Agriculture. Its monumental investigation of the public utilities was the basis for much regulatory legislation after 1933. Commissioner Garland S. Ferguson declares that "the Commission has investigated or studied practically every line of business activity in the country."

The Commission has made little use of its powers under section 6 (h) of the Federal Trade Commission Act to investigate trade conditions in and with foreign countries, although one of the first investigations by the Commission was an inquiry in 1916 into the reasons for the high cost of binder twine which involved the study of the regulation by the government of the State of Yucatan of the production and marketing of sisal. One reason for the meagerness of this branch of the Commission's work appears to be that the study of foreign trade conditions has been carried on not by the Economic Division but by the Export Trade Section which has neither funds nor personnel for adequate investi-

[75] See *Fifth Annual Report of the Securities and Exchange Commission* (1940), pp. 117-21.

gation along this line. Except for two valuable reports on anti-dumping regulations,[76] the Export Trade Section has been obliged to content itself with publishing in the Annual Reports of the Commission a few pages of summaries of foreign legislation affecting trade.

TEMPORARY NATIONAL ECONOMIC COMMITTEE

The Temporary National Economic Committee (Senator Joseph C. O'Mahoney, Chairman) was established by Joint Resolution of Congress, approved June 16, 1938 (Public No. 113, 75th Congress), to make

. . . a full and complete study and investigation with respect to . . . monopoly and the concentration of economic power in and financial control over production and distribution of goods and services . . . with a view to determining, but without limitation, (1) the causes of such concentration and control and their effect upon competition; (2) the effect of the existing price system and the price policies of industry upon the general level of trade, upon employment, upon long-term profits, and upon consumption; and (3) the effect of existing tax, patent, and other Government policies upon competition, price levels, unemployment, profits, and consumption; and shall investigate the subject of governmental adjustment of the purchasing power of the dollar so as to obtain 1926 commodity price levels; and (b) To make recommendations to Congress with respect to legislation upon the foregoing subjects, including the improvement of anti-trust policy and procedure and the establishment of national standards for corporations engaged in commerce among the States and with foreign nations.

---

[76] See below, p. 272.

The Committee is composed of three members of the Senate, three members of the House, and one representative of each of the following: Department of Justice, Department of the Treasury, Department of Labor, Department of Commerce, Securities and Exchange Commission, and the Federal Trade Commission. Other agencies have also coöperated; for example, the Tariff Commission, the Marketing Laws Survey of WPA, and others. An initial appropriation of $500,000 for expenses of investigation has since been supplemented by a further grant of $510,000.

Leon Henderson was, until his appointment as a member of the Securities and Exchange Commission, Executive Secretary of the Committee. His successor was James R. Brackett, who was succeeded in July, 1940, by Dewey Anderson. The Committee's Economic Adviser until September, 1940, was Theodore J. Kreps of Stanford University.

The research of the Committee is conducted by the several government agencies represented on it. The member agencies make their several investigations and present the results at public hearings for which the researches constitute a preparation. At the hearings government officials, businessmen, economists, and others testify.

The public hearings of the Temporary National Economic Committee opened in December, 1938, with a three-day factual survey of the problems of the national economy. Mr. Lubin of the Bureau of Labor Statistics, Mr. Thorp of the Department of Commerce, and Mr. Henderson, then executive secretary of the Committee, described the failure of the national economy to produce enough goods and services since 1929 to maintain an adequate standard of living for the American people, analyzed the structure of the

American economic system, and listed some of the problems for which the Committee would seek an answer. Mr. Henderson set forth the main lines of study at the hearing on December 3, 1938, as follows:

A. Concentration and control
B. Price system and price policies
C. Effect of Government policies
    1. Specific policies; as named by resolution
        (a) Taxation
        (b) Patents, pools, specific abuses
        (c) Adjustment of purchasing power to 1926 level
    2. Government policies not specifically named by resolution
        (a) Compensatory fiscal policies
        (b) Governmental Intervention
        (c) Foreign Trade, reciprocal trade agreements
        (d) Agricultural program
        (e) Housing
        (f) Governmental regulation
        (g) Social Security
        (h) Results of other legislative committee studies: Munitions, holding companies, etc.
D. Bureau of Industrial Economics
E. Socially and economically harmful competition
F. Improvement of antitrust policy and procedure
G. National standards for corporations
H. Mergers, interlocking relationships, industrial, utility and bank holding companies, investment trusts
I. Insurance companies
J. Corporate practices
K. Distribution, Marketing Laws
L. Credit mechanism for Small Enterprises
M. Over-all economic data and special studies

Publication of the hearings of the Committee was begun at the end of April, 1939, under the omnibus title: *Investigation of Concentration of Economic Power*. Fourteen parts had been published by June, 1940, and there has been a flood of fugitive mimeographed material.

The parts published thus far are: Part 1: *Economic Prologue* (December 1–3, 1938), Part 2: *Patents—Automobile Industry, Glass Container Industry* (December 5–16, 1938), Part 3: *Patents-Proposals for Changes in Law and Procedure* (January 16–20, 1939), Part 4: *Life Insurance* (February 6–17, 1939), Part 5: *Monopolistic Practices in Industries—Development of the Beryllium Industry* (February 28, March 1–8, 14, May 8–9, 1939), Part 5A: *Federal Trade Commission Report on Monopolistic Practices in Industries* (March 2, 1939), Part 6: *Liquor Industry* (March 14–17, 1939), Part 7: *Milk Industry—Poultry Industry* (March 9–11, May 1–3, 1939), Part 8: *Problems of the Consumer* (May 10–12, 1939), Part 9: *Savings and Investment* (May 16–26, 1939), Part 10: *Life Insurance* (June 6–21, 1939), Part 11: *Construction Industry* (June 27–July 14, 1939), Part 12: *Industrial Insurance* (August 23–September 7, 1939), Part 13: *Life Insurance* (September 11–December 22, 1939), Part 14: *Petroleum Industry* (September 25–30, 1939).[77] A brief preliminary report to Congress was made in July, 1939 (76th Congress, 1st Session, Senate Document No. 95).

The Committee is required by Section 4 of the act to submit its final reports before the termination of the 76th Congress (1940). A brief preliminary report in the form of a

[77] The hearings on the Petroleum Industry are contained in four volumes, Parts 14–17. The Executive Secretary of the Committee has issued a tentative list of the hearings and monographs to be published.

letter from the chairman was transmitted to Congress in July, 1939 (76th Congress, 1st Session, Senate Document No. 95). Senator O'Mahoney announced on February 7, 1940, that the Committee "expects to complete hearings and research by about June 1, 1940, and thereafter to carry out a thorough job of analysis and summarization of the hearings and reports which are expected to run to some 80 volumes." The final hearings will be "a general economic 'free-for-all'" at which employers, employees, the investing public, and the public generally will have an opportunity to be heard, after which the final report will be drawn up. Some of the studies made for the Committee will be published by the agencies making them, although most of the material will be published by the Committee itself in a monograph series.

Federal Works Agency

WORK PROJECTS ADMINISTRATION

The Work Projects Administration was formerly the Works Progress Administration which was created by Executive Order No. 7034 of May 6, 1935, under the authority of the Emergency Relief Appropriation Act of 1935 (since extended by successive annual Acts). Under the President's Reorganization Plan No. I, the Works Progress Administration was consolidated under changed name together with other agencies in the Federal Works Agency.

WPA operates, in coöperation with local, state, and Federal sponsors, a program of useful public work projects to aid needy unemployed persons by providing work on such projects. Projects might formerly be sponsored by WPA itself; all projects must now be independently sponsored.

As the three volume WPA *Index of Research Projects* shows, many research programs have been sponsored by Federal, state, and local agencies and have qualified as useful public works projects. Some of the projects formerly sponsored by WPA have now been transferred to other sponsorship in order to comply with the changed requirements of the law. WPA resources of funds and personnel have been a major source of aid to other Federal agencies in the conduct of researches which their own limitations of funds and personnel prevented them from undertaking unaided. Under the 1939 Emergency Relief Appropriation Act the Commissioner of Work Projects is authorized to allocate to other Federal agencies an amount not to exceed $60,000,000 for the purpose of operating projects of the types specified for the Work Projects Administration.

The Division of Research, formerly the Division of Social Research (Howard B. Myers, Director), conducts nonsponsored researches which are directly related to problems of relief. They include the collection and analysis of economic and social data as the basis for development of principles and policies for the unemployment relief program and the collection and analysis of data pertinent to operating problems. The first type of activity involves general studies in the fields of unemployment and dependency. The general studies are published in the form of monographs. In addition, the Division has begun to issue popular presentations of research data in pamphlet form.[78]

[78] Four of these have been issued to date. A list of researches completed under WPA auspices may be found in *Subject Index of Research Bulletins and Monographs issued by Federal Emergency Relief Administration and Works Progress Administration Division of Social Research,* September, 1937; *Catalog of Research Bulletins issued by WPA,* October,

Some of the studies made by WPA bear quite directly on the international economic relations of the United States. Such are the technological and the state trade barrier studies described in Part II.

SECURITIES AND EXCHANGE COMMISSION

The Securities and Exchange Commission was established by the Securities and Exchange Act of 1934 and took over from the Federal Trade Commission the administration of the Securities Act of 1933. The Commission supervises the registration of new issues of securities and regulates practices in the sale of securities under the 1933 Act.[79] It supervises and regulates transactions and trading in outstanding securities on the stock exchanges and in over-the-counter markets, regulates public utility holding companies, prepares advis-

---

1938; and in *Index of Research Projects* (3 vols.) edited by Harold R. Hosea. Each of these is published by WPA.

[79] Title II of the Securities Act of 1933 created a "Corporation of Foreign Security Holders" for the purpose of "protecting, conserving, and advancing the interests of the holders of foreign securities in default." Sec. 210 of the act made it unlawful for the Corporation to represent that it acted or spoke for the Department of State or the United States government or to do anything "which could interfere with or obstruct or hinder or which might be calculated to obstruct, hinder or interfere with the policy or policies of the said Department of State or the Government of the United States or any pending or contemplated diplomatic negotiations, arrangements, business or exchanges between the Government of the United States or said Department of State and any foreign government or any political subdivision thereof." Title II was not to take effect until proclaimed by the President. The difficulties in the establishment of a government corporation to represent holders of foreign securities foreseen by sec. 210 could not be overcome. Instead a private organization, Foreign Bondholders' Protective Council, Inc., was set up over which the Department of State and the Securities and Exchange Commission have certain visitorial powers.

ory reports on corporate reorganization plans, participates as a party in the judicial proceedings concerning such plans under the Bankruptcy Act, supervises the trust indentures used in public offerings of new security issues, and regulates investment companies and investment advisers in accordance with the act of August 22, 1940.

In the course of registration with the Commission of security issues, the fullest disclosure of all circumstances bearing on the proposed financing must be made. Hence, the Commission's files are rich in material concerning the economic and financial details of corporate structure. By the use of WPA funds the Commission has been enabled since 1937 to make available to the public generalized data drawn from the individual files of security registrations in the so-called *Survey of American Corporations*. There is a Research and Statistics Section which is part of the Trading and Exchange Division of the Commission. Not all the Commission's research activities, or even the most important ones, are centered here, however. Since its establishment the Commission has engaged in a series of noteworthy investigations, such as that on protective committees and on investment trusts, for which it has set up *ad hoc* research units. A noteworthy part of the protective committee study was the volume dealing with foreign bondholders' committees. These investigations involved not only research but viva voce hearings and were undertaken with a view to remedial legislation. The Commission is one of the agencies represented on the Temporary National Economic Committee and has established a special Monopoly Study Division to carry out its part of the task of investigation.[80]

[80] The Commission has made investigations and studies for the Com-

FEDERAL SECURITY AGENCY

SOCIAL SECURITY BOARD

The Social Security Board was established under the provisions of the Social Security Act of August 14, 1935 (49 Stat. 620). By the President's Reorganization Plans I and II, effective July 1, 1939, the Board became a part of the Federal Security Agency. At the same time the United States Employment Service was transferred from the Department of Labor to the Board and its functions were consolidated with the unemployment compensation functions of the Board in the Bureau of Employment Security.

The Board's purpose is to promote economic security through social insurance. In execution of this aim it exercises various administrative and supervisory functions in respect to old age benefits, old age assistance, aid to dependents and the blind, unemployment compensation, and employment service. In addition, one of the Board's primary duties is the conduct of research with a view to making recommendations concerning the most effective methods of providing economic security through social insurance. In this a Federal Advisory Council on Social Security composed of representatives of labor, employers, and the general public which was established to formulate policies and discuss problems relating to employment assisted the Board.[81]

---

mittee of the functioning of the capital and securities markets and the significance of the present financial organization in relation to the control of industry. The studies fall into three major parts: insurance, investment banking, and corporate practices. See the *Fifth Annual Report of the Securities and Exchange Commission,* 1939, pp. 123–26.

[81] The Council, which was an adjunct of the Board's Bureau of Employment Security, is not to be confused with the Committee on Economic

The Bureau of Research and Statistics (I. S. Falk, Director) makes studies of the causes of economic insecurity, the adequacy of existing social security measures, and improved adaptation of Federal and state programs to the different needs of various groups. The Bureau performs important functions of statistical compilation and analysis, provides consultation service to other welfare agencies, and prepares, edits, or reviews material for the Annual Report of the Board, for the *Social Security Bulletin* (the monthly periodical issued by the Board since March, 1938, which is the vehicle for the publication of most of the researches of the Board and contains much other economic data of importance), and for other professional and technical publications. The Bureau has made many inquiries into foreign experience in the field of social security.

The Bureau of Old-Age and Survivors Insurance (John J. Corson, Director), the Bureau of Employment Security (Ewan Clague, Director) and the Office of the Actuary also make numerous economic studies, the researches of the first two being largely concerned with the planning of operations, the appraisal of performance, and the analysis of proposals relating to their respective programs.

The ramifications of the Board's research are aptly illustrated in the following passage from its *Annual Report* for 1939:

Research in the field of economic and social studies is intended to complement that which deals primarily with specific types of

Security, created by Executive Order No. 6757 of June 29, 1934, and composed of the Secretaries of Labor, Treasury, Agriculture, and Commerce, the Attorney General, and the Chairman of the Social Security Board, which is charged with studying the whole problem of economic and social security and developing an appropriate legislative program. Its work resulted in the enactment of the present Social Security Act.

social security or specific programs already established. In general terms, the purpose of these studies is to analyze the economic structure within which social security measures must operate, and to study phenomena which touch upon two or more phases of social security or cut across the different operating programs. Such analyses are essential to the formulation of specific policies and lines of development in connection with particular measures for social security. Emphasis is laid not upon devising administrative techniques but rather upon providing a basis of judgment for determining their feasibility.

Considerable attention has been given to analysis of the problems involved in the allocation of Federal grants to the States. The present preliminary findings indicate that there are large differences in the financial resources of the States in relation to their population. An arrangement whereby the Federal Government matches State funds at a ratio uniform for each State is likely, therefore, to be less effective in attaining the objectives for which Federal funds are granted than would be an arrangement whereby the Federal percentages could be varied according to some measure of the differences in State economic capacities. At this stage of the analysis it appears that the amount of income received currently by the inhabitants of the different States affords, when adjusted for differences in population, a reasonable basis for measuring these differences in economic capacity. Consideration of a number of other measures has tended to confirm the validity of the judgment that per capita income constitutes the best single measurement. Research on the possibility of using per capita income adjusted by related factors or of devising other measures which might constitute a better basis will continue.

Among related studies in progress are analyses of the fiscal structure, with special reference to that of States and localities; of the current distribution of income, both with respect to individuals and to geographical areas; of the population structure, with special reference to the internal movement of the population; of differences in the costs and standards of living; of the production structure; and of social legislation and institutions, with particular emphasis on the modifications which such legislation has produced in the factors affecting the security and insecurity of individual groups and areas.

From the time of its establishment, one of the most important problems confronting the Board has been the education of the public in the understanding of its program in order that the Board may obtain voluntary informed coöperation. The Office of Informational Service is charged with the performance of this task. While the Board's activity in this regard derives primarily from the need to ensure efficient and economical administration of its programs, the activity of this office may be expected to become an increasingly important means of promoting public enlightenment on socio-economic questions.

The Board's activities of liaison and coöperation with other agencies, Federal, state, and local, governmental and private, and with such international bodies as the I.L.O., are too many to enumerate here. They are detailed in its annual reports.

UNITED STATES PUBLIC HEALTH SERVICE

The Public Health Service dates from 1798. Created originally as an aid in the medical care of American merchant seamen, its functions were expanded in the course of years until now it constitutes a national health service. Its present name was acquired in 1912. It was transferred from the Treasury Department to the Federal Security Agency by the President's Reorganization Plan No. I. Its functions include research in the causes, in methods of prevention, and in control of disease, and the dissemination of public health information. It has various regulatory duties in relation to the manufacture and sale in interstate commerce of biologic products, the prevention of the introduction of disease from abroad (examination and inspection of persons arriving from abroad, quarantine, and so forth), and the prevention of the spread of communicable diseases between states. It participates in the work of the Interdepartmental Committee to Coördinate Health and Welfare Activities. Its relations with the Social Security Board are particularly close. Its functions in relation to public health have led it, latterly, to engage in economic research of great importance in filling in gaps in the knowledge of the predisposing environmental and socio-economic factors of disease. It undertook, between October, 1935, and March, 1936, a national health survey to discover, among other things, the incidence and nature of disabling illnesses; the duration of such illnesses; the relation between disease and social, economic, and other status; the relation of mortality to income and other social and economic circumstances. For this purpose about 5,000 WPA workers made a house-to-house canvas of 776,000 families (2,800,000 persons) in 84 cities in 19 States. In addition, 23 rural counties were surveyed. A related study covered occupational morbidity and mortality.[82]

FEDERAL COMMUNICATIONS COMMISSION

The Federal Communications Commission was created in 1934 to regulate interstate and foreign communication by

[82] The foregoing account of the National Health Survey is based on the description in *Report on Progress of the WPA Program, June 30, 1938,* pp. 95–100. The family schedules obtained by the Public Health Service

wire or radio. There are two research units: (1) the Accounting, Statistical, and Tariff Department, and (2) the Engineering Department. The latter is charged with the handling of international matters and interdepartmental relations, such as those with the State Department. Collaboration with the State Department on the international aspects of radio, wire, and cable services is close and constant. Representatives of the Commission have participated in various international communications conferences and in the preparatory work for future conferences. Records of international communications statistics are maintained. The Commission plays an important part in the execution of the government's program of coöperation with the other American republics. Its exhaustive studies of the telephone and telegraph industries in the United States have necessarily led it to examine the international economic position [83] of these industries and their foreign affiliations, and the relations between American and foreign-controlled communications services.[84]

In September, 1940, the President appointed a Defense Communications Board, of which James L. Fly, Chairman of the Communications Commission, is chairman, to prepare plans for the control and coördination of all communications in connection with defense needs in time of national

have been used by the Social Security Board in a study of family composition, one of the purposes of which was to estimate the extent of economic insecurity according to composition and size of family. See *Fourth Annual Report of the Social Security Board, 1939*, p. 143.

[83] See, e. g., Federal Communications Commission, *Supplemental Report on the Telegraphs Industry (International Telegraph Service)*, submitted to the Senate Committee on Interstate Commerce, February, 1940.

[84] See *Report of the Federal Communications Commission on the Investigation of the Telephone Industry in the United States*, 76th Cong. 1st Sess., House Doc. No. 340 (1939), pp. 376 ff.

emergency. The Board will have no power to impose censorship or to take over facilities.

Federal Power Commission

The Federal Power Commission, as organized in 1920, consisted of the Secretaries of War, Interior, and Agriculture. Since its reorganization at the end of 1930 it has been composed of five commissioners appointed by the President. Under the Public Utility Act of August 26, 1935 (49 Stat. 838), it possesses broad powers over water-power projects on navigable streams or affecting interstate or foreign commerce or public lands, and also over the interstate transmission of electrical energy. Its jurisdiction has been further enlarged by various statutes in relation to the power project side of flood control and the transportation and sale in interstate commerce of natural gas. It also possesses certain powers affecting the Tennessee Valley Authority and the Bonneville Dam.

A large part of the Commission's work is the conduct of economic investigations through its Bureau of Engineering and its Bureau of Accounts, Finance and Rates. In addition to numerous special studies, the Commission compiles and issues statistics of rates, utilities, and power.

The National Power Survey, instituted in accordance with the President's Executive Order No. 6251 of August 19, 1933, was the first investigation ever undertaken of "the water resources of the United States as they relate to the conservation, development, control, and utilization of water power, of the relation of water power to other industries and to interstate and foreign commerce, and of the transmission of electrical energy in the United States and its distribution to consumers." The survey contributed to the enactment of the Public Utility Act of 1935, from title II of which most of the Commission's present powers are derived. Other subjects dealt with were the need for an enlargement of generating capacity—a matter of much interest in connection with the present defense program, especially as affects the location of industry—and the growing power requirements of the electro-process industries.

Developed and potential power resources have been surveyed in a number of special and general reports. In these studies close coöperation is maintained with the War Department. The Flood Control Act of 1938 (52 Stat. 1215) directs the Secretary of War to install in the flood-control projects under his jurisdiction facilities that will make them useful for eventual power devolopment. In furtherance of this aim the Power Commission is required to investigate the hydroelectric power potentialities of all authorized Federal flood-control dam and reservoir projects and to make recommendations to the Secretary of War concerning power installations. One hundred and sixteen projects had been studied by the Commission up to June 30, 1939, a number much increased since then. This branch of the Commission's work has important conservation aspects which require the Commission to work not only with the War Department but also with the Departments of Interior and Agriculture, the National Resources Planning Board, and other Federal and state agencies.

Power requirements for national defense in case of war or other emergency have been studied by the Commission for the past seven years. The Interim Report of the National

Power Survey, published in 1935, urged the increase of generating capacity in order to avoid shortages of power such as occurred during the World War. Subsequently, special studies were made to determine the power increases that would be required in wartime, the points at which shortages might occur, and means of preventing them. In 1937 the War Department and the Commission made joint studies of these problems for the National Defense Power Committee, and these were continued by the Commission for the successor organization, the National Power Policy Committee, of which the chairman of the Commission, Leland Olds, is vice chairman.

In June, 1940, the President requested that the Commission coöperate with the National Power Policy Committee and the Advisory Commission to the Council of National Defense in maintaining a check on the adequacy of the power supply to meet the demands created by national defense production. To carry out this instruction the Commission established a new National Defense Power Unit, which performs most of the technical work of the National Power Policy Committee. The importance of this work has been accentuated by the revival of the St. Lawrence Waterway Plan.

Among the Commission's annual publications are a *National Electric Rate Book* (the first issue of which appeared in 1939), *Statistics of Electric Utilities in the United States*, and *Electric Power Statistics*, the last named being a summary of the Commission's monthly reports of the production of electricity for public use in the United States by plants of all types and also of their generating capacities.

The Assistant Secretary of War, under the National Defense Act of 1920 is responsible for supervising the procurement of military supplies. The supervision of procurement plans of the supply arms and services concerns the Planning Branch of his office, while the supervision of actual procurement is the task of the Current Procurement Branch. Neither branch makes purchases. Responsibility for procurement planning and supervision in the Navy is not centralized by law, but the same end is accomplished by administrative arrangement. The National Defense Act of 1920 also charges the Assistant Secretary of War with the task of assuring "adequate provision for the mobilization of material and industrial organizations essential to wartime needs." The experience of the World War showed that this function was a necessary accompaniment of responsibility for procurement planning.

To train personnel for the procurement agencies of the armed services, the Army Industrial College was organized in 1924 as part of the office of the Assistant Secretary of War. The course of study is concerned with the interrelation of military activity and the national economy. Navy as well as Army officers attend. The former Assistant Secretary of War has stressed the need for such training.

It is clear as a result of recent national experience in economic adjustments and readjustments that industrial activity must be thoroughly understood to accomplish national aims even in peace time. Then, with the maladjustments incident to war to further complicate the national economy, the increasing importance of

study by those responsible for the intrusions of military requirements into this economic picture must be self-evident.[85]

As set forth in the Annual Reports of the Assistant Secretary of War, the problems of procurement planning fall into
four major categories, the last two of which provide a rather
direct transit to problems of industrial mobilization. These
categories are (1) standardization and specification of design, (2) determination of requirements, (3) surveys and
allocation of facilities for production, and (4) determination
of contributory requirements.[86]

With the passage from planning to actual procurement,
statistical controls of accomplishment are needed. These are
provided by the Statistics Branch established late in 1939.
Colonel Leonard Ayres of the Cleveland Trust Company,
who served as Director of the Statistical Branch of the General Staff in the World War, was recalled in June, 1940, to
serve as head of the new organization.

ARMY AND NAVY MUNITIONS BOARD

The following account relates to the period before the initiation of the present defense effort. With the vast appropriations for the defense program actual procurement
operations have, of course, displaced the planning func-

---

[85] *Annual Report of the Secretary of War*, 1938, p. 25. Tobin and Bid-
well state that the students of the Army Industrial College have made numerous reports for the use of the Army and Navy Munitions Board, *Mobil-
izing Civilian America* (1940), p. 62. The graduates of the school would
presumably be employed as aides to the War Resources Administration provided for in the Industrial Mobilization Plan.

[86] Contributory requirements are those factors, such as raw materials,
power and fuel, transportation, facilities, and labor supply, needed to
assure the supply of primary requirements. Plans for industrial mobilization relate principally to contributory requirements.

tions of the War and Navy Departments in relative importance.

Each department determines its military requirements separately and makes its own arrangements for procurement. Without provision for coördination, their plans would tangle. Such coördination is the task of the Army and Navy Munitions Board, established in 1922.

This agency is one of four joint army-navy boards, which, by military order of the President effective July 1, 1939, exercise their functions under his direction and supervision as Commander in Chief. The Board is to

1) Formulate and keep up to date such pertinent plans and policies as in the opinion of the two departments should be adopted by the Federal Government for coördinating and controlling national industrial effort in an emergency

2) Assure the necessary coördination in the procurement war plans of the Army and Navy, and in all plans, studies, and appendixes thereto intended to facilitate the Government's efforts to promote orderly mobilization of industry in an emergency

3) Coördinate, when a war emergency is imminent and until the War Resources Administration is functioning, all Army and Navy procurement programs [87]

The Board is composed of the Assistant Secretaries of War and the Navy, to whom is attached an Executive Committee of three officers from each department, themselves assisted by a number of committees and coördinating divi-

[87] *Industrial Mobilization Plan, Revision of 1939* (76th Cong., 2d Sess., Sen. Doc. No. 134). The general progress of the Board's work can be followed in the reports of the Assistant Secretary of War. Occasional references to it are also found in the annual reports of the Bureau of Mines, the Bureau of Foreign and Domestic Commerce, and the Tariff Commission.

sions of army and navy officers. With the establishment of the Advisory Defense Commission in May, 1940, the committees and divisions were rearranged to stress the Board's operating functions in time of emergency. Standards and requirements are dealt with by a Plans, Programs and Requirements Committee. Problems of priority between Army and Navy orders are handled by a Priorities Committee. There is a Clearance Committee to coördinate foreign and domestic munitions orders. A special group maintains liaison with the Advisory Defense Commission. The Administrative Division maintains relations with the peacetime agencies concerned with labor, trade, price control, and finance. There is a Transportation Division and a Power and Fuel Division. The plans of the two services for the utilization of facilities (that is, industrial plants and manufacturing establishments) are coördinated by the Facilities Division, which maintains central allocation records for the army and navy.

The Commodities Division studies problems of contributory requirements of raw materials, that is, the availability and distribution of, and the development of substitutes for, the so-called "strategic and critical raw materials" in which wartime shortages are likely to occur. This Division includes a minerals and metallic materials section, a chemicals section, and an animal and vegetable materials section. Each of these embraces numerous committees, as, abrasives, ferro-alloys, glass, medical supplies, rubber and rubber goods, vegetable and animal oils, and others. As of January 30, 1940, fourteen materials were listed as "strategic" and fifteen as "critical." Others are under surveillance. This Division has made a systematic effort to obtain the cooperation of other government agencies and of industrial and other civilian experts for service on advisory committees.[88]

As part of its task of coördinating procurement plans the Board is charged with

1) Determination of measures to be employed to insure the proper coördination and use of the Nation's resources

2) Development of plans for the organization of administrative machinery that will execute these control measures

Proposals to these ends are embodied in the so-called Industrial Mobilization Plan, of which drafts were issued in 1931, 1933, 1936, and 1939. The latest draft differs from earlier ones in the omission of the annexes of draft legislation and administrative schemes.

The 1939 Plan would establish, immediately on the outbreak of war, an emergency civilian-administered War Resources Administration outside the regular framework of government to effect industrial coördination for war purposes by means of priority measures such as classification ratings, allocation of facilities, licenses, embargoes, permits, and warrants. Agencies for the control of prices and of foreign trade would be set up from time to time as required. If

[88] Relations with the Bureau of Mines have been very close and have resulted in passage of the act of June 7, 1939 (Public 117, 76th Congress), which authorized the Bureau to conduct a special strategic minerals investigation. Authorization was also given by the act for the expenditure of $100,000,000 on stockpiles of certain deficiency minerals, but the inclusion of "Buy American" provisions has rather stultified that part of the act. The Reconstruction Finance Corporation, acting under authorization granted by act of Congress, June 25, 1940 (Public 664, 76th Congress), has established two government corporations to acquire needed raw materials reserves.

necessary, additional organizations would be established to formulate policies concerning labor, finance, and other matters, to be carried out through the appropriate permanent agencies of government. All these proposals operate within the frame of a continued system of private enterprise, which would, however, be subject to more extensive and better integrated controls than during the World War.

Procurement planning and industrial mobilization plans involve economic judgments which must be based on studies covering such diverse matters as productive capacity, labor supply and skill, costs of production, contract methods, prices, location of manufactures, transportation, power and fuel, foreign trade, civilian requirements, standards of living, public relations, and others. Neither the extent nor the adequacy of the inquiries made into such problems can be judged, for such studies are necessarily confidential and, as stated above, the annexes to the latest Industrial Mobilization Plan were not published. Inferences can perhaps be drawn from omissions remarked by critics. Professor Tobin has pointed to the "lack of any provision for war financing." [89] Charles O. Hardy of the Brookings Institution, in a study made at the instance of the War Department, comments on the neglect to consider import policy as a means of conserving labor in wartime or the need to coördinate fiscal and banking policy with measures of price control.[90] The scope of the Board's plans is, of course, also determined by strategic directives settled by the Army-Navy Joint Board, and, in these, hemisphere defense and a two-ocean navy

[89] "Preparing Civilian America for War," *Foreign Affairs* (July, 1939), p. 694. His remark relates to the 1936 Plan. The 1939 draft can hardly be said to deal adequately with the problem.

[90] *Wartime Control of Prices* (1940), pp. 46, 84.

would appear to have introduced revolutionary innovations which involve corollary changes in underlying economic considerations.

According to the Board itself, its task has been "to anticipate the difficulties experienced by the United States during the World War." Such a view of the problem suggests an excessive reliance on precedent in a field where rigidity of thought and failure to allow for the contingency of experience may be costly. It seems unfortunate, therefore, that adequate provision for civilian participation in the Board's work was not made.[91] Civilian scrapping of the Board's proposals may be, as Professor Tobin has pointed out, the consequence of military exclusiveness in drawing them up.

In any case, present measures of defense preparation are being taken in circumstances different from those foreseen in the Industrial Mobilization Plan. The latter looked to a situation of imminent war and made no provision for a "limited national emergency" of indefinite duration. Accordingly, the administrative arrangements recently made to "mobilize" industry differ substantially from the proposals in the Plan. Then too, the need for measures of industrial control appears, in the official view, to be not now so urgent as in the period preceding American entrance into the World War. As then, a Council of National Defense and an Advisory Commission have been established. It is

---

[91] On August 10, 1939, a civilian War Resources Board, headed by Edward R. Stettinius, Jr., was appointed to work with the Army and Navy Munitions Board on questions of industrial mobilization. The submission to the President on November 4, 1939, of a still unpublished report was followed, on November 25, 1939, by the disbandment of the War Resources Board. Joint War and Navy press releases of August 9 and 17, 1939, had rather created the expectation that the War Resources Board would eventually become the War Resources Administration.

hardly overstating the situation to say that the superior effectiveness of the Advisory Commission set up in May, 1940, in getting a vast defense program under way is the result of the availability of efficient resources of government research, which the earlier organization lacked. The conclusion appears to be justified that, in existing circumstances, mandatory controls are less important than adequate and efficiently organized data in the hands of men thoroughly familiar with the workings of industry and able to use this knowledge to muster the effective support of public opinion in obtaining the necessary coöperation.[92] Present problems also differ sensibly from those of the earlier period. Governmental pronouncements emphasize that existing conditions of unemployment and under-utilization of resources permit expansion of existing production to meet the requirements of the defense program and that such adjustments as are required in civilian and military production may be made as circumstances change. In other words, until existing production capacity is fully taken up there would appear to be no need to establish priorities except in connection with special capacity problems, such as those in the machine tool industry, of which it is worth noting that bottlenecks are being dealt with at present by means of a voluntary system of preferences. In the long run, to be sure, rationing of any kind connotes an unsatisfactory condition of supply. The belief appears to be held, however, that existing strains are temporary. The use of coöperative methods of speeding up

[92] Mr. Bernard Baruch testifies that "The greatest deterrent to effective action in administration of the Government's business during the war was a lack of facts." For a brief analysis of the shaky legal foundation of the War Industries Board's authority, see Randall B. Kester, "The War Industries Board, 1917–1918," *American Political Science Review*, August, 1940, p. 655.

production and supply and the creation of agencies of surveillance are probably in better accord with such a situation than the establishment of instruments of control possessed of mandatory powers would be.

ADVISORY COMMISSION TO THE COUNCIL OF NATIONAL DEFENSE

The Army Appropriation Act of August 29, 1916 (39 Stat. 649) which authorized the establishment of a Council of National Defense and of an Advisory Commission to the Council, was still on the statute books when the provision of machinery to coördinate the industrial effort required for the execution of the present defense program became urgent. The Council, which is composed of the Secretaries of War, Navy, Interior, Agriculture, Commerce, and Labor, was nominally reconstituted to nominate the persons to be appointed members of the Commission by the President. The appointments were made on May 28, 1940 (*Federal Register*, June 3, 1940).

The functions of the Council of National Defense are, in effect, exercised by the Advisory Commission, which, although nominally responsible to the Council, in fact reports directly to the President. The statute requires that the Commission shall be composed of not more than seven persons, having special knowledge of some industry, public utility, or the development of some natural resource, or otherwise specially qualified. Each member of the Commission bears the official title of Adviser and is in charge of and responsible "for investigation, research, and coördination in his designated field."

The members of the Advisory Commission and their fields

of work are: William S. Knudsen (industrial production), Edward R. Stettinius, Jr. (industrial materials), Sidney Hillman (employment), Chester C. Davis (farm products), Leon Henderson (price stabilization), Ralph Budd (transportation), and Harriet Elliott (consumer protection). William H. McReynolds, administrative assistant to the President, combines the office of Secretary to the Advisory Commission with that of Secretary to the Council of National Defense. The statutory limitation of the membership of the Advisory Commission to seven persons has made necessary the "association" with it of other persons whose services were required for the discharge of similar functions in allied fields. A Coördinator of National Defense Purchases (Donald M. Nelson), a Coördinator of Housing (Charles F. Palmer), a Coördinator of Commercial and Cultural Relations between the American Republics (Nelson A. Rockefeller), and a Director of State and Local Cooperation (Frank Bane) were appointed by the Council of National Defense with the approval of the President.

The objects for which the Commission was established are officially described as follows:

To supervise and direct investigations and make recommendations to the President and the heads of executive departments as to

1) The mobilization of military and naval resources and defense

2) The increase of domestic production of articles and materials essential to the support of armies and of the people during the interruption of foreign commerce

3) Data as to the amounts, location, method, and means of production, and availability of military supplies

4) The giving of information to producers and manufacturers as to the class of supplies needed by the military and other services of the Government, the requirements relating thereto; and

5) The creation of relations which will render possible in time of need the immediate concentration and utilization of the resources of the Nation

The statute gives the Commission no powers of compulsion; it can only advise and recommend. Its recommendations are not, however, without sanction. The President has instructed the War and Navy Departments to clear all contracts which will involve amounts of more than $500,000 with the Adviser on Industrial Production and to clear all plant sites with the Commission. The situation is not without difficulty, for only the President, over whose busy desk the Commission's recommendations must pass and with whom it meets only once a week, can settle differences between the armed services and the Commission.[93] But so far as concerns the relation of the Commission with industry, critics of the failure of the Administration to endow the Commission with a share of power (these critics appear usually to have in mind the Industrial Mobilization Plan) have not

[93] On January 7, 1941, the President established an Office of Production Management, composed of a Director General (Knudsen), Associate Director General (Hillman), and the Secretaries of War and Navy, under whom are three divisions, viz., production (John D. Biggers), purchases (Donald M. Nelson, whose previous office of coördinator of defense purchases was abolished), and priorities (Edward R. Stettinius, Jr.). The Presidential delegation of authority to the new agency, which forms part of the Office for Emergency Management in the Executive Office of the President, is large. The Defense Commission continues; in effect it now has a collegial executive whose members "have the power to make all decisions without reference to the President" and are thus under pressure to agree. The Priorities Board has been reconstituted as an advisory organ of the OPM (to which its powers have been transferred), composed of the five men named in this note and Leon Henderson.

demonstrated that a want of power is felt at this stage of the Commission's work, when the making of contract awards has not been completed and full use of production facilities is still some way off. The Commission is now backed up by a supplementary organization, the Priorities Board, establishment of which was recommended by the Commission and approved by the President in an Executive Order of October 21, 1940. The members of the Board are the Adviser on Industrial Production (Knudsen), the Adviser on Industrial Materials (Stettinius), and the Adviser on Price Stabilization (Henderson). With the approval of the President, the Board designated Donald M. Nelson to be Administrator of Priorities. The Executive Order establishing the Board is based on Section 2 (a) of the act of June 28, 1940 (Public 671, 76th Congress), and authorizes the Administrator of Priorities and the Priorities Board "to require . . . persons with whom naval and Army contracts and orders have been or are placed, to grant priority for deliveries pursuant thereto over all deliveries for private account or for export." Originally by no means so broad a control as the industrial ratings used in the World War, this power was enlarged on December 15, to cover subcontractors. The President has also given the OPM, new holder of the priorities power, authority to take over uncoöperative plants.

Supplementing the work of the Commission is also the Administrator of Export Control (Lieutenant Colonel Russell L. Maxwell), appointed by the President to administer the act of July 2, 1940 (Public 703, 76th Congress), which authorizes the President to prohibit or curtail, by proclamation, the exportation of munitions, equipment, machinery, tools, or materials needed for the national defense.

Congress has authorized the expenditure by the Army and Navy of about nineteen billion dollars for defense; of that amount about half is to cover the cost of equipment and facilities of all kinds and of pay and subsistence for an army of 1,400,000 men and reserves of 600,000 more, while the other half is for a 70 percent expansion of the Navy. In addition, well over a billion dollars of the funds of agencies, such as WPA, RFC, the Office of Education, and others, is available for various defense purposes, such as the provision of housing, purchase of raw materials, imports, vocational training, and the like.

The actual letting of contracts for supplies is done by the Army and the Navy; the Commission's function is to clear the contracts. This has been the most spectacular and widely noticed activity of the Commission, principally because of the huge sums involved. The import of that function is not clear, however, without some analysis of the activities which are channeled into it and of the activities which flow from it.

Contract clearance proper—that is, guidance to the Army and Navy in letting the contracts and to industry in undertaking to execute them—is the task of the Adviser on Industrial Production. His aim is to translate the specifications and requirements of the armed services into a coordinated schedule of production contracts framed, so far as possible, in terms of standard industrial practice and designed by the maximum and efficient utilization of existing production capacity and, where the latter is inadequate, by enlarging it or by creating new facilities, to insure that supplies in required quantity and of proper quality will flow together smoothly and speedily through the various stages of manufacture until they reach the government warehouse.

Chief among the problems involved is the elimination of bottlenecks caused, on the demand side, by the conflict of counsels of military perfection with commercial standards and, on the supply side, by the lack or inadequacy of facilities and of machine tools.

Speed, quality, and quantity, the principal desiderata in the program of defense production, depend also on the timely provision of raw materials in sufficient amounts. The elimination of bottlenecks in materials supplies, whether by stockpiling, by developing domestic sources of supply, or by the use of substitutes, is the care of the Adviser on Industrial Materials. The Adviser on Transportation deals with difficulties that arise out of such matters as improper freight-car use, excessive fluctuations in traffic load, and lack of warehousing facilities.

Problems of labor supply are the province of the Adviser on Employment. Labor requirements must be determined by appraising defense contracts in terms of the nature, amounts, and time requirements of the labor skills needed for their performance. Shortage of essential skills develops even in the face of much unemployment, and often because of it; problems of supplying labor requirements cannot be dealt with merely by putting the unemployed back to work, although reëmployment is a major factor in the Commission's plans to avoid dislocation of civilian production. Manpower must be inventoried by skill: reserves of required skill must be uncovered by canvasses of unskilled occupations which have absorbed the men who were, during depression years, lost to industries important to defense; and trade-union rolls and employment office registers must likewise be scrutinized. Finally, "refresher" courses must be provided and additional resources of skilled labor developed through apprenticeship training by industry and through vocational training by schools.

Under some conditions competitive bidding becomes more or less illusory. It is ill-suited where facilities must be created *ad hoc* and is not easily adapted to such peculiar requirements of defense policy as spreading production loads. Congress has, accordingly, permitted the War and Navy Departments to negotiate contracts. Negotiated contracts present delicate questions of price—that problem of problems in munitions contracts, which are complicated even more by difficult problems of the financing of plant expansion, of amortization of capital expenditures, and of taxation.

In the endeavor to separate problems of price from problems of plant depreciation as an element of cost, a major development has been the so-called Emergency Plant Facilities Contract worked out by the Commission in collaboration with the Treasury, the Army, and the Navy. It provides for repayment by government in sixty monthly installments of costs incurred in enlarging or creating plant facilities for defense. An important consideration in this connection has been to make the contract "bankable in order to get private finance to take a hand in the program." Supply contracts are now assignable, but their financing involves considerable difficulty, particularly when they are held by small businessmen. The Commission has designated the Coördinator of Defense Purchases to be Director of Small Business Activities. He has obtained the aid of the Federal Reserve Board, which acts as operating agent in helping small business to obtain access to sources of needed credit.

The purchasing activities of government agencies are kept

in perspective by the Coördinator of Defense Purchases who is charged with maintaining liaison among them as a means of coördinating their purchases. He is also required to determine the most economical and effective methods of purchase of repetitive items common to several agencies with a view to avoiding the besetting sin of our earlier war procurement effort, competition for available supplies. He has also to "determine and keep current combined immediate material requirements of all Federal agencies, and estimate future requirements so as to facilitate purchases and to cushion the impact of such orders on the national economy." It is evident that these functions are closely related to his duties as Administrator of Priorities.

Production planning is, in its technical aspects, a job for industrial experts. Messrs. Knudsen, Stettinius, Budd, and Nelson have staffed their sections with industrialist aides whose names make up a partial roster of leading American businessmen. Mr. Hillman has the coöperation of a labor policy advisory committee of leaders of organized labor and of Owen D. Young as advisory aide on labor training. Army and Navy officers also serve on the Commission's staff.

Technical and economic problems interlace at every point in the Commission's studies and require the collaboration of production experts and economists for their solution. Production bottlenecks occur because of conflicts between strategic considerations of geographic decentralization of orders and the usual economic determinants of the location of industry. The endeavor to contribute through the defense program to the rehabilitation of disadvantaged agricultural areas and so-called "ghost towns" makes for additional difficulty in determining the location of plants. In turn, these problems complicate the provision of labor supply and the maintenance of labor standards, as does the matter of adequate housing for workers.

The problems involved in defense contracts of financing plant expansion, of price, of amortization of capital expenditures, and of taxation lead quite directly to such large questions of policy as the methods by which the defense program is to be financed, the fiscal policies to be adopted, the means of preventing inflationary price advances, the proper balance between savings and consumption.

Mention has already been made of the official view that defense requirements can be met by adding munitions production to civilian production and adjusting any conflicts as they arise. That theory is the basis for efforts to utilize off-season production periods for defense production wherever possible, a method which commends itself also as reducing costs by evening out production levels. The recent establishment of the Priorities Board may signify, however, that difficulties are already foreseen in maintaining "business as usual." For the time being, it is announced, voluntary preference ratings will continue.

The President's radio talk on national security of December 29, 1940, appears to express this altered viewpoint. He said:

But all of our present efforts are not enough. We must have more ships, more guns, more planes—more of everything. And this can be accomplished only if we discard the notion of "business as usual." This job cannot be done merely by superimposing on the existing productive facilities the added requirements of the nation for defense.

Our defense efforts must not be blocked by those who fear the future consequences of surplus plant capacity. The possible consequences of failure of our defense efforts now are much more to be feared.

And after the present needs of our defense are past, a proper handling of the country's peacetime needs will require all of the new productive capacity, if not still more.

No pessimistic policy about the future of America shall delay the immediate expansion of those industries essential to defense. We need them.

I want to make it clear that it is the purpose of the nation to build now with all possible speed every machine, every arsenal, every factory that we need to manufacture our defense material. We have the men—the skill—the wealth—and above all, the will.

I am confident that if and when production of consumer or luxury goods in certain industries requires the use of machines and raw materials that are essential for defense purposes, then such production must yield, and will gladly yield, to our primary and compelling purpose.

The presence on the Priorities Board of the Adviser on Price Stabilization is a reminder that priorities serve not only to accelerate defense production but also as a means of price control. The present priority power is perhaps not altogether apt as a means of price control and would probably have to be widened in scope to be effective in the civilian sector as well as the governmental. As the defense program proceeds, however, some form of price control seems likely to come, and the spotlight will then focus brightly on Mr. Henderson's office. His activities of price surveillance, reenforced by the use of publicity, have already been effective.

Regard for civilian needs must be shown. The Commission is, of course, absorbed in the problem of speeding up production. During the World War similar preoccupation was accompanied by neglect of consumer interest, an almost inevitable result of emergency improvisation in time of pressing need. Any large-scale diversion of national resources to purposes of defense is bound to affect the consumer by forcing a reduction of the standard of living upon him. Consumer protection can, at most, only mitigate the hardships of sacrifice and defend the population against unnecessary, excessive, and inequitable burdens. The general ineffectiveness of consumer organizations in achieving more limited objectives than these makes clear the need for provision in the defense organization itself of means of systematic consideration of consumer interests. In the present situation such provision has been made by establishing the office of Adviser on Consumer Protection, headed by Miss Harriet Elliott, who has had long experience in this field. Her program appears to aim at setting higher standards of nutrition and health and so to improve the quality of the nation's human resources for defense, an objective which may also be stated in terms of more effective use, through consumer organizations and other means, of the income and resources not preëmpted by defense needs. In a sense, this part of the defense organization stands closest to the New Deal and its concern with the "common man." As yet, no imperative of saving and taxes as means of restricting consumption challenges the claim of the common man to a higher standard of living. If such an antinomy, however, should be presented in the future, it may be resolved in part, at least, by the efforts at consumer protection now being planned. The likelihood that all such plans will be overborne by the "terrible urgency" of defense requirements must be kept in mind, however.

Hemisphere defense complicates enormously the economic problems of preparedness. Outside our borders questions of defense economics become problems of economic defense against commercial policies used in the service of political aspirations. In the southern part of this hemisphere the United States encounters the disadvantageous strategic circumstance that Argentina, Chile, and, in smaller degree, Brazil depend on European markets. Economic affiliations which the United States has, on the whole, seen with indifference in the past, appear in the light of present happenings to run counter to the increased political intimacy insistently and successfully developed since 1933 by Secretary of State Cordell Hull through measures of inter-American coöperation and friendship. Attention was first turned to economic defense by the difficulties made for the reciprocal trade agreement policy because of barter systems of trade. When the existence of a new autarkic instrument of war was understood, measures of economic coöperation acquired a larger, if belated, importance in the inter-American program.

The cardinal fact is, however, that the economic structures of the United States and of some of the more important South American countries are less complementary than competitive. That circumstance does not warrant the conclusion that, to the extent that their interests appear to be at odds, economic accommodation in the interest of political association is impossible. Not only the conclusion but also the viewpoint is faulty. Political association is needed to insure the maintenance of liberal principles of trade which alone make possible the continuance of equal competition in the world's markets. It is not by suppressing honest economic rivalry but rather by seeking in political accord the power to continue it that economic defense is, in all the circumstances, to be perfected. The principle was recognized at Havana in July, 1940, in the resolution that "the American nations continue to adhere to the liberal principles of international trade."

Events overseas have strengthened the desire for hemisphere solidarity in the economic as well as the political domains. The forced severance of trade with most of Europe affords the opportunity, while making it urgently necessary as well, to frame plans of inter-American economic defense involving rearrangement of traditional patterns of production and trade to accord better with hemispheric solidarity and to stiffen the resistance of the American republics against the commercial instruments of expansionist policy before which some of them are now relatively defenseless. Such plans look, in the main, to increases of inter-American exchange and to growth in home production of consumer goods which will make South America less dependent on foreign supplies. Ideally, what is involved is more rational use of the resources of the Western Hemisphere, with the United States in the role of supplier of funds, knowledge, and technical skill. It is ironic, if characteristic, that this revolution in economic policy should have come as part of a program of national defense.

In this complex of activity the Commission plays an important part, both through the Coördinator of Commercial and Cultural Relations between the American Republics, who is also chairman of the Inter-American Development Commission and of the Interdepartmental Committee on Inter-American Affairs, and through its Adviser on Farm Products (Chester C. Davis), who has in charge the problems of hemispheric agricultural surpluses and of changes in agricultural trade relationships and methods which the present European disaster may force upon us.

Most of the commissioners have appointed economic and statistical specialists to organize for their specific use data obtained from a wide range of governmental and private sources. The staff of the Adviser on Price Stabilization includes two important research sections: one on price economics, headed by Richard V. Gilbert, and the other on defense finance, headed by F. Taylor Ostrander. The staff of the Adviser on Consumer Protection also includes an economics section of some size headed by Ben W. Lewis.

The entire Commission is served by a staff agency, the Bureau of Research and Statistics (Stacy May, Director), which, although attached to the office of the Secretary of the Commission, in practice clears questions of policy and jurisdiction with a subcommittee headed by the Adviser on Price Stabilization. The Bureau was organized originally "to provide a channel assuring the orderly flow of requests from the various defense commissioners to the existing research and statistical agencies of Federal, state and local governments as well as to trade associations and business enterprises." The Bureau is staffed at the top by liaison officers "having intimate knowledge of all research activities of the Federal Government," who have been detailed to the Bureau by their respective agencies for either part-time or full-time service. Many of them are division chiefs or executive officers in their agencies of origin. They come from the Bureau of Foreign and Domestic Commerce, the Bureau of the Census, the Bureau of Agricultural Economics, the Bureau of Mines, the Budget Bureau, the Bureau of Internal Revenue, the Securities and Exchange Commission, and the Tariff Commission.

The Bureau's functions of research proper have come to overshadow its duties of spot information, although the latter continue. It is in the requirements studies and capacity surveys conducted here that the limits of validity of the theory that the defense program can be superimposed on the civilian production load are being tested. Studies are being made of military requirements (including British orders) in terms of items, components, and raw materials, and of time schedules. Parallel with these go estimates in terms of finished products and raw materials of the total civilian requirements which correspond to total military requirements at successive stages.

Just as military requirements change with each shift in the prospective defense effort required, so civilian requirements change with each shift in the level of activity. Consumers' demands expand with each increase in the level of incomes. The needs of industry for materials and productive facilities change with these demands, as with the demands of the fighting forces for arms and equipment.

What are the total civilian requirements which at any moment correspond to the military requirements? Studies under the direction of Mr. V. Lewis Bassie are designed to answer this question. These studies cover both finished products and raw materials. The former are estimated in terms of consumer expenditures at the expected level of national income. The latter are estimated from their past relation to the level of general activity. It is hoped eventually to trace the flow of materials from source to finished product and thus to complete the picture. At the moment the central problem turns upon the extent of the probable expansion under the defense program in this and the next fiscal years.[94]

The ultimate test of the expansibility of military and civilian production together is found in the confrontation of the combined military requirements and presumed derived civilian requirements with the estimates of industry and commodity capacity being developed in the Bureau under the supervision of Howard Piquet. Starting with data concerning the capacity of industry to produce any given commodity, these surveys then examine the relation between capacity in industries producing components and those turning out the finished product. From all these studies it is hoped that it may be possible to determine where, in the expansion of production, bottlenecks may arise and to adopt policies for avoiding them. An important by-product of these studies should be better knowledge of the conditions of maximal employment of the national resources. The task of coördinating the several steps in this program of determining Army, Navy, British, and civilian requirements and of measuring them against capacity is in charge of Robert Nathan.

Another important research activity of the Bureau, closely allied with that just described, is the making of progress reports on the operation of the Commission's programs of production of airplanes, tanks, ships, and other munitions, and of stockpiling industrial materials.

[94] *Defense* (October 25, 1940), p. 8. The publication cited is the weekly bulletin issued by the Commission to keep members of state and local defense councils advised of the progress of the defense program.

Typical of the Bureau's spot information activity is an inventory of the cost information available in twenty Federal agencies. The Bureau has also served as host to academic economists, who served on its staff temporarily to organize special studies for the Commission.

OTHER AGENCIES

As must already be clear, almost all the permanent agencies of government have had to undertake new research burdens, either to aid the Defense Commission or independently. Some new research units have been established, but the added work is being carried for the most part by existing organizations. Some of the Departments have designated officers or committees to coördinate defense activities and to maintain liaison with other agencies. Finally, there has been considerable growth in interdepartmental committees concerned with defense problems.

Among new research units are the Statistics Branch in the office of the Assistant Secretary of War and the National Defense Power Unit of the Federal Power Commission, both of which were mentioned earlier. A new Division of Special Latin American Investigations in the Office of Foreign Agricultural Relations has been set up to coördinate all phases of the program for encouraging the production of complementary products in Latin America, particularly rubber.

Coördinating groups include an Agricultural Advisory Council set up in September, 1939, by the Department of Agriculture, which also designated a full-time officer to coördinate the defense activities of the Department and to maintain liaison with other agencies. The Defense Resources

Committee established in June, 1940, by the Department of Interior has already been mentioned. Special advisory committees attached to the Department of Labor deal with questions of apprenticeship, conservation of manpower, and standards for the employment of women in defense industries.

The State Department group which has been studying questions of economic defense and post-war economic policy and reconstruction has become interdepartmental. Related to its work is that of the Interdepartmental Committee on Inter-American Affairs. Another interdepartmental group has been organized by the Adviser on Farm Products of the Defense Commission to inventory food supply, including production, processing, warehousing, and distribution, as a basis for further planning. Activities of the health and welfare services are coördinated by an interdepartmental committee which maintains contact with the office of the Adviser on Consumer Protection.

It is appropriate to point here to some evidences of the reliance placed by the Defense Commission on the services of the regular agencies of government. The work on labor requirements of the Adviser on Employment and the work of continuous price observation of the Adviser on Price Stabilization are done partly with the facilities of the Bureau of Labor Statistics. For data used in the requirements and capacities studies of the Defense Commission's Bureau of Research and Statistics levy is being made for the most part on the resources of the National Income Division of the Bureau of Foreign and Domestic Commerce, the Tariff Commission, the Bureau of Labor Statistics and the Bureau of Home Economics (consumer purchases studies), the

Bureau of the Census, and the Army and Navy Munitions Board. The stockpiling activities of the Adviser on Industrial Materials rest on the foundation of the Bureau of Mines and the Department of Agriculture. Increased appropriations have permitted the Bureau of Mines to enlarge its inquiries at every point of interest to the Defense Commission. Its contribution to the scrap metals and non-ferrous metals price surveys recently made by the Adviser on Price Stabilization are fundamental. The foregoing are merely samples of a collaboration which appears in many other domains.

II: FIELDS OF RESEARCH

Explanatory Note

THE FOLLOWING inventory of American official researches bearing upon international economic relations covers the years 1933 to 1940. Occasional citation of earlier studies will also be found, while there are bound to be some oversights in the period covered. The problem of exclusion has been resolved by listing studies, even when their interest was rather particular and local, if it appeared that they were part of a larger program of study which bore, even indirectly, on international economic relations. The aim has been, as indicated earlier, to cover the principal domestic factors affecting our foreign relations as well as the principal international influences on our domestic economy.

While most of the researches described in the following pages relate to the economy of the United States, some of them are studies of the economic situation and practices of foreign countries. When practicable these have been grouped together at the end of the appropriate section. The headings of the latter, therefore, are to be taken in a comprehensive sense as including the United States and foreign countries. To escape avoidable duplication complete bibliographical data are given only in the finding list which follows Part II.

The inventory here presented is organized in accordance with the following analysis of the fields of research:

A. The Structure of National Economy
 1. Resources and Their Use
    General.–Land Utilization.–Minerals
 2. Population Factors
 3. Production Factors
    Agricultural.–Industrial.–Labor
 4. Distribution Factors
    Marketing and Transportation.–Income and Expenditures
B. The Structure of International Economic Organization
 1. The Organization of National Enterprise for External Operations
 2. International Business Organization
 3. Monetary and Financial Organization
 4. International Economic Access
 5. Interdependence of National Economies for Raw Materials
C. International Economic Relations
 1. Rationale of International Trade
 2. Process of International Exchange
    Transportation.–The Course of Trade.–Trade Opportunities Abroad.–Finance and Investment
 3. Governmental Controls
    Tariffs, Subsidies and Trade Regulations
 4. Relations with Dependencies
 5. War Problems
    Defense Economics.–Economic Defense

A. The Structure of National Economy

I. RESOURCES AND THEIR USE

General

The Report of the National Resources Board, December 1, 1934, is an omnibus report prepared by committees of government and non-government experts. The work deals comprehensively with the national land, water, and mineral resources, and presents the basic data concerning them which are needed in planning.

The National Resources Committee has issued a study of *Regional Factors in National Planning and Development* (December, 1935), and a series of eight reports (May, 1936–May, 1939) on regional planning covering the Pacific Northwest, the St. Louis region, New England, the Baltimore-Washington-Annapolis area, the Red River of the North, the Upper Rio Grande, Alaska, and the Northern Lakes States. It has also issued a study of the *State Conservation of Resources.*[1]

Land utilization

The many materials relating to agriculture which were synthesized in the *Report of the National Resources Board* mentioned above were later published as a *Supplementary Report of the Land Planning Committee* in 11 parts, as follows: (1) *General Land Requirements*, (2) *Agricultural Exports in Relation to Land Policy*, (3) *Agricultural Land*

---

[1] See also the study of *Rural Regions of the United States* (1940), prepared by the Division of Research of WPA.

Requirements and Resources, (4) *Agricultural Land Available through Reclamation,* (5) *Soil Erosion,* (6) *Maladjustments in Land Use,* (7) *Forest Resources and Policy,* (8) *Land Problems and Government Land Policies,* (9) *Planning for Wildlife in the United States,* (10) *Indian Land Problems,* (11) *Recreational Use of Land.* The studies prepared by the Land Planning Committee, of which Lewis C. Gray, then assistant administrator of the Resettlement Administration, was director, constitute the basic statement of the philosophy of the Department of Agriculture.[2]

Concerning these studies the National Resources Committee remarks: [3]

The report of the Land Planning Committee, issued in 1934, constituted the most comprehensive body of materials ever assembled in the United States on land policy. In the preparation of the report, the Committee took stock of the probable future requirements for the various products of the Nation's lands, inventoried the available land which might be used to satisfy these requirements, pointed out maladjustments in land use, and proposed public policies for the correction of these maladjustments and for the direction of land uses into the most productive channels.

Although various public and private agencies had given attention to segments of land policy prior to the appearance of this report, the work of the Land Planning Committee furnished the first comprehensive view of the land situation, produced a balanced and coördinated plan for action, and served to focus

---

[2] See Gray, *Land Planning,* Public Policy Pamphlet No. 19 (1936); *idem, Evolution of the Land Program of the United States Department of Agriculture* (1939, mimeographed).

[3] National Resources Committee: *Progress Report,* December, 1938, pp. 26–27.

popular attention on the necessity for a departure from the practice of heedless land exploitation.

Since the preparation of the Report of the Land Planning Committee, substantial progress along the lines there indicated as desirable has been made by the various administrative agencies of the Government. New and supplemental legislation has been adopted by the Congress in harmony with the general suggestions of the committee. The land use program has not always moved as rapidly as the committee recommended; the movement is uneven on the various fronts; there are important gaps. Still, greater headway in soil conservation, retirement of submarginal land, control of grazing, and other policies has been made than in any other like period in the history of the Nation. The Land Planning Committee would not assert that its efforts have been the sole moving force in recent land planning measures. Yet the Committee's work focussed public attention on the problems of the land, stimulated a reorientation of policies of many administrative units of the Federal Government, and defined broad objectives to serve as a general frame of reference for the work of the members of the committee in their capacity as administrative officers of various agencies of the Government concerned with land.

The advisory and coördinating work in the field of land planning adumbrated by the Land Planning Committee has been taken up by the Land Committee of the National Resources Planning Board formed in November, 1938. This Committee has given particular study to problems of land classification and acquisition. Its first published report is *Public Land Acquisition, Part 1: Rural Lands* (June, 1940).

The Department of Agriculture has lately completed its fourth *Graphic Summary of American Agriculture*. The first was published in 1915 and was largely based on the 1910 census. The second was published in 1921, based on the 1920 census. The third was published in 1931 and was based on the 1925 agricultural census and on annual estimates of the Bureau of Agricultural Economics. The present series, publication of which extended from December, 1936, to February, 1939, is by far the most elaborate and devotes special attention to economic and social conditions. It is based on the 1930 and 1935 census reports as well as on annual estimates of the Bureau of Agricultural Economics. The series was prepared under the general direction of O. E. Baker, Senior Agricultural Economist, and consists of (1) *Graphic Summary of Physical Features and Land Utilization in the United States*, (2) *Graphic Summary of Farm Tenure*, (3) *Graphic Summary of Farm Taxation*, (4) *Graphic Summary of the Value of Farm Property*, (5) *Graphic Summary of Farm Machinery, Facilities, Roads, and Expenditures*, (6) *Graphic Summary of Farm Labor and Population*, (7) *Graphic Summary of the Number, Size, and Type of Farm, and Value of Products*, (8) *Graphic Summary of Farm Crops*, (9) *Graphic Summary of Farm Animals and Animal Products*, and (10) *Graphic Summary of Agricultural Credit*.

Since 1936 the Department of Agriculture's Yearbooks have been devoted to the comprehensive treatment of major aspects of modern agriculture. The Yearbook for 1938, issued under the title *Soils and Men*, is an effort to see the problem of better land use as a whole in its scientific, practical, social, and economic aspects. It represents the collaboration of one hundred authors, and is described as "another step toward coöperation between the natural sciences and the social sciences."

The Department of Agriculture has long been noteworthy for its policy of publishing leaflets embodying practical directions for the improvement of agricultural practices. With the adoption of the Agricultural Adjustment Program by the present Administration, there was a marked expansion of this effort of education into new fields, and particularly in respect to flood control, soil conservation, and soil erosion. The Department has issued a noteworthy group of scientific studies of these subjects phrased in nontechnical and vigorous language. Among them are *Little Waters*, issued by the National Resources Committee in November, 1935, which is a study of headwater streams and other little waters, their use and relations to the land; [4] *The Land in Flood Control* (Miscellaneous Publication No. 331, 1938); and *To Hold This Soil* (Miscellaneous Publication No. 321, 1938), which is an account of the abuse of the land and the need for remedy.[5]

The *Bibliography of Land Utilization, 1918–1936*, issued in 1938 by the Department of Agriculture (Miscellaneous Publication No. 284), is the product of collaboration between the staff of the library of the Bureau of Agricultural Eco-

[4] This study was prepared by the Soil Conservation Service, the Resettlement Administration, and the Rural Electrification Administration, all of the Department of Agriculture.

[5] See also *Report of the Mississippi Valley Committee of the Public Works Administration* (October 1, 1934); Great Plains Drought Committee, *Future of the Great Plains* (1936); National Resources Committee, *Inventory of the Water Resources of the United States* (June, 1935); *Bibliography on Soil Erosion and Water Conservation* (Miscellaneous Publication No. 312, 1938); and *Soil Conservation*, the monthly issued by the Soil Conservation Service of the Department of Agriculture.

nomics and the Land Utilization Division of the former Resettlement Administration. An earlier bibliography of related interest covered *Land Settlement* (Miscellaneous Publication No. 172, 1934). Both bibliographies survey the literature relating to foreign countries as well as to the United States.

The Farm Security Administration (formerly the Resettlement Administration) of the Department of Agriculture and the Bureau of Agricultural Economics, in coöperation, have issued a series of *Social Research Reports,* among which the studies of agricultural tenure are of interest here. These are published under the title of *Tenure of New Agricultural Holdings in Several European Countries* (Social Research Report No. II, September, 1937, processed publication). Three earlier studies were issued by the Resettlement Administration in mimeographed form under the head of *Land Settlement Technique Abroad* (Land Policy Circular Supplement, July, 1935, and October, 1935, and Land Use Planning Publication No. 5, July, 1936). These covered the organization of land settlement activities in England, Germany, and Italy, the financing of land settlement, and the selection of settlers.

Minerals

The section on mineral policy contained in the December, 1934, *Report of the National Resources Board* was prepared by a Planning Committee for Mineral Policy which was discontinued when its functions were turned over to the National Resources Committee. The subjects dealt with included surplus production, deficiency of supply, depletion, consumption, forecasts, monopoly, submarginal minerals and mineral lands, monopoly, taxation, scrap metal, foreign trade in surplus and deficient minerals, national defense, tariffs, cartels, and foreign investments. Further studies were projected but could not be completed because of the disbandment of the Planning Committee for Mineral Policy.[6]

The National Resources Committee, in coöperation with other interested official agencies, and acting on the instructions of the President, has made a study of the energy resources of the United States, covering particularly coal, oil, gas, and water power. The report of their findings was published in January, 1939, under the title *Energy Resources and National Policy*.[7] Included in the study are an economic analysis of the energy resources industries, and studies of energy resources, of technology and conservation, of public policy, and of foreign experience in the use of substitute and synthetic motor fuels. It is perhaps not altogether inappropriate to mention here The National Power Survey conducted by the Federal Power Commission.

A study was made for the National Resources Committee in 1936 by C. K. Leith and Donald M. Liddell of the *Mineral Reserves of the United States and Its Capacity for Production* (processed publication).

[6] The Energy Resources Committee of the National Resources Committee has recommended the establishment of an advisory planning agency for the formulation of a coördinated national policy toward the energy resources industries. This field of study is noteworthy for the extent to which private agencies have collaborated with public agencies in the study of the problems involved. Much of the function of offering fertilizing suggestions has been performed by private groups, e. g., the Science Advisory Board of the National Research Council, whose reports were cited in Part I, Note 41. Various organizations of mining and metallurgical experts have coöperated as has the American Iron and Steel Institute.

[7] A digest of this study has been issued by the National Resources Committee: *Our Energy Resources* (1939).

The Army and Navy Munitions Board, the Bureau of Mines, and the Senate Military Affairs Committee, in collaboration with various other official agencies, have been making studies of American requirements of strategic raw materials. Various associations of mining engineers are participating in some of these studies. One result has been the passage by Congress of a law authorizing the appropriation of funds for stockpiling certain deficiency minerals, such as manganese, and the investigation of domestic resources of such minerals.[8] Under that law the Bureau of Mines has made investigations of ores and other mineral substances in order to discover and develop domestic sources of supply, devise new methods for the treatment and utilization of low grade reserves, and create substitutes for essential ores and mineral products. Eight projects have already been started relating to antimony, chromite, manganese, tin, and tungsten. Comprehensive reports have been prepared by the Bureau of Mines for the Army and Navy Munitions Board on various mineral commodities of potential military importance.[9] Monthly canvasses of production, stocks, and consumption in the United States of manganese, tin, tungsten, chrome, and mercury are now being conducted. Similar canvasses are in prospect for aluminum and antimony. Bimonthly surveys of the iron and steel scrap situation, sponsored by the American Iron and Steel Institute, are under way in the Bureau of Mines. A secondary metals section has

[8] Public 117, 76th Cong., 1st Sess. June 7, 1939. In this connection, see National Resources Committee, *Energy Resources and National Policy*, pp. 23–24.

[9] One member of the Bureau serves on the Mineral Advisory Committee to the Army and Navy Munitions Board, and three others serve on five of its commodity subcommittees.

been set up by the Bureau at Pittsburgh. The problems dealt with in the strategic minerals inquiries include, among others, the following: form (ore, metal, or alloys) and derivation (domestic or import) of present consumption, national emergency requirements and sources from which they can be met (as stocks, scrap, substitutes, foreign sources), deficiencies and amounts to be stock piled, reserves, effects of domestic policies on life of reserves, dependence on and problems of access to foreign supplies, and position of foreign countries in relation to all the foregoing problems.

In this connection note should be made of the studies made by the Economics and Statistics Branch of the Bureau of Mines in coöperation with WPA of technologic changes and output per man in selected mineral industries in the United States. These are part of the National Research Project described below. While oriented principally toward the problems of reëmployment, they have an important bearing on the question of the comparative position of mineral industries of different countries, since output per man is frequently of use in making such comparison. The most recent of these is an over-all study of *Production, Employment and Productivity in the Mineral Extractive Industries, 1880–1938* (Report No. S-2, June, 1940).

The Bureau of Mines has for some years maintained a foreign minerals specialist in Europe. Many of the studies made by him have been published at irregular intervals as supplements to the Bureau's periodical, *Mineral Trade Notes*. He has analyzed various aspects of the raw materials situation of Italy, Russia, Germany, and Poland. In 1939 he completed a study of *The Iron and Steel Industries of Europe* (Bureau of Mines Economic Paper 19), which dealt principally with the distribution of resources of iron ore supply in the individual countries of Europe, and with the dependence of those countries on each other and on countries outside Europe for their requirements in the manufacture of iron and steel products.[10] The Bureau's foreign minerals specialist has now been transferred to South America where, in the course of the next two years, he will make an economic survey of the mineral resources, production, and trade of the twenty Latin American countries to the south of us. This work is part of the government's program of coöperation with the American Republics and the assignment was made at the request of the State Department.

There have been numerous raw-materials investigations by Congressional committees, some of which have been specially appointed as, for example, the Joint Committee to Investigate the Adequacy and Use of the Phosphate Resources of the United States.[11] These can be conveniently traced in the *Raw Materials Bibliography* (mimeographed), issued by the Tariff Commission in December, 1939, a special section of which is devoted to legislative activity in the field since 1930.

The Tariff Commission has made studies of the following raw materials industries: *Chemical Nitrogen* (Report No. 114, 2d series, 1937), *Iron and Steel* (Report No. 128, 2d series, 1938), *Mica Industry* (Report No. 130, 2d series, 1938), *Sodium Sulphate* (Report No. 124, 2d series, 1937), and *Synthetic Resins* (Report No. 131, 2d series, 1938). The Temporary National Economic Committee has studied the

[10] See also Bureau of Mines, *Coal Mining in Europe* (Bulletin 414, 1939), a study of coal-mining practices under various economic and regulatory conditions.

[11] Public 112, 75th Cong.

development of the beryllium industry (*Hearings*, Part 5). In May, 1940, the Department of Commerce completed a study of the potash industry in this country.

The Minerals Division of the Bureau of Foreign and Domestic Commerce, before the transfer in 1935 of certain of its activities to the Bureau of Mines, had made several important studies in mineral economics, among which are the following: *Mineral Raw Materials* (1929), which was a survey of commerce and sources of mineral raw materials in major industrial countries, and *Charts of World Production, Imports, and Exports of Major Minerals of Industry, 1929*, published in 1933.[12] Researches relating to the interdependence of national economies for raw materials are described below under that head.

2. POPULATION FACTORS IN NATIONAL ECONOMY

The Bureau of the Census has published several analytical studies of population problems: *Increase of Population in the United States, 1910–1920* (Census Monograph No. 1, 1922); *Farm Population of the United States* (Census Monograph No. 6, 1926), which is an analysis of the 1920 farm population figures in comparison with urban figures, and also contains an analysis of the principal economic factors affecting farm population; *Immigrants and Their Children, 1920* (Census Monograph No. 7, 1927); and *Introduction to the Vital Statistics of the United States* (1933).

---

[12] Note also the volume on *Mineral Raw Materials* (1937) written by the Foreign Minerals Division of the Economics and Statistics Branch of the Bureau of Mines. The files of the Commodities Division of the Planning Branch of the Office of the Assistant Secretary of War constituted, according to Emeny, "the most valuable single source" used in his work on *The Strategy of Raw Materials* (1934).

In a report entitled *Problems of a Changing Population*,[13] published in May, 1938, the Committee on Population Problems of the National Resources Committee undertook to offer a systematic survey of the human resources and internal population problems of the United States which should parallel for the field of population the presentation of basic data on natural resources in the *Report of the National Resources Board* of December, 1934. The statistical data had been published earlier in three volumes, *Population Statistics* (October, 1937). The first volume covers national data, and the second offers state data. The third volume is analytical and contains a discussion of urban population changes and of metropolitan regions.[14] The role of urban areas in the national economy was examined by the National Resources Committee in *Our Cities* (June, 1937).

On the basis of figures turned in by crop reporters, the Division of Farm Population and Rural Life of the Bureau of Agricultural Economics had for some years been making annual estimates of farm-to-city and city-to-farm movements; but these estimates were felt to be unsatisfactory. Accordingly, the Division of Research of WPA and the Bureau of Agricultural Economics collaborated in a comprehensive analysis of rural population mobility in the United States which was published in May, 1939, as *Rural Migration in*

---

[13] A digest of the findings is offered in a pamphlet issued by the Committee, *Population Problems* (1938). A new population study is now being planned.

[14] The material on urban population changes was prepared for the Committee by Warren S. Thompson of the Scripps Foundation for Research in Population Problems; the material on metropolitan regions was prepared by Louis Wirth and Lewis Copeland of the University of Chicago. A study of *Urban Planning and Land Policies* is promised for early publication.

the United States (WPA Division of Research, Research Monograph XIX, 1939).[15] New estimates as of January 1, 1940, were released in July, 1940. The Bureau of Agricultural Economics, in January, 1940, issued an *Inventory of Reports and Research Studies Completed and in Progress, Relating to Adjustments of Population to Resources in the Northern Great Plains States* (processed). It may be noted here that, in an appendix to *Problems of a Changing Population,* the National Resources Committee has evaluated the work of existing official agencies for the compilation of population data, and has indicated important research needs.

In *Agricultural Exports in Relation to Land Policy* (Part II of the *Supplementary Report of the Land Planning Committee* cited above) is a noteworthy analysis of the effect of population changes on demand.

3. PRODUCTION FACTORS IN THE NATIONAL ECONOMY

Agricultural

A fundamental aim of the Department of Agriculture and the one most stressed today is to establish the income of the farmer on a basis of "parity" with the income of the non-farm sector of the community; this aim the present Administration seeks to accomplish by "closing the gap" between the prices of the things the farmer sells and the prices of the things he buys—a conception which assumes that there is a "normal" relationship between them, and which does in fact take the period 1909–1914 as one in which the assumed

---

[15] Compare Goodrich *et al., Migration and Economic Opportunity* (1936); Thompson, *Research Memorandum on Internal Migration in the Depression* (1937); Vance, *Research Memorandum on Population Redistribution within the United States* (1938); Thomas, *Research Memorandum on Migration Differentials* (1938).

"normal" ratio prevailed.[16] Testifying before the Senate Appropriations Committee in February, 1940, Secretary Wallace defined "parity income" for agriculture as follows:

Parity income for agriculture, as defined by law, is that net income from farming operations per person living on farms which bears the same relation to the income per person not living on farms as prevailed in the 5 years before the World War. Or to state it another way, parity income for agriculture is the same share of the total per capita income available for living that agriculture received in the 1909–14 period. The farm income available for living includes cash received from the sale of farm commodities, plus the estimated value of products consumed on the farm, minus the principal business operating expenses of the farmer. Nonfarm income available for living is the comparable income received by the individual making up the nonfarm population.

"Price parity" or "fair exchange value" he defined thus:

Fair exchange value is, generally speaking, that price for farm commodities which has the same purchasing power in terms of things farmers buy as those commodities had in the 5 years before the first World War.

Most of the members of this committee were Senators in 1933 when Congress first selected this 5-year period as the base period for price and income comparisons. Whether or not you were in Congress at that time, you will all recall the reasons why this period was selected. From 1909 to 1914 farm and city incomes were in balance with each other and farm goods flowed freely to the cities while city goods flowed freely to the farm;

---

[16] The economic philosophy of the present agricultural program was stated in 1933 by Mordecai Ezekiel and Louis H. Bean, advisers to the Secretary of Agriculture, in *The Economic Basis for the Agricultural Adjustment Act.*

never since then has there been such a stable balance of incomes and general well-being.

Using parity income for comparative purposes, farm income overbalanced city income during the war and immediately afterward; in the past 2 decades city income and buying power have overbalanced farm income and buying power. For the 4 years ending with 1919 farmers got their full share of the national income. But these 4 fat years were followed by 20 lean ones and the end is not yet in sight.

. . . I have with me today two mail-order catalogs—one dated 1913 and one dated 1940, issued by the same company. Let us look at a few items which the farmer customarily buys and see how much he now has to pay for them, compared with 1913.

Take work shirts for example. Work shirts could be ordered from the 1913 catalog for an average price of 57 cents. The average price in the 1940 catalog is 73 cents, an increase of 28 percent. At January 15 prices in 1913 it took 4.7 pounds of cotton to buy a work shirt. The cost now is the equivalent of 7.2 pounds of cotton, based on January 15 prices, or 53 percent more than in 1913. The cost of bib overalls has increased 39 percent in dollars and cents. In terms of cotton, the cost has increased from 5.8 pounds to 9.6 pounds, or 66 percent.

In each of these examples I have tried to pick articles that are essentially the same now as in 1913. Common nails have not changed much, if any, since 1913, but the price has gone up 74 percent. At January 15 prices for hogs in 1913 it took 31 pounds of hogs to buy 100 pounds of eight-penny nails. But at January 15 prices in 1940, it took 70 pounds of hogs to buy 100 pounds of eight-penny nails, an increase of 126 percent.

These aims of restoring agricultural-industrial balance are stated and restated in the successive Annual Reports of the Secretary of Agriculture which contain comprehensive analyses of national agricultural problems and are indispensable in understanding governmental policies and programs relating to agriculture.[17] The accomplishments of the Department of Agriculture in giving effect to these aims are recorded in the voluminous reports of the Agricultural Adjustment Administration of which six have been issued since 1934. The reports of the Agricultural Adjustment Administration, of the Chief of the Bureau of Agricultural Economics and of the Chief of the Soil Conservation Service, throw particular light on the relation between action programs and research. The means used to accomplish the Administration's basic aims in relation to agriculture, the problem of which is visualized as the elimination of the "menace of recurring surpluses," have been many: commodity-adjustment, acreage restriction, marketing agreements, licenses, and orders reenforced by processing and other taxes, crop insurance, soil conservation, land-use planning, subsistence farming, ever-normal granary, surplus diversion, export subsidies, and others. The use of each of these has involved research and planning.

The problem of agricultural-industrial "balance" is the subject of coöperative investigation by the Department of Agriculture and the National Bureau of Economic Research which have been studying the trends and causes of long-term changes in agricultural-industrial relationships. The National Bureau of Economic Research has already published some of the results in its Bulletin 78 (April 28, 1940), entitled *The Composition of Gross Farm Income since the Civil War.* The Department of Agriculture will publish the main body of the study in two technical bulletins: *Gross Farm Income,*

[17] See the *Report of the Secretary of Agriculture,* 1939, p. 34.

Indexes of Farm Production and of Farm Prices in the United States, 1869–1937, and *Changing Trends of Farm Production, Farm Prices, and Gross Farm Income since the Civil War.*

The Soil Conservation and Domestic Allotment Act of February 29, 1936, which aimed at reëstablishing "the ratio between the purchasing power of the net income per person on farms and the income per person not on farms that prevailed during the five-year period August 1909– July 1914, inclusive," was modified in 1938 by defining parity as the relationship between farm and nonfarm per capita incomes without regard to purchasing power. One of the major research tasks of the Department of Agriculture has grown out of this statutory definition. The Agricultural Adjustment Administration, the Bureau of Home Economics, and the Bureau of Agricultural Economics (Division of Historical and Statistical Research) are coöperating in the development of income parity estimates.[18] The four major areas in which estimates are being developed are: farm income, expenses of agricultural production, prices paid by farmers for commodities and services, and income to farmers from nonfarm sources. A series of preliminary reports under the head of *Income Parity for Agriculture* is now being issued; these will later be summarized and compared with the available data of income to nonfarmers. Already there have been issued: estimates of farm income from twelve agricultural products; one section of the estimates of expenses of agricultural production (covering the cost of hired farm labor)—three more are in press; five sections of esti-

[18] The Central Statistical Board has participated in planning and developing the project.

mates of prices paid by farmers; and a study of population, farms and farmers. The period covered is, in general, from 1909 to date.[19]

Related to this work are the studies by the Bureau of Agricultural Economics of the spread between prices received by farmers and prices paid by city consumers for foods. A report was issued in July, 1936, and another in February, 1939, entitled *Price Spreads Between the Farmer and the Consumer* (processed). These studies have been utilized by the International Institute of Agriculture in an investigation of the margin between producers' and consumers' prices of certain foodstuffs.[20]

The researches touching the agricultural adjustment program in its successive forms are most extensive of all. There

[19] See *Agricultural Economics Bibliography* No. 73 on the concept of income and methods of obtaining income statistics (May, 1938). The studies of price-production relationship made by the Department of Agriculture up to October, 1935, are listed in *Agricultural Economics Bibliography* No. 58.

[20] The *Agricultural Income Inquiry* completed by the Federal Trade Commission in 1937 (74th Cong., 2d Sess., House Doc. No. 380; 75th Cong., 1st Sess., Sen. Doc. No. 17; 75th Cong. 1st Sess., Sen. Doc. No. 54; two later parts of the report were printed by the Commission: *Fruits, Vegetables and Grapes* [June 10, 1937]; and *Supplementary Report* [November 8, 1937]), contains important data on the division of the consumer's dollar among farmers, manufacturers, and distributors, increases or decreases in the income of the principal corporations engaged in the manufacture and distribution of the principal farm products; rates of return on investment; decline in farmers' incomes; conditions in terminal grain markets; producer coöperative groups; and concentration of control. See also the important study made by the Bureau of Agricultural Economics and issued by the Bureau of Internal Revenue of the Treasury Department, *An Analysis of the Effects of the Processing Taxes Levied under the Agricultural Adjustment Act* (1937); and *Regional Variations in Prices Received by Farmers 1925–1934 for Ten Selected Commodities* (May, 1939, processed). The Library of the Bureau of Agricultural Economics has issued a bibliography of studies of *Price Fixing by Government in the United States, 1926–1939* (July, 1939).

has been since 1933 a progressively closer integration of research and adjustment planning in the Department of Agriculture. This process, beginning with informal agreements of coördination between the Agricultural Adjustment Administration and the Bureau of Agricultural Economics, has now reached its high point in the reorganization of the Department and the transfer of program planning from AAA to the Bureau of Agricultural Economics. Relations between the research of the Bureau of Agricultural Economics and the land-use activities of the Soil Conservation Service in which all the action phases of the physical land-use adjustment programs on agricultural land were grouped together in October, 1938, have likewise steadily grown closer.

As the Secretary of Agriculture has frankly avowed, the aims of soil conservation and agricultural adjustment are the same. When the 1933 Agricultural Adjustment Act was struck down in the *Hoosac Mills* case in January, 1936, the Soil Conservation and Domestic Allotment Act of February 29, 1936, came along to continue the basic aim of the invalidated statute, namely, to control the production of commodities in oversupply. Technically, however, this result is a by-product of the soil conservation program. The close relation between the regional adjustment survey undertaken by the Bureau of Agricultural Economics in 1935, in connection with the Agricultural Adjustment program, and its research in the economics of soil conservation is indicated in the report of the Bureau of Agricultural Economics for 1935.

It has been recognized that adjustments in acreage and production in all areas, by a given percentage from a base period, present certain difficulties, although as a basis for an emergency program, such adjustments proved markedly successful in meeting the acute surplus problem confronting the Agricultural Adjustment Administration at its inception . . . The project on regional adjustment . . . conducted in coöperation with the agricultural experiment stations of all the States and with the Agricultural Adjustment Administration, aimed to secure a more definite basis for agricultural adjustment in accordance with conditions prevailing in the different types of farming areas . . . The project set out to determine what would be the resulting approximate acreage and production in the different States and sections if those changes in farming were made which are indicated as desirable in the light of good farm management and soil conservation. The results thus far brought together indicate that the adjustments shown to be desirable in the light of good farm management and soil conservation are, to a substantial degree, in general harmony with the adjustments sought by the agricultural adjustment program.[21]

In 1935 the Soil Erosion Service was transferred from the Department of Interior to the Department of Agriculture, where it was renamed the Soil Conservation Service. The Soil Conservation Act of 1936 enlarged its powers from the prevention of soil erosion to the stimulation of soil conserving practices, in aid of which Congress authorized the making of various payments to farmers.[22]

In the 1936 Report of the Chief of the Soil Conservation Service appears the following:

In the final analysis all activities of the Soil Conservation Service may be challenged with the queries: "Are they eco-

[21] See also Bureau of Agricultural Economics, *Analysis of the Present Program of Research in the Economics of Soil Conservation and Suggestions for its Improvement* (March, 1940, processed).

[22] The Chief of the Soil Conservation Service, Hugh H. Bennett, has recently written an extensive work on soil conservation.

nomically and socially justifiable? Will they yield a dividend, not only to the farmer, but to society as well? In short, will they pay?"

In order to answer questions of this sort, economic research is essential. Studies on the economic and rural-life aspects of soil conservation are necessary. Out of these economic studies will come the answers to many questions such as the effect of the operation of soil-conservation measures upon farm practices, upon the organization and operation of the farm, upon farm income, and upon farm-family living. Out of these economic studies will come, also, answers to questions in regard to the economic and social effects of soil-conservation measures, upon the operations of the farmers, and also upon groups of farms, communities, counties, and finally, the Nation.

. . . in April 1936, 98 studies of an economic character were started on 52 demonstration project areas in 25 States. These studies included general economic surveys to obtain a cross section of the background of economic and rural-life conditions in existence when the soil-conservation measures were inaugurated, repeat surveys to record the effects of a planned program of soil-conservation measures upon the economic and rural-life aspects of farms. For the same purpose farm-record and account books were installed and supervised. Special features were investigated, such as the man- and power-time spent on field operations under the influence of soil-conservation measures as contrasted with the time spent under previous conditions. Studies were also made of erosion history, soil erosion, and tax delinquency, the influence of erosion on yields and the economic consequences thereof, and land depreciation . . .

To insure a coördinated program, it was agreed in a memorandum of understanding that specialists approved by the Bureau of Agricultural Economics are to be employed by the Soil Conservation Service to conduct, under the direction of a liaison officer, the essential research in the economic and social aspects of soil conservation. Insofar as possible, all such research activities of the Service are to be coördinated with the other research activities of the Bureau of Agricultural Economics.

The lines of attack are two: What is the effect of agricultural adjustment and soil conservation (1) on private or individual farm management, and (2) on the general public.

In the 1939 Report of the Chief of the Soil Conservation Service it was said that this research was utilized in the preparation of advance estimates showing the probable economic and social consequences of soil- and water-conserving farming as compared with the probable economic and social consequences of the conventional system of farming. As a basis for these estimates, it was necessary to acquire information on yields, production, labor time, power and equipment used, materials used, livestock feeds and feeding, livestock changes in kinds and numbers, cash receipts and expenditures, and, finally, farm income.

The advance estimates have been considered the final product of much of the research in the economics of soil conservation. As prepared for farms operating under soil and water conservation programs and for the same farms assuming their operation under conventional systems of farming, they have offered an effective basis for comparison of the recommended systems with the farmers' previous systems. In turn, the comparisons have constituted a basis for appraisal of the economic feasibility of the recommended soil and water conservation programs. From such appraisals, suggestions can be made for their improvement.

These advance estimates are still in process of development and most of the reports on which they are founded are still unpublished.[23]

[23] See, however, Bureau of Agricultural Economics, *Operation of Agricultural Adjustment Programs in Illinois* (January, 1940, processed).

The problem of the most remunerative use of the farmer's resources from his point of view and that of the nation involves not only the physical but the economic study of land utilization, land classification, rural zoning, grazing legislation, tax delinquent lands, flood control, farm management and organization, farm classification by size, physical and economic resources, tenure,[24] type of farming, alternative production possibilities in view of conservation and income expectancy, the latter determined by considerations of general economic conditions, interregional competition, and welfare of the farm population, which in turn raises problems of migration and tenure.[25] Each of these problems is the subject of continuing study by the Department of Agriculture which, as the Brookings Institution has aptly pointed

---

The Soil Conservation Service has also undertaken studies of foreign experience in the field of land use. A survey is being made of ancient and modern land utilization in European and Mediterranean countries, with special reference to soil conservation and flood-control work. Historical studies of those foreign countries from which the United States has derived its crops or traditional methods of farming were also made.

[24] For studies of this subject see *Farm Tenancy in the United States*, (Agricultural Economics Bibliography No. 70, June, 1937, and No. 85, April, 1940, issued by the Library of the Bureau of Agricultural Economics).

[25] See Bureau of Agricultural Economics and Agricultural Extension Service, *Report on the Progress of Land-Use Planning during 1939* (January 31, 1940, processed). *Land Policy Review*, a monthly issued by the Bureau of Agricultural Economics (obtainable from the Superintendent of Documents at 50 cents per year), affords perhaps the best insight into the land-use problems which are continuously before the Department for analysis. While most of its contributors are Department officials, many are drawn from outside the Department. The material is presented in a lively style under provocative captions, such as "Square Meals from Spare Acres," a study of farm self-sufficiency, and "Idle Men—Idle Plants—and the Farmer," a study of the relation of the business cycle to chronic underemployment, and of both to the agricultural adjustment program. Excellent book reviews round out the journal. Until September, 1940, the *Land Policy Review* was a bimonthly.

out, has now come to be a Department of Rural Welfare.

The objectives of the research in types of farming [26] are described in the 1935 Annual Report of the Chief of the Bureau of Agricultural Economics as follows:

> . . . (1) to depict the agriculture of the United States as it varies from region to region and area to area throughout the country and to characterize the farming thus geographically differentiated in terms of selection of enterprise, size of operating units, sources of income, and methods of operation; and (2) to analyze the relations between the farming thus described and the forces and conditions that have shaped it. These conditions consist of the peculiarities of soil, surface, climate, and other physical conditions, on the one hand, and the economic forces that tend to influence agriculture primarily through prices of products and the prices of cost goods and services, on the other. . . . Results of these type-of-farming studies have already proved of value through the use that has been made of them by workers in the land-use planning project, in studies on farm reorganization, in the regional agricultural adjustment project now in progress, and as a basis for orientating other research projects and extension work.

In 1937 the Bureau of Agricultural Economics announced that projects were in progress dealing with farm organization and soil management in forty-four states, and with farm tenancy in relation to agricultural adjustment in eight states.

Studies have been made of farm organization and production methods in all the specialized wheat areas of the country to determine what are normal yields, the frequency of different rates of yield, the basis of successful wheat production, the incidence of success and failure, and the need for

[26] An earlier study is the Census Monograph, *Types of Farming in the United States* (1933), based on data obtained in the 1930 census.

readjustment area by area throughout the entire Wheat Belt.[27] Localized studies in farm management have been many. Farm-to-farm surveys of representative livestock producing sections in the Corn Belt have been made to determine the relationship between farm practices and crop and livestock production.[28] Commodity studies and special projects in the field of farm management concerned primarily with production costs, farm incomes, and farm practices relate to a wide variety of particular problems as, for example, hogs in Georgia; the efficiency of dairy farming [29] and the yields, prices, and returns of apple varieties in the Cumberland-Shenandoah and neighboring areas; [30] the cost of producing corn, wheat, oats, and cotton,[31] of producing fruit and truck crops; the farm return,[32] and coördination of farm—busi-

[27] For example, *Organization and Crop Production Practices on Grain Farms in Selected Areas of the Pacific Northwest* (October, 1939, processed); a similar study for the Northern Great Plains (December, 1939, processed); *Size of Farm in Relation to Family Requirements in the Northern Plains* (preliminary edition, June, 1939, processed).

[28] *Probable Effects of the Agricultural Conservation Program on Livestock Production in the Midwest Dairy Region* (January, 1940, processed). Part I is a summary of the studies of selected areas, of which four have appeared thus far.

[29] A typical series of production studies now in progress concerns the relation between feed input and milk output. The research is described in a paper by Einar Jensen, "Determining Input-Output Relationships in Milk Production" (Bureau of Agricultural Economics, *Farm Management Reports, No. 5*, January, 1940). The Bureau of Agricultural Economics, the Bureau of Dairy Industry, and ten state agricultural experiment stations are coöperating in the study.

[30] *Orchard Farming in Pennsylvania, Virginia and West Virginia* (March, 1938, processed).

[31] The Bureau of Agricultural Economics makes an annual inquiry into the cost of producing corn, wheat, oats, and cotton.

[32] The Bureau is making studies of farm returns and exploring the possibility of constructing index numbers to show changes in farmers' costs and returns.

ness—analysis studies; and wildlife as a supplementary farm enterprise.

Designed as an aid to lay understanding is *Production Costs and Returns* (processed) issued in June, 1939, by the Bureau of Agricultural Economics, a general discussion of the major features of the cost-of-production problem. It deals with "public and private interest in farm-production costs, cost objectives, methods and problems of computing costs, three types of cost-price relationship, considerations in determining a 'fair' cost-price relationship, the influence of price if set at different cost levels, the relationship between costs and prices, and historical costs as a basis for price fixing."

The problem of alternative uses for land released from its original production under the Agricultural Adjustment Program has resulted in a series of studies of which the first was published in November, 1939: *Food, Feed, and Southern Farms* (Farm Management Reports No. 1, processed). This is a study of production in relation to farm needs in the South, and attempts to "estimate the acreage that would be needed to provide a minimum-adequate diet of farm-grown products for the farm people and to produce feed for workstock." [33]

The problem of the best land use has also led the Bureau of Agricultural Economics into an extensive exploration of problems of interregional competition. In April, 1939, was issued an *Analysis of Interregional Competition in Agriculture* (processed), which is a discussion of the economic theory involved in coöperative studies of interregional competi-

[33] See also National Emergency Council (now the Office of Government Reports), *Report on Economic Conditions of the South* (1935); and Department of Agriculture, *Economic and Social Problems and Conditions of the Southern Appalachians* (1935).

tion which the Bureau of Agricultural Economics had been making for two years previously in the dairy regions of the Northeast and the Midwest. The use made of economic theories developed in the context of international trade is one of the striking features of these studies. The authors observe that

> The study of international trade has concerned economists more than trade within national boundaries. Yet international trade may be regarded logically as only a special case of inter-regional trade. . . . International trade theory has much to say about exchanges, currencies, tariffs, and other barriers to the free movement of both products and resources of production. The study of interregional trade within national boundaries is largely freed from these complications. Attention may be directed to more fundamental causes for trade between regions.
>
> Perhaps the most obvious thing about interregional trade in the United States is its multi-lateral nature.

It is illuminating to read what the authors write about the practical bearing of their study:

> The Farm Credit Administration, the Forest Service, the Agricultural Adjustment Administration, the Soil Conservation Service, the Land Use Program, the Farm Security Administration, and other agencies have all been shifting the emphasis of their efforts toward longer-term planning. The recent administrative reorganization of the work of the Department of Agriculture and realignment in coöperative relationships with the agricultural colleges, with the increased emphasis on planning of agricultural programs, have further focussed attention in this direction.
>
> With the increased importance of the institutional structure represented by these Government agencies and by private agencies in the marketing and distribution fields, considerable modi-

fications in individual farmers' reactions and plans of production have occurred. The farmer still remains much more nearly a freely competitive agent than producers in most other fields of economic endeavor—yet the production choices he makes have been conditioned and limited in new ways. Grave questions have arisen with respect to whether the new choices open to him are reasonably effective in achieving the maximum economic utilization of agricultural resources and the lowest social cost.

This question has arisen to plague administrators most seriously in its interregional aspects. Programs that lean on historical bases (as has been the case, for example, in the Agricultural Adjustment Administration with respect to bases, quotas, allotments, and goals, and has been true of the Farm Credit Administration system of appraisal with reference to 1910–14 price levels) may ignore divergent regional trends and retard desirable interregional adjustment. Marketing agreements and orders tend to give differential advantages to certain areas which may or may not be justified on a long-time basis if maximization of the national income be taken as a criterion.

Another problem which has affected agriculture equally with industry in recent years arises out of technological change, the attendant growth of large scale organization and the displacement of labor. The results of studies made by the Department of Agriculture and WPA are interpreted in an article by C. Horace Hamilton, "The Social Effects of Recent Trends in the Mechanization of Agriculture" (*Rural Sociology*, March, 1939).

In December, 1935, the Works Progress Administration organized a study, known as the National Research Project on Reëmployment Opportunities and Recent Changes in Industrial Techniques, the results of which are now in course of publication. In that study, conducted in coöperation with other public agencies and with numerous private agencies, inquiry was made into the extent of recent changes in industrial technique and the effect of such changes on the volume of employment and unemployment. While oriented in the field of employment, the studies throw much light on the position of the industries involved. The entire program is described in the *Research Program of the National Research Project* (August, 1937), published by WPA. A *Summary of Findings to Date, March, 1938,* has been issued. Among the agricultural studies published (prepared in collaboration with the Department of Agriculture) are *Selected References on Practices and Use of Labor on Farms* (2 parts, October, 1937, Report No. A-3), *Trends in Size and Production of the Aggregate Farm Enterprise, 1909–1936* (July, 1938, Report No. A-6), *Mechanical Cotton Picker* (August, 1937, Report No. A-2), *Field Implements* (August, 1939, Report No. A-11), *Tractors, Trucks and Automobiles* (December, 1938, Report No. A-9), *Trends in Employment in Agriculture, 1909–1936* (November, 1938, Report No. A-8), *Sugar Beets* (August, 1937, Report No. A-1), *Potatoes* (March, 1938, Report No. A-4), *Corn* (June, 1938, Report No. A-5), *Cotton* (September, 1938, Report No. A-7), *Wheat and Oats* (April, 1939, Report No. A-10), and *Vegetables* (September, 1939, Report No. A-12). A related study is that on the *Beet Sugar Industry* (October, 1938, Report No. N-1), which contains a noteworthy analysis of the effect of the tariff on sugar beet production.

In April, 1939, the Bureau of Agricultural Economics began a "study of the consequences of current technological and related developments with a view to forecasting result-

ant changes in agriculture in the next ten years . . . The
primary objective is to determine the incidence of benefits
derived from these developments, to ascertain which groups
in agriculture will be placed at a disadvantage as a result, and
to suggest ameliorative programs if possible." In response to
a questionnaire sent to crop reporters, 25,000 reports relative
to the extent of combine use, binder use, and other methods
of harvesting wheat and oats, and the custom rates for com-
bining and threshing were received by the Bureau. Similarly,
data on the extent of use and custom rates for the use of
the mechanical corn picker were obtained. Another study
deals with the effect of the use of tractors on farm organization and management. The general study was published in
August, 1940, as *Technology on the Farm*. Abstracts appeared in *Agricultural Situation* for September, 1940.

Other studies of the mechanization of agriculture include
Power and Machinery in Agriculture (Department of Agriculture Miscellaneous Publication 157, Government Printing Office, Washington, 1933), and, in progress, *A Study
of Farm Mechanization and Farm Labor Changes: 1938*.
The latter study is being conducted jointly by the Texas
Agricultural Experiment Station, WPA, and the Farm Security Administration. Related in interest is the Federal
Trade Commission's investigation, completed in 1938, of
the *Agricultural Implement and Machinery Industry*. The
Federal Trade Commission submitted its report to Congress
on June 6, 1938 (75th Congress, 3d Session, House Document No. 702).

Large scale agricultural organization is dealt with in the
Bureau of Agricultural Economics' studies of *Large Scale*

Farming in the United States (April, 1938, processed), *Large Scale Organization in the Dairy Industry* (Department of Agriculture Circular No. 527, July, 1939), and *Plantation Organization and Operation in the Yazoo-Mississippi Delta Area* (Department of Agriculture Technical Bulletin 682, May, 1939). Related in interest is a study of *Dollar Sales, Capitalization and Earnings of Leading Food and Tobacco Corporations* (February, 1938, processed).

WPA has issued an important study of cotton plantation organization in the seven southeastern cotton states: *Landlord and Tenant on the Cotton Plantation* (Research Monograph V., 1936). A survey of plantation organization similar to the one analyzed in that report is now being made for the crop year 1937 and for the situation at the time of the field enumeration in 1938. See also the Bureau of Agricultural Economics report on *Tenure Status and Land Use Patterns in the Corn Belt* (Land Economics Report No. 5, August, 1939).

The Bureau of Agricultural Economics has, since 1924, been making surveys of the agricultural situation of particular foreign countries and foreign producing regions. Its studies have covered geographic and population factors, land tenure, technological changes, the effect of post-war economic and territorial readjustments, and competitive position in world markets. In 1930 this work was concentrated in the Foreign Agricultural Service of the Department of Agriculture (now the Office of Foreign Agricultural Relations). Earlier surveys were published as *Technical Bulletins* of the Department of Agriculture. Since 1937 most of them have been published in *Foreign Agriculture*, a processed monthly publication of the Office of Foreign Agricultural Relations.

However, the Bureau of Agricultural Economics continues to make important international economic studies. In March, 1939, the Secretary of Agriculture transmitted to Congress a report on *Export Trade in and Byproducts Uses of Tobacco* (76th Congress, 1st Session, Senate Document No. 39), and in April, 1939, he transmitted to Congress a report on *Flaxseed Prices and the Tariff* (76th Congress, 1st Session, Senate Document No. 62), both of which had been prepared in the Bureau of Agricultural Economics.[34]

The Office of Foreign Agricultural Relations has made a series of studies dealing with the rise of modern textile industries in the Orient and the effects on the oriental market for American cotton: "Japanese Cotton Textile Industry and American Cotton" (*Foreign Agriculture*, December, 1937), "Trends and Possibilities of Cotton Production in China" (*idem*, March, 1938), "The Indian Textile Industry and American Cotton" (*idem*, April, 1938), and "The Chinese Textile Industry and American Cotton" (*idem*, September, 1938). Other cotton studies appearing in *Foreign Agriculture* are "Cotton Growing in the Soviet Union" (August, 1938), "British Cotton Textile Industry and Demand for Raw Cotton" (April, 1939), and "Production of

[34] According to Memorandum No. 804 of the Secretary of Agriculture, January 28, 1939, the Bureau of Agricultural Economics remains "primarily responsible for the preparation and dissemination of analytical reports on the world situation and outlook, including domestic and foreign factors," e. g., *Statistics on Cotton and Related Data* (December, 1939, processed), *World Production and International Trade in Butter and Cheese* (May, 1939, processed), and the numerous periodic commodity situation reports.

Cotton in Latin America" (September, 1939). There were special reports on *Cotton Production in Egypt* (Technical Bulletin No. 451, October, 1934), *Cotton Production in Southern Brazil* (September, 1939, processed), and *Cotton Production in Northeastern Brazil* (December, 1939, processed). A report on *The Tariff on Long Staple Cotton and Its Effect* (processed) was issued in 1938.

The results of an intensive investigation of foreign hog and pork industries have been published in *Foreign Agriculture* at intervals in the past three years. Studies have been made of the foreign trade of the United States in meats and livestock and of the downward trend in exports of meats and livestock in the last thirty years.

There have been numerous studies of wheat: "An Appraisal of Recent French Wheat Policy" (*Foreign Agriculture*, June, 1937), "Effect of Subsidies on British Wheat Acreage and on Returns to Growers" (*idem*, December, 1937), "Argentine Wheat" (*idem*, July, 1938), "Soviet State Grain Farms" (*idem*, October, 1938), "Government Aid to Wheat Producers" (*idem*, November, 1938), "European Wheat Requirements and Policies" (*idem*, January, 1939), and "The Australian Wheat Assistance Scheme" (*idem*, November, 1939).

Tobacco has been the subject of important studies: "British Imperial Preference in Relation to United States Leaf Tobacco Exports" (*idem*, November, 1937), "The Market for American Tobacco in the Scandinavian and Baltic Countries" (*idem*, June, 1939), "The Market for American Tobacco in Switzerland" (*idem*, September, 1939), and "Tobacco in Principal Producing Countries of the Far East" (*idem*, May, 1940). There have also been special reports on *To-*

bacco Production and Consumption in China and the *Tobacco Market in the British Isles* (processed publications). A special report of some importance is *The Citrus Industry of Palestine* (December, 1938, processed).

In addition to the studies of particular agricultural industries in foreign countries there have been several important studies of the agriculture of particular foreign countries: "The Soviet Ukraine—Its People and Agriculture" (*Foreign Agriculture*, July, 1939), "Agricultural Problems of India" (*idem*, August, 1939), "Agriculture in China" (*idem*, October, 1939), "Agriculture in Haiti" (*idem*, December, 1939), "Norwegian Agriculture" (*idem*, February, 1940), "Chosen's Agriculture and Its Problems" (*idem*, February, 1940), "Finland's Agriculture" (*idem*, March, 1940), "Turkish Agriculture—Changing Agro-economic Policy" (*idem*, April, 1940), and "Denmark's Agriculture as Affected by War" (*idem*, May, 1940). The land problems of various foreign countries have been studied: "The Land Problem in Mexico" (*idem*, March, 1939), "The Russian Peasant Household under the Mir and the Collective Farm System" (*idem*, March, 1940), and others. The latest studies to appear in *Foreign Agriculture* relate to the Netherlands Indies (September, 1940), Sweden (October, 1940), and Italy (November, 1940).

In addition to omnibus reviews of agricultural policy and brief discussions of current developments in agriculture abroad, there have been many studies of the agricultural policy of particular foreign countries, including South Africa, New Zealand, Sweden, Britain, Japan, and others. There have been studies of "Agricultural price control in foreign countries" (*idem*, January and February, 1939), "The

Brazilian Coffee-Defense Experiment" (*idem*, December, 1937), and others. Analyses have been made of the treatment accorded agriculture in some of the reciprocal trade agreements and in the trade agreements between foreign countries. A timely study is "Inter-American Agricultural Coöperation" (*idem*, May, 1940).

German agriculture and agricultural policies have long been the subject of study by the Office of Foreign Agricultural Relations and its predecessor: "German Agriculture in the Four-Year Plan" (*Foreign Agriculture*, March, 1937), "Germany's Capacity to Produce Agricultural Products" (*idem*, May, 1937), "Certain Economic Implications of the Austro-German Union" (*idem*, April, 1938), "Farm-Labor Shortage in Germany" (*idem*, August, 1938), "The German-Rumanian Economic Agreement" (*idem*, April, 1939), and "Southeastern Europe's Trade Increasingly Dominated by Germany" (*idem*, May, 1939). An earlier study dealt with the crucial *Edible Fat Problem in Germany* (June, 1934, processed).

War has brought new governmental controls, and intensive study of these is now being made: "Wartime Control of Agricultural Trade and Production in Belligerent Countries" (*Foreign Agriculture*, November, 1939), "French Wartime Control of Agriculture" (*idem*, January, 1940), "British Price Policy and Price Developments in Wartime" (*idem*, February, 1940), "Wartime Agricultural and Food Control in Germany" (*idem*, April, 1940), "Canada's Wartime Agricultural Measures" (*idem*, January, 1940), and, related in interest since Japan is also at war, "Japan's Food Self-Sufficiency" (*idem*, June, 1940). At the same time the Bureau of Agricultural Economics has issued a series of brief studies in processed form comparing the supply of the following agricultural commodities in the World War and at the outbreak of the present war: cotton, wheat (September, 1939), corn, dairy products, fats and oils, fruits, livestock, wool (October, 1939), rice, tobacco (November, 1939), and sugar (January, 1940).

Industrial

Patterns of Resource Use, a technical report prepared under the direction of Dr. Gardiner C. Means by the Industrial Section of the Industrial Committee of the National Resources Committee, and issued in 1939, presents the unusual feature of having been issued in a preliminary edition for technical criticism by a selected group of official and unofficial experts among whom the document was circulated for study and comment. The introduction to the preliminary edition of the report contains the following explanation of the questions to which it is addressed:

Under prevailing technical conditions, what is the level of economic activity which would absorb practically all of the great army of unemployed? What would be the market for commodities and services, industry by industry, at such a level? Is it possible to lay a foundation for answering these questions through the discovery of continuing relationships between such factors as employment, production, and consumer incomes? On the basis of such relationships can coherent patterns of resource use be developed which would show for the different parts of the national economy the volume of production and employment most likely to arise at any given level of national activity?

The foregoing study is remarkable for the absence from it of any consideration of the international setting of the

American economy. The implicit assumption of the study appears to be that little if any weight is to be assigned to international influences in the analysis of changes in the domestic economy. Except in the field of energy resources and in the early report of the Land Planning Committee the National Resources Committee has given little attention to the effect the resources of the rest of the world have on the optimum use of American resources—a line of study which would surely have been pertinent for a planning body to consider.

In addition to the effort just described to ascertain the volume of goods produced and of employment provided by the various segments of American industry at different levels of national income, two other studies have been made under Dr. Means's direction. The first is a study of the *Structure of the American Economy* in which the attempt is made to outline "the basic nature of the wants of American consumers, the national resources, and the organization of industry and government by which resources are utilized to satisfy human wants." Part 1, "Basic Characteristics," has already been issued (June, 1939). The second study covers "capital equipment requirements at different levels of production and the bottlenecks in these requirements which might develop in selected industries at various rates of increased production." [35]

The Bureau of Agricultural Economics and the Bureau of the Census (Census of Manufactures) are making a study of the location and migration of industry. This study will

---

[35] "The Problem of Manufacturing Capacity" is the title of an article by George Terborgh in the July, 1940, issue of the *Federal Reserve Bulletin*.

present a historical account of the growth of industry from 1889 to 1937 and an analysis of the location of individual industries in 1929 by counties and types of communities, of new, dead, and idle plants in industry from 1932 to 1937, and of the location of industry in 1937. For each of about forty selected industries three maps will be prepared showing (1) the location of establishments, (2) the relative size of establishments as measured by the number of wage carriers, and (3) relative size as measured by value added by manufacture.[36]

Many statistical series and indexes touching production, employment, trade, and so forth, are published in the *Federal Reserve Bulletin*, the *Monthly Labor Review*, the *Treasury Bulletin*, and the *Survey of Current Business*.[37]

The Federal Reserve index of industrial production was revised this year. The revision covers the period from 1919 to 1940 on a monthly basis. The revised indexes for total industrial production and for individual industries and groups of related industries have been published together with explanatory matter in the August, 1940, issue of the *Federal Reserve Bulletin*. Some of the problems involved in measuring the course of production are treated in the September issue of the Bulletin. A chart book of the new indexes for total industrial production, 33 groups and 81 individual series, is being prepared.[38]

[36] In connection with these studies it is appropriate to recall the important studies by the Bureau of the Census of the *Growth of Manufactures, 1899 to 1923* (Census Monograph VIII, 1928), and of *The Location of Manufactures, 1899 to 1929* (1933).

[37] Concerning the statistical series maintained by various government agencies, see the works cited in the Introduction.

[38] See also Frank R. Garfield, "General Indexes of Business Activity," *Federal Reserve Bulletin* (June, 1940).

In 1932, 1936, 1938, and 1940, supplements to the *Survey of Current Business* were issued containing cumulative statistical records covering the same materials as are presented in the monthly index series. One issue of the *Survey* each year (usually the March or April issue) is devoted to an analytical economic review of domestic business.[39] Limitations of space prevent the enumeration here of the many statistical series and analytical reviews issued by the various Divisions of the Bureau of Foreign and Domestic Commerce. Under an agreement between the Bureau of the Census and the Bureau of Foreign and Domestic Commerce the function of reporting current trade figures was recently transferred from the latter to the former. The agreement looks to the eventual centralization of the collection of trade statistics in the Bureau of the Census. The recently-transferred trade reporting service is based on monthly sales reports from 30,000 independent retail stores, monthly reports from 3,300 wholesale firms on sales, accounts receivable, collections and inventories, monthly reports from 2,000 manufacturing establishments on sales, accounts receivable, and collections, et cetera. Compiled at longer intervals than the foregoing are the Biennial Census of Manufactures, the Census of Business (irregular), which has been taken for the years 1929, 1933, 1935, and 1939, and the annual *Statistical Abstract of the United States*.

Under the Securities and Exchange Act of 1934, issuers of securities listed on national exchanges are required to file with the Securities and Exchange Commission much detailed information covering their corporate and financial structure

---

[39] This was formerly published as part of the annual *World Economic Review*.

and business. Such information is required to be kept up to date by annual supplements. In 1935 the Securities and Exchange Commission decided that the more significant data available only from this unique source of information should be published in tabular form in a *Census of American Listed Corporations.* Work was begun in January, 1936, with WPA funds and personnel under the supervision of officers of the Commission. The first eighteen reports were published in processed form and distributed free. Thirty-one further reports were made but these are available only at the offices of the Commission. Each report covers a particular industry. The reports have now been supplemented by three volumes called a *Survey of American Listed Corporations* (processed), covering twenty-seven of the same industries but containing figures of later date. Supplementary reports containing figures of later date are issued from time to time. The matters covered in the reports, in which no attempt is made to draw conclusions or to indicate opinion, are described by the Commission as follows:

Included in the data on individual companies are a general survey, the names of the parents and subsidiaries of each company, the outstanding security issues of each company, sixteen financial and operating ratios for each company, salary data for each company, and individual balance sheets, profit and loss statements and surplus reconciliations. The combined data for each group as a whole include a balance sheet, a profit and loss statement, a surplus reconciliation, totals of selected expense items, and sixteen financial and operating ratios.

The industries covered include automobiles, meat packing, chain stores, steel, tires, agricultural machinery, cigarettes, sugar refining, mail order houses, oil refining, office machinery, cement, department stores, chemicals and fertilizers, motion pictures, containers, chain groceries, automobile parts, bakers of biscuits and bread, cereals, quarrying, cigars, snuff, stockyards, dairy products, beverages, sulphur and salt, drugs, shoes, furniture, specialties, restaurants, candy, industrial machinery, paint and varnish, vegetable oil, toilet preparations, tanning, bricks, building materials, textiles, hosiery, apparel, canning, chewing gum, lumber, paper, railroad equipment, commercial cars and trucks. A statistical summary of this data is being prepared.

In January, 1933, the Tariff Commission was directed by Senate Resolution 334 (72d Congress, 2d Session), to revise its earlier *Summaries of Tariff Information*.[40] Holding that the principal value of the latter was in their being kept up to date, the Commission decided in 1934 not to print them until such time as they might be needed by Congress, especially since the revision of such a volume of data would be much easier and less costly while it was in manuscript form. Drafts have been prepared for about 1,700 out of a probable total of 2,000 summaries. Nevertheless, parts of the work have been made public from time to time in two forms: (1) trade agreement digests of the data on articles on which the United States has made concessions by trade agreements, and (2) comprehensive industrial surveys utilizing the materials in the summaries of tariff information on groups of closely related commodities. *Digests of Trade Data* have been published covering articles on which concessions have been made by the United States in its agreements with Belgium, Brazil, Canada (1st and 2d agreements), Czechoslovakia, Finland,

[40] Described above, p. 92.

The Netherlands, Sweden, Switzerland, Turkey, and the United Kingdom.

The preparation of industry surveys embodying the data in the summaries of tariff information was begun in 1936. When completed, these surveys will cover about twenty groups of commodities important from the point of view of the tariff. Others will probably be added from time to time. Surveys have already been issued covering *Chemical Nitrogen* (2d Series, Report 114, 1937), *Flat Glass* (2d Series, Report 123, 1938), *Sodium Sulphate* (2d Series, Report 124, 1937), *Iron and Steel* (2d Series, Report 128, 1938), *Mica* (2d Series, Report 130, 1938), *Synthetic Resins and Their Raw Materials* (2d Series, Report 131, 1938), *Cutlery Products* (2d Series, Report 129, 1938)—supplemented by a multilithed report on *Pocket Cutlery* (1939)—*Incandescent Electric Lamps* (2d Series, Report 133, 1939), *Grapes, Raisins, and Wines* (2d Series, Report 134, 1939), *Glues, Gelatines and Related Products* (2d Series, Report 135, 1940), *Starches and Dextrines* (2d Series, Report 138, 1940), and *Silverware* (2d Series, Report 139, 1940). Other studies well advanced touch rayon, earthen tile (in press), handkerchiefs, razors and electric dry shavers, cattle, beef, and canned beef, and hogs and hog products.

Related studies under paragraph 332 of the Tariff Act of 1930 have been the following: *Cigar Industry and the Tariff* (2d Series, Report 62, 1933), *Fishery Products* (2d Series, Report 69, 1933), *Long-Staple Cotton* [41] (2d Series, Report 85, 1935), *Laces and Lace Articles* (2d Series, Report 83, 1934), *Whiskey, Wine, Beer, etc.* (2d Series, Re-

---

[41] This study of the effect of the 1930 duty on long-staple cotton was made at the request of the State Department.

port 90, 1935), *Wool Prices,* (2d Series, Report 120, 1937).

Among surveys issued in response to Senate resolutions are studies of *Wood Pulp and Pulpwood* (2d Series, Report 126, 1938), *Tuna Fish* (2d Series, Report 109, 1936), *Nets and Netting and Other Fishing Gear* (2d Series, Report 117, 1937); *Salmon and Other Fish* (2d Series, Report 121, 1937), and *Phosphates and Superphosphates* (2d Series, Report 100, 1935).

The Commission makes an annual report on the production and sale of synthetic organic chemicals in the United States. Such reports have been made each year since 1917.

Since 1932 the Tariff Commission has completed cost of production investigations under section 336 of the Tariff Act of 1930 covering the following commodities: sperm oil and spermaceti wax, barley malt, blown-glass tableware, agricultural hand tools, folding rules, precision drawing instruments, optical fire-control instruments, upholsterers' nails, chair glides, thumb tacks, cocoa-fiber mats, crab meat, rubber-soled and rubber footwear, cotton velveteens and velvets, fish packed in oil, candied fruits, laminated products, canned clams, cut flowers, cotton ties, meat and food choppers, cotton fishing nets and netting, grass and straw rugs, toothbrushes and other toilet brushes, pins, beer, wool knit gloves and mittens, slide fasteners, frozen swordfish, plate glass, and dressed or dyed furs. Of more permanent interest are the Commission's cost-of-production investigations of *Sugar* (2d Series, Report 73, 1934) [42] and *Cotton Cloth* (2d Series, Report 112, 1936).

Investigations under section 3e of the National Industrial Recovery Act, closely akin to the cost-of-production investi-

[42] See also the Commission's *Statistics on Sugar* (1939, processed).

gations, have covered wood-cased lead pencils, quicksilver, wool-felt hat bodies, matches, cotton rugs, red cedar shingles, hat braids and bodies containing synthetic textiles, sun glasses, household pottery.

Investigations under paragraph 22 of the Agricultural Adjustment Act of 1933, as amended, cover *Cotton and Cotton Waste* (2d Series, Report 137, 1939) and *Wheat and Wheat Products* (in progress).

The only attempt at synthesis of the Commission's work in investigating costs of production was a report prepared in 1933 in response to Senate Resolution, entitled *Range and Variety of Costs of Production*, which summed up the findings in forty-four investigations made by the Commission since 1920.

After the decision of the Supreme Court in May, 1935, invalidating the National Industrial Recovery Act, a Division of Review of the National Recovery Administration headed by Leon Carroll Marshall was set up by Executive Order No. 7075, dated June 15, 1935. The Executive Order directed that

The Division of Review shall assemble, analyze, and report upon the statistical information and records of experience of the operations of the various trades and industries heretofore subject to codes of fair competition, shall study the effects of such codes upon trade, industrial and labor conditions in general, and other related matters, shall make available for the protection and promotion of the public interest an adequate review of the effects of the Administration of Title I of the National Industrial Recovery Act, and the principles and policies put into effect thereunder, and shall otherwise aid the President in carrying out his functions under the said Title.

Separate sections were set up in the Division of Review to make

. . . industry studies, foreign trade studies, labor studies, trade practice studies, statistical studies, legal studies, administrative studies, miscellaneous studies, and to write code histories.

Several series of studies were made: (1) Code Histories, (2) Works Materials (which included industry studies, trade practice studies, labor studies, administrative studies, and legal studies), (3) Evidence Studies, and (4) Statistical Materials. This exploration of the materials in the files of NRA constituted, according to Mr. Marshall, "the largest and richest single body of information concerning the problems and operations of industry ever assembled in any nation."

The studies made were too many to detail here. The industries covered (concerning each of which one or more voluminous processed monographs was prepared) [43] included, among others, *Industry Studies:* automobiles, bituminous coal, electrical, fertilizer, fishing, forest products, iron and steel, knitting, leather and shoes, lumber and timber products, men's clothing, millinery, motion pictures, needle trades (a study of the migration of industry), paper, rubber, textile yarns and fabrics, tobacco, wholesale trades, women's neckwear, and women's apparel; *Evidence Studies* (so called because the material was originally gathered for pending court cases) covering forty-eight industries: automobiles, automobile parts and equipment, baking, boots and shoes, bottled soft drink, builders' supplies, canning, chemicals,

[43] These are available at the NRA Records Section of the Department of Commerce, at the district offices of the Department of Commerce, and in some of the larger libraries of the country.

cigars, coat and suit, construction, cotton garments, dresses, electrical contracting, electric manufacturing, fabricated metals, fishery, furniture, general contractors, graphic arts, gray iron foundries, hosiery, infants' and children's wear, iron and steel, leather, lumber and timber products, mason contractors, men's clothing, motion picture, motor vehicle retailing, needlework industry of Puerto Rico, painting and paperhanging, photoengraving, plumbing contracting, retail lumber, retail trade, retail tire and battery trade, rubber, shipbuilding, silk textile, structural clay products, throwing, trucking waste materials, wholesale and retail food, wholesale fresh fruit and vegetable, and wool textile; *Statistical Materials*, studies covering nineteen industries: asphalt shingle and roofing, business furniture, candy, carpet and rug, cement, cleaning and dyeing, coffee, copper and brass mill products, cotton textile, electrical manufacturing, fertilizer, funeral supply, glass container, ice manufacturing, knitted outerwear, paint, varnish and lacquer, plumbing fixtures, rayon and synthetic yarn, and salt.

The foreign trade studies may be singled out for special mention. Work Materials No. 37, *Foreign Trade under the National Industrial Recovery Act*, in two volumes and a separate appendix, is described in the foreword as an attempt

. . . (a) to indicate the relative importance of foreign trade in the commerce of the United States, the extent to which it has declined, and the effect of that decline on the problem of recovery to which the National Industrial Recovery Act was addressed; (b) to analyse the provisions of the Act relating to foreign trade; (c) to provide a review of the administration of Section 3 (e) of the Act and to evaluate that section as a method of dealing with the problem of import competition in connection with the program of industrial recovery; (d) to survey NRA experience in the regulation of import and export trade by means of code provisions, and (e) to study the problems of industrial regulation to which foreign trade gave rise, particularly the changing competitive relationships between domestic and foreign commerce.

Other foreign trade studies covered forest products, cotton textiles, and automotive industries. There was also an important comparative study of the *Textile Industry in the United Kingdom, France, Germany, Italy, and Japan* (Work Materials No. 28).

The existence of the Division of Review ended on March 31, 1936. On April 1, 1936, a Committee of Industrial Analysis, composed of the Secretaries of Commerce, Agriculture, and Labor, and of Professor John M. Clark, Mr. William H. Davis, Mr. George M. Harrison, and Mr. George H. Mead, was created by Executive Order to complete the summary of the results of the National Recovery Administration. A Division of Industrial Economics was created in the office of the Secretary of Commerce to aid the Committee in this work. The *Report of the President's Committee of Industrial Analysis* (processed) was presented to the President on February 17, 1937.[44]

Economic analyses of technological changes in production are many. The studies made by the Department of Agriculture have already been cited. The most extensive research in this field is the WPA National Research Project on Reëmployment Opportunities and Recent Changes in Industrial Techniques. This investigation covers the whole field of

[44] Available at the places indicated in note 43.

technological change in manufacturing (in which the principal collaborator is the Bureau of Labor Statistics), the extractive industries (in which the principal collaborator is the Bureau of Mines), and agriculture (with the collaboration of the Department of Agriculture). In addition, a number of studies of economic theory relating to technological change have been made. Many agencies have coöperated in the investigation. The official agencies which collaborate are the WPA, the Department of Agriculture, the Bureau of Mines, the Bureau of Labor Statistics, the Railroad Retirement Board, the Social Security Board, the Bureau of Internal Revenue, the Department of Commerce, the Federal Trade Commission, and the Tariff Commission. The private agencies which collaborate are the Industrial Research Department of the University of Pennsylvania, the National Bureau of Economic Research, Inc., the Employment Stabilization Research Institute of the University of Minnesota, and the Agricultural Experiment Stations of California, Illinois, Iowa, and New York. The headquarters of the National Research Project are in Philadelphia.

The studies included in the National Research Project fall under four main heads: (1) "General," (2) "Types and Rates of Technological Change," (3) "Production, Productivity, and Employment," and (4) "Effects of Industrial Change on Labor Markets." Up to June, 1940, sixty-five studies had been published. The titles of the National Research Project studies of changes in farm power and equipment have been listed above under *Agriculture* and the labor market studies will be found below under *Labor*. Among the general studies the following require separate mention: *Industrial Change and Employment Opportunity—Selected*

Bibliography (Report G-5, July, 1939), *Survey of Economic Theory on Technological Change and Employment* (Report G-6, May, 1940), and *Effects of Technological Developments upon Capital Formation* (Report G-4, March, 1939). Of the studies in types and rates of technological change the following are of most general interest: *Industrial Instruments and Changing Technology* (Report M-1, October, 1939), and *Industrial Research and Changing Technology* (Report M-4, January, 1940).[45] Other studies in this group relate to the following industries: cotton garment, cotton textile, woolen and worsted, brick, cement, and mineral. Of the studies in production, productivity, and employment, the investigation of *Production, Employment, and Productivity in 59 Manufacturing Industries, 1919–1936*, 3 volumes (Report S-1, May, 1939), is particularly worthy of note. It is a study of the volume of output of the worker in industry.[46] Detail studies in this group relate to beet sugar, brick and tile, leather, cigar manufacture, boots and shoes, coal, phosphate rock, copper, petroleum, iron, and other minerals.[46a]

[45] On this subject see also Federal Communications Commission, *Report on the Investigation of the Telephone Industry*, 76th Cong. 1st Sess., House Doc. No. 340 (1939), chaps. 7 and ff. The National Research Council has completed a study of industrial laboratories for the National Resources Planning Board, which is soon to be published. See also Temporary National Economic Committee, *Hearings* (Part 8, "Problems of the Consumer"), pp. 3475 ff., for a description of the functions of the Bureau of Standards by its Director.

[46] Compare the study of "Unemployment and Increasing Productivity" prepared by the director of the National Research Project in March, 1937, for the National Resources Committee's symposium on *Technological Trends and National Policy* (1938).

[46a] In this connection, it is worthy of note that by Joint Resolution approved June 7, 1940 (Public 77, 76th Congress), the Bureau of Labor Statistics was authorized to make continuing studies of productivity and

A symposium on *Technological Trends and National Policy* was prepared for the National Resources Committee and published by it in 1938. On April 8, 1940, the Temporary National Economic Committee began hearings on the economic effects of technological change. An over-all picture of the problem was drawn for the Committee by Theodore J. Kreps, economic adviser to the Committee. An interesting feature of Mr. Kreps's statement was his discussion of the tendency of technological advance to make an economic unit of the world.

The Bureau of Foreign and Domestic Commerce has lately made various studies turning about the problems of cyclical fluctuations in industry. The Division of Business Review of the Bureau of Foreign and Domestic Commerce has made a study of changes in the size of manufacturing establishments. Another study by the Bureau of Foreign and Domestic Commerce is described in a press release of July 22, 1940, as "a survey of plant and equipment expenditures of manufacturing concerns throughout the United States covering the past twenty years as well as current expenditures of this nature. The purpose of this study is to provide basic statistical measures of total plant and equipment expenditures by all manufacturing industries on a quarterly basis as well as separate data on an annual basis for each of 12 selected industries, such as foodstuffs, textiles, forest products, chemicals and metal working, etc." The study supplements the new capital formation research undertaken by the National Income Division.[47]

labor costs in manufacturing, mining, transportation, distribution, and other industries. For the studies to be made in the present fiscal year $100,000 was appropriated.

[47] See, in that connection, the income studies described below under "Income and Expenditures."

Several studies of industrial concentration have been made by the Bureau of Foreign and Domestic Commerce for the Temporary National Economic Committee. They are described by Ernest A. Tupper, Chief Statistician of the Bureau, as follows:

The first study, entitled "The Integration of Manufacturing Operations," is concerned with the analysis of the extent and significance of central-office operations, as measured by the number of establishments, wage earners, value of product, etc. The functional relations of establishments within central offices are classified and analyzed.

In the second study, "The Concentration of Production in Manufacturing," 1807 census products have been analyzed and the concentration in the manufacture of these products has been measured in terms of the proportion of the total value of each product accounted for by the four largest producers. The products have been selected to give a cross-section picture of product concentration as it existed in 1937, and are being studied to determine the factors with which concentration is associated.

The third project relates to "The Product Structures of Large Corporations." Production statistics for the fifty largest manufacturing corporations (selected on the basis of their value of product) have been analyzed to determine the number of products manufactured, the proportion of total United States value of each product accounted for by each company and the contribution of each product to the companies' total value of products. In addition the significance of these fifty companies in relation to all manufacturing has been evaluated.[48]

---

[48] *Journal of the American Statistical Association*, June, 1940, p. 391. This periodical runs regularly a section entitled "Statistical News and Notes" which offers much information on statistical research projects conducted by the government. With the studies mentioned in the text compare Willard L. Thorp's *Integration of Industrial Operation* (Census Monograph III, 1924).

In May, 1940, the Department of Commerce completed a study of the domestic potash industry which was undertaken at the joint suggestion of the Department of Justice and the industry.[49]

The Federal Trade Commission's investigations of industry and commerce have been numerous. A list with brief descriptions will be found in the Annual Reports of the Commission. Moreover, as is the practice of several other agencies, such as the Tariff Commission and the National Resources Planning Board, the Annual Reports contain more or less extensive summaries of investigations completed in the year under review. Since 1932 the Federal Trade Commission has published exhaustive studies of the following industries: *Agricultural Implement and Machinery Industry* (75th Congress, 3d Session, House Document No. 702), *Cement Industry* (73d Congress, 1st Session, Senate Document No. 71), *Cottonseed Industry* (71st Congress, 2d Session, Senate Document No. 209), *Milk and Dairy Products* (74th Congress, 1st Session, House Document No. 152; 2d Session, House Documents Nos. 387, 451, 501, 506; 75th Congress, 1st Session, House Documents Nos. 94 and 95), *Motor Vehicle Industry* (76th Congress, 1st Session, House Document No. 468), *Steel Code Inquiry* (73d Congress, 2d Session, Senate Document No. 159), *Utility Corporations* (70th Congress, 1st Session, Senate Document No. 92, in 95 volumes). An extensive study was also made of the *Textile Industry* which was published by the Commission in many parts from 1934 to 1937.[50]

[49] Professor Clifford L. James of Ohio State University has prepared a study on the relation of the tariff to industrial concentration for the Temporary National Economic Committee (Monograph 10, 1940).

[50] Compare International Labour Office, *The World Textile Industry*

The numerous studies of unlawful monopolistic practices and restraints of trade made by the Federal Trade Commission are conveniently reviewed in the report prepared by the Commission, in connection with its participation in the work of the Temporary National Economic Committee, on the cases in which it had taken formal action against offenders. The report was published as Part 5-A of the *Hearings* of the Temporary National Economic Committee. From February 28 to May 9, 1939, the Federal Trade Commission presented the results of its studies of monopolistic practices in industries in hearings before the Temporary National Economic Committee (Part 5 of the *Hearings*).[51] These included a noteworthy study of the development of the beryllium industry, and various monographs, such as "Monopoly and Competition in Steel, an exposition of the basing-point system and its economic consequences on the capitalistic system" (*Hearings*, Part 5, p. 2192), and "Concentration of Control over Sales and Distribution of Milk and Dairy Products" (mimeographed, Release T.N.E.C.— 14, 10/25/39). Of special interest is the material on the sulphur industry and its international relations presented

---

(Geneva, 1937); and the NRA study of foreign textile industries mentioned above, p. 199. The Textile Foundation, Inc., created by act of Congress, June 10, 1930, and administered by a Board of Directors of which the Secretaries of Commerce and Agriculture are members, makes investigations of scientific and economic problems affecting the textile industries. Several publications of economic interest, including one entitled, *The Textile Industries—an Economic Analysis*, have appeared.

[51] Earlier, the Federal Trade Commission had published two studies of the basing-point system, one in relation to cement prices (1932), the other in relation to steel prices (1934). See also the study of the basing point system made by it for the Temporary National Economic Committee (Release T.N.E.C. No. 28, 1/26/40).

at the hearings (Part 5, pp. 1983 ff. and exhibits, pp. 2200 ff.).[52]

The Securities and Exchange Commission has made studies for the Temporary National Economic Committee of present financial organization in relation to the control of industry. The studies fall into three divisions: insurance, investment banking, and corporate practices. Part 4 of the Hearings of the Temporary National Economic Committee was devoted to the presentation by the Securities and Exchange Commission of facts relating to the use made by the great insurance companies of their investments as "an instrument of economic power." Part 10-A of the *Hearings* of the Temporary National Economic Committee is a statistical compilation, prepared by the Securities and Exchange Commission, of "Operating Results and Investments of the Twenty-Six Largest Legal Reserve Life Insurance Companies Domiciled in the United States 1929–1938." Parts 10, 12, and 13 of the *Hearings* also deal with insurance.

In this connection note should be made of the exhaustive *Report on the Study of Investment Trusts and Investment Companies* made by the Securities and Exchange Commission. Of that study, the following parts have already been published by the Securities and Exchange Commission: Part One, *The Nature, Classification, and Origins of Investment Companies,* and Part Two, *Statistical Survey of Investment Trusts and Investment Companies.* Of Part Three, *Abuses and Deficiencies in the Organization and Operation of Investment Trusts and Investment Companies,* the following chapters have been published: Chapter I, "Background of Investment Company Industry in Rela-

[52] Compare Montgomery's *The Brimstone Game* (1940).

tion to Abuses"; Chapter II, "Detailed Histories of Various Investment Trusts and Investment Companies"; Chapter III, "Problems in Connection with the Distribution and Repurchase of Shares of Open-end and Closed-end Management Investment Trusts and Investment Companies"; and Chapter IV, "Problems in Connection with Shifts in Control, Mergers and Consolidations of Management Investment Companies." The following supplementary reports have also been issued in connection with the Investment Trust study: *Investment Trusts in Great Britain; Investment Counsel, Investment Management, Investment Supervisory and Investment Advisory Services;* and *Commingled or Common Trust Funds Administered by Banks and Trust Companies.*

The Securities and Exchange Commission began the presentation to the Temporary National Economic Committee of material on the concentration of control in the investment banking industry in December, 1939.

Material on savings and investment was presented by the Securities and Exchange Commission at the Temporary National Economic Committee hearings in May, 1939, and published as Part 9 (1940).[53] The analysis relates to the importance of expenditures for capital goods in producing the national income, major changes in the proportion of national production devoted to capital equipment, the occurrence of capital expansion and of gaps in capital expendi-

[53] In the same connection the Bureau of Foreign and Domestic Commerce made an analysis of the financial statements of large and small corporations for the purpose of determining the source of funds flowing to business enterprise from various channels, and the use and disposal made of such funds by corporations. Emphasis is placed on capital expenditures and their relationships to depreciation, security flotations, earnings, liquidity, and other factors.

tures, sources of savings, and the relative importance of private enterprise and government undertakings as outlets for savings.[54] The Commission has issued a study of the *Cost of Flotation for Small Issues 1925–29 and 1935–38.*

The Department of Commerce in coöperation with WPA is making a study of the investment habits of people of various wealth classes. The data is obtained from the inventories of gross estates in twelve or thirteen states and from inventories filed with Federal estate tax returns.

Related in interest are studies of durable goods expenditures.[55] The Bureau of Foreign and Domestic Commerce has for some years been engaged in continuous research on the construction industry in the United States. A report on the subject, *Construction Activity in the United States, 1915–1937* (Domestic Commerce Series No. 99), was issued in 1938. That was "primarily a statistical account of the volume of construction activity" and covered "the design, production, and maintenance of field works and structures" for residential, commercial, governmental, manufacturing,

---

[54] In connection with public works see the following studies made for the National Resources Committee: *Public Works Planning* (December 1, 1936); *Criteria and Planning for Public Works* (June, 1934); *Economics of Planning Public Works* (1935); and Gayer, *Public Works in Prosperity and Depression* (New York: National Bureau of Economic Research, 1935). The Public Works Committee of the National Resources Planning Board in coöperation with the Bureau of the Budget and the Planning and Federal Projects Division of the Public Works Administration prepares the 6-year programs of public works authorized by the Employment Stabilization Act of 1931. One of its subcommittees has made a study of the public works experience of the United States in recent years in order to measure the effect of public works activity upon employment and income in the United States (November, 1940).

[55] See Terborgh, "Estimated Expenditures for New Durable Goods 1919–1938," *Federal Reserve Bulletin*, September, 1939, and his "Present Position of the Durable Goods Inventory," *idem*, October, 1940.

transportation, storage, and commodity-transmission purposes, as well as river and harbor improvements. Supplements to that study appeared in the *Survey of Current Business*, December, 1938, and March, 1940. An analysis of fluctuations in residential building prepared by Mr. Chawner of the Department of Commerce was published by the National Resources Committee.[56] That study forms part of a long-term project of analysis of the fluctuations in various types of construction which is being made by the Department of Commerce. Another project of that Department is an analysis of the economic organization of the construction industry.[57] In 1937 the Department of Commerce published the first volume of a *Financial Survey of Urban Housing* (processed). The second volume is to be published this year.[58]

The Bureau of Labor Statistics, with the coöperation of the Federal Housing Administration, the Home Loan Bank Board, and the Works Progress Administration, undertook a survey of building permit records of more than eight hundred cities for the period 1929 to 1935 to supplement data

[56] National Resources Committee, *Residential Building*, Housing Monograph Series No. 1 (1939). Besides Mr. Chawner's study, the National Resources Committee has published two other studies in its Housing Monograph Series: *Legal Problems in the Housing Field* (May, 1939), and *Land, Materials, and Labor Costs* (1939). FHA has issued an account of the *Structure and Growth of Residential Neighborhoods in American Cities* (1939). The United States Housing Authority is also engaged in studies of low-cost housing.

[57] Hearings on the construction industry and its relation to the problem of savings and investment were held by the Temporary National Economic Committee in June and July, 1939. The record was published as Part 11 of the *Hearings*. Material on the major economic factors influencing the volume of residential construction was presented at the T.N.E.C. hearings by the Department of Commerce.

[58] See also WPA, *Urban Housing* (1938).

collected annually since 1920. The results were published in *Statistics of Building Construction, 1920 to 1937* (Bureau of Labor Statistics Bulletin No. 650, 1938, 2 parts), and in summary form in *Building Construction, 1921 to 1938* (Bulletin No. 668, 1940). A second survey covering building cycles previous to the World War, residential building by cost groups and by types of construction material for 1936 through 1938, suburban dwellings, and relationship between permit valuation and selling price, was undertaken in 1938 with WPA funds but the results are not yet available. Further surveys of this kind will be made.

A line of continuing study by the Department of Commerce concerns public and private debt in the United States. "A general historical picture of the changes in the debt structure in the United States" since 1912, together with "a detailed analysis of these changes since 1929" was published by the Department in 1937 under the title, *Long-Term Debts in the United States* (Domestic Commerce Series No. 96).[59] A supplementary study appeared in *Survey of Current Business*, January, 1939. A study of gross and net debt in the United States for the period 1929–1939 is soon to be issued in bulletin form. A preliminary statement appeared in the June, 1940, issue of the *Survey of Current Business*.

Of interest is *Industrial Prices and Their Relative Inflexibility* (74th Congress, 1st Session, Senate Document No. 13), a report made in 1935 by Gardiner C. Means, then economic adviser on finance of the Department of Agriculture. The report contains

[59] The suggestion for the study came from the Twentieth Century Fund, Inc., a research organization, which in 1933 had published *The Internal Debts of the United States*, edited by Evans Clark.

. . . the results of (1) a study into the behavior of prices during the depression and (2) an interpretation of the meaning of the price inflexibilities which the study disclosed. The study was undertaken to throw light on the disparities which existed between agricultural and industrial prices. Its results cast light on the character of the maladjustments which burden our whole American economy and suggest the route toward basic economic readjustment.

In submitting Mr. Means's report to the Senate, Secretary of Agriculture Wallace took pains to point out that the report "places particular emphasis on the inflexibility of prices in industries in which active competition is present."

On September 29, 1939, President Roosevelt wrote Chairman O'Mahoney, of the Temporary National Economic Committee, asking that organization to maintain a "constant surveillance" over price movements. The Committee has from time to time issued analyses of price movements. In addition, extensive price studies were begun which were presented at public hearings in December, 1939. Professor M. G. de Chazeau presented a study of "Steel Prices in War Time" (T.N.E.C. Release No. S-13). Willard L. Thorp and Commissioner of Labor Statistics Isador Lubin offered noteworthy price analyses.[60]

Prices indices are maintained by the Department of Com-

[60] The Bureau of Labor Statistics has prepared for the Temporary National Economic Committee a four-volume report on price behavior and business policy. The study deals with the relation of policy decisions of businessmen to competition, the level and movement of prices, and the goods produced for consumption. It explores the concept of price flexibility, the effect of market characteristics and business policy decisions on price and of these on depression and recovery. Price lines, brands, advertising, trade marks and the direction and redirection of competitive effort are dealt with. There are two technical appendices. The report has been published by the Committee as Monograph Series No. 1 (1940).

merce (*Survey of Current Business*), Federal Reserve Board (*Federal Reserve Bulletin*), and the Department of Labor (*Monthly Labor Review*). The Bureau of Labor Statistics is assembling a handbook containing the specifications of each of the commodities for which wholesale prices are collected by the Bureau, including those which enter into its wholesale price index. This will be issued under the title, *Specifications for Wholesale Commodity Prices*.

The publications issued by the Division of Regional Information and the Industrial Divisions of the Bureau of Foreign and Domestic Commerce which bear upon the situation of specific industries abroad are many. No systematic enumeration of them is undertaken here, since much of the material is found in reports which are not primarily concerned with the analysis of the foreign industrial situation, and which discuss the latter only in connection with problems of marketing, and the like. Among specific foreign industry studies are those on iron and steel, chemicals, motion pictures, leather goods, industrial machinery, printing, and so forth. These can easily be identified in the *List of Publications of the Department of Commerce* (June, 1940).

The principal unit of the Bureau of Foreign and Domestic Commerce charged with the study of general economic conditions abroad is the Division of Regional Information. Its major published contributions are the weekly report of "The Business Situation Abroad" in *Commerce Reports*, and its annuals: *Foreign Commerce Yearbook*, and *Economic Review of Foreign Countries*. *Foreign Commerce Yearbook* is a compilation of "all the principal statistics of area and population, agriculture, mineral and industrial production, transportation and communication, trade and finance of the principal foreign countries and their important colonies, as well as several world production and trade tables." *Economic Review of Foreign Countries* is "largely nonstatistical, containing analyses and interpretation of basic economic developments in individual foreign countries in each successive year."

From time to time, as current events make it opportune, the Division issues mimeographed surveys of the economic situation in various foreign countries. While not so extensive as the reports on economic conditions for various countries issued by the British Department of Overseas Trade, they are more timely. In earlier years, commercial and industrial handbooks of some size were occasionally issued for various foreign countries, but it was not possible to keep them up to date, and the practice appears to have been discontinued. It should not be supposed that the somewhat meager publication program signifies that the field is not being thoroughly explored or that the compilation and analysis of pertinent data is neglected. As is the case with so many other agencies in the Bureau, that Division is overwhelmed with requests from all quarters, official and private, for data. Its studies, therefore, while continual are hardly consecutive. Limitations of time and personnel and the urgency of current work prevent the preparation of well-rounded presentations which would justify publication.

Labor

In this field the studies of the Bureau of Labor Statistics are preëminent. They are so many that only a sample of the rich production of the Bureau can be given here. It is to be noted also that many of its researches are published only in summary form in the *Monthly Labor Review*, or in mimeographed form. The following sampling of Bulletins published by the Bureau, therefore, represents only a fraction of the results of its study. Among its studies of wages, hours, and working conditions may be mentioned the following: *History of Wages in the United States from Colonial Times to 1928*, with Supplement, 1929–1933 (Bulletin No. 604, 1934), *Union Scales of Wages and Hours in the Printing Trades* (Bulletin No. 655, 1938), *Union Scales of Wages and Hours in the Building Trades in 70 Cities* (Bulletin No. 657, 1938), and *Wages in Cotton-Goods Manufacturing* (Bulletin No. 663, 1938). Each year there is a survey of union wages and hours of labor, the results of which are published in the *Monthly Labor Review*. The 1938 survey covered seventy-two cities and sixty-nine trades and subdivisions of trades in the baking, building construction, transportation, and printing industries, and in barber shops. Among detailed surveys of wages, hours, and working conditions in particular industries, which are undertaken from time to time, those completed lately covered hosiery, knit goods, men's apparel, men's hats, boots and shoes, electrical manufacturing, radio transmitters, foundries and machine shops, iron and steel, furniture, and fertilizer. In progress are surveys of the lumber industry, of rubber manufacturing, of the motor vehicle industry, and one of labor and industry in Hawaii. Special wage studies in the shipbuilding industry were made for the Maritime Commission.

The labor productivity surveys of the National Research Project of WPA, mentioned earlier, were conducted by the Bureau in coöperation with the National Research Project and other agencies.

Problems connected with labor organization, collective bargaining, and industrial disputes have been the subject of major research effort by the Bureau.[61] Among studies in this field are *Strikes in the United States 1880–1936* (Bulletin No. 651, 1938), and *Characteristics of Company Unions, 1935* (Bulletin No. 634, 1938). A *Handbook of American Trade-Unions* (Bulletin No. 618, 1936) is revised from time to time as is the invaluable *Handbook of Labor Statistics* (Bulletin No. 616, 1936). Note should be made of the important researches in this field conducted by the Division of Economic Research, later the Technical Service Division (David J. Saposs, Chief Economist) of the National Labor Relations Board. They include *Governmental Protection of Labor's Right to Organize* (Bulletin No. 1, 1936), and *Written Trade Agreements in Collective Bargaining* (Bulletin No. 4, November, 1939).

Perhaps the most extensive single inquiry into industrial relations is the inquiry into violations of free speech and labor made by a subcommittee (usually known as the Senate Civil Liberties Committee) of the Senate Committee on Education and Labor, headed by Senator La Follette. Over

[61] See the report on *Methods of Collaboration between the Public Authorities, Workers' Organizations and Employers' Organizations* (Geneva, 1940), submitted by the International Labour Office to the Twenty-Sixth Session of the International Labour Conference. In this connection it is of interest to note that in June, 1940, twenty-one national and international unions, the A.F.L., and the C.I.O. sent their research directors to a conference at Washington called by the Bureau. A temporary committee of three A.F.L. and three C.I.O. research directors was appointed to consider how to coördinate the research of the Bureau and the unions. A standing committee of nine, including one representative of the railroad brotherhoods, was appointed to maintain "closer coöperation and consultation" with the Bureau. See *Labor Information Bulletin*, August, 1940.

sixty volumes of *Hearings* have appeared. The Committee reports are ten in number (75th Congress, 1st Session, Senate Report 46; 76th Congress, 1st Session, Senate Report No. 6). On March 1, 1940, the Maritime Labor Board submitted to the President and to Congress a report dealing with the history of labor relations and union organization in the maritime industry and embodying recommendations on future methods of dealing with employer-labor relations in the merchant marine service.

Other studies of the Bureau of Labor Statistics include *Labor Offices in the United States and in Canada* (Bulletin No. 632, 1938),[62] *State Labor Legislation, 1937* (Bulletin No. 654, 1938), and *Labor Laws and Their Administration*

---

[62] The United States Employment Service, formerly in the Department of Labor and now in the Social Security Board, has been engaged for many years in the publication of so-called "Job Descriptions" which are descriptions of various industrial occupations. There are now separate Job Descriptions for each of the following: Automobile Manufacturing Industry (3 vols., June, 1935); Construction Industry (5 vols., July, 1936); Cotton-Textile Industry (June, 1935); Laundry Industry (June, 1937); Hotels and Restaurants (2 vols., April, 1938); Job Foundries April, 1938); Job Machine Shops (April, 1938); Retail Trade (3 vols., April, 1938); Cleaning, Dyeing and Pressing Industry (October, 1938); Bakery Products Industry (June, 1939). The Cotton Textile and Automobile Manufacturing volumes are now out of print. A *Dictionary of Occupational Titles* (3 parts, June, 1939) has also been published. Because heightened activity in lines of work especially affected by national defense may produce shortages of specific types of labor, this unit of the Social Security Board began in June, 1940, a monthly reporting scheme on professional, skilled, and semiskilled occupations designed to locate and measure such shortages. The work is based on an existing inventory of more than 5,000,000 active job-seekers registered in April with Federal and State employment services. Through this survey it is hoped to determine the skills for which training programs should be developed. See *Hearings before the Subcommittee of the Committee on Appropriations, United States Senate, Seventy-sixth Congress, Third Session on H. R. 10104* (Second Deficiency Appropriation Bill for 1940), testimony of A. J. Altmeyer, pp. 124 ff.

Bulletin No. 653, 1938), which is the record of the Proceedings of the Convention of the International Association of Governmental Labor Officials and is published each year.

The Women's Bureau of the Department of Labor has lately made extensive studies of *Women in the Economy of the United States* (Bulletin No. 155, 1937), *Differences in Earnings of Women and Men* (Bulletin No. 152, 1938), *Trends in the Employment of Women, 1928–1936* (Bulletin No. 159, 1938), *Women at Work* (Bulletin No. 161, 1939), *Employed Women and Family Support* (Bulletin No. 168, 1939), *Conditions in the Millinery Industry in the United States* (Bulletin No. 169, 1939), and *The Woman Wage Earner: Her Situation Today* (Bulletin No. 172, 1940). Studies in progress deal with women in canning and dried fruit packing in the United States and Hawaii, with the necessity of the money contribution of women to the family budget, and with industrial injuries and occupational diseases affecting women. The Women's Bureau publishes *The Woman Worker*, a bimonthly periodical.

The Bureau of Labor Statistics has collaborated extensively with the Temporary National Economic Committee. Among other studies made for the latter by the Bureau are investigations of the relationship of size of plant and regularity of employment, the effect of wage changes upon production costs, geographical wage and price spreads, and so forth.

In the field of employment, according to the 1939 Annual Report of the Commissioner of Labor Statistics,

The monthly reports issued by the Bureau of Labor Statistics are the only official figures currently available indicating the fluctuation in employment, earnings, and hours worked for any considerable portion of the wage earners of the country. In addition to covering a very large number of manufacturing and nonmanufacturing industries, employing nearly 50 percent of the total wage earners of the country, these reports cover all forms of Federal employment . . . During the intervals between censuses the Bureau's reports furnish a barometer from which reliable approximations of total employment and weekly payrolls in the industrial groups covered can be arrived at. These estimates, based on the reporting sample, are revised periodically as census data become available.

The results of the monthly studies are made available to the public in mimeographed form during the month following that to which the pay period covered relates. More detailed information on employment and pay rolls, as well as data on hourly and weekly earnings and hours worked per week for each of the industries covered, is presented in pamphlet form each month . . .

The reports referred to are extensively used by various governmental and nongovernmental agencies as a basis for current estimates of unemployment and national income . . .

Ninety separate manufacturing industries and 16 nonmanufacturing industries are covered in the regular monthly survey, the 14 major groups into which the manufacturing industries are classified being divided into two larger divisions, "durable goods" and "nondurable goods." The 16 nonmanufacturing industries are: Anthracite mining, bituminous-coal mining, metalliferous mining, quarrying and non-metallic mining, crude petroleum producing, telephone and telegraph, electric light and power and manufactured gas, electric railroad and motorbus operation and maintenance, wholesale trade, retail trade, hotels, laundries, dyeing and cleaning, brokerage, insurance and private building construction. The reporting sample in a number of industries is recognized as not being as complete as desirable, and additional contacts are made from time to time to enlarge the coverage, particularly in the various lines of wholesale and retail trade and in private building construction.

In keeping with an established policy of revising its indexes from census totals as such data become available, the indexes of employment and pay rolls for manufacturing industries were adjusted during the past year to the levels of the 1937 manufacturing census.

The reports on average hours and earnings were further improved during the year by the construction of weighted averages for specific industries and by the reclassification of certain firms. A bulletin presenting average weekly and hourly earnings and average hours per week by years from 1932 to 1938 and by months from January 1932 to the latest month available is now in course of preparation. A companion bulletin containing the revised indexes of employment and pay rolls is also now being prepared for publication. This latter bulletin will furnish a continuation of the data contained in Bulletin 610, entitled "Revised Indexes of Factory Employment and Pay Rolls, 1919–1933." [63]

In addition to a continuation of the Bureau's regular studies on changes in clerical employment, weighted indexes of employment and pay rolls for retail trades were constructed during the past year and will be released in the near future. Work is also under way on the compilation of a similar index for wholesale trade.

Since January, 1940, labor turnover rates have been published for twenty-nine states and for thirty-three industries as well as combined rates for one hundred and forty-four industries and all states. A survey of state, county, and municipal employment was organized by the Bureau of Labor Statistics in December, 1938, and is now being conducted

[63] See also "Revised Indexes of Factory Employment," *Federal Reserve Bulletin*, October, 1938.

on a nation-wide basis with the assistance of WPA. This study, which covers the period 1929 to 1938, will fill the last major gap in the Bureau's series on nonagricultural employment.

An analysis was made for the Wage and Hour Administration of labor conditions and the impact of wages on costs in the textile industry.

Part of the National Research Project consists of studies of the effect of industrial change on labor markets. Under that head the following studies have been published by WPA: *Farm-City Migration and Industry's Labor Reserve* (Report L-7, August, 1939), and *Trade-Union Policy and Technological Change* (Report L-8, April, 1940). In addition, there have been fifteen studies of particular urban labor markets, nine of which relate to Philadelphia.

Important labor studies have been made by the Division of Research of WPA, principally in connection with problems of relief and rehabilitation. These include, among others, *The Transient Unemployed* [64] (Research Monograph III, 1935), *Urban Workers on Relief*, May, 1934 (Research Monograph IV, 1936, 2 parts), *Chronology of the Federal Emergency Relief Administration, 1933–1935* (Research Monograph VI, 1937), *The Migratory-Casual Worker* (Research Monograph VII, 1937), *Farmers on Relief and Rehabilitation* (Research Monograph VIII, 1937), *Part-Time Farming in the Southeast* (Research Monograph IX, 1937), *Rural Youth on Relief* (Research Monograph XI, 1937), *Effects of the Works Program on*

[64] See also the exhaustive study by the Department of Labor, *Migration of Workers: Preliminary Report of the Secretary of Labor*, 2 vols. (Washington, 1939, mimeographed).

Rural Relief (Research Monograph XIII, 1938), *Migrant Families* (Research Monograph XVIII, 1938), and *Youth in Agricultural Villages* (Research Monograph XXI, 1940). The study of rural population mobility, *Rural Migration in the United States* (Research Monograph XIX, 1939) was mentioned earlier. A useful summary of other government studies is *Seasonal Employment in Agriculture* (September, 1939). The Division of Research of WPA has, likewise, made various special reports from time to time on such questions as the problems of the drought areas, the usual occupations of workers on relief, and so forth. The results of a survey of youth in the labor market are partly available in preliminary form in *Urban Youth: Their Characteristics and Economic Problems* (processed, 1939), and *Disadvantaged Youth in the Labor Market* (processed, 1940). An interesting feature of the WPA publication program has been the issuance of pamphlets presenting in simple language summaries of the result of its major researches. In the labor field the following have been issued: *Depression Pioneers* (Social Problems No. 1, 1939), based on the study of *Migrant Families*, mentioned earlier; *Rural Relief and Recovery* (Social Problems No. 3, 1939); and *Facts About Unemployment* (Social Problems No. 4, 1939).

The *Social Security Bulletin* published monthly by the Social Security Board is the vehicle for numerous studies of employment security, public assistance, and old age and survivors' insurance. Among special reports by the Board are *Unemployment and Health Insurance in Great Britain, 1911–1937* (1939), *Seasonal Workers and Unemployment Insurance in Great Britain, Germany and Austria* (1940) and *Old Age in Sweden* (1940). In 1938 the Bureau of the

Census published a new kind of classification of gainful labor arranged in the following categories: (1) professional, (2) proprietors, managers and officials, (3) clerks, (4) skilled workers, (5) semiskilled and (6) unskilled workers: *A Social-Economic Grouping of the Gainful Workers of the United States.*[65]

Studies of social insurance in foreign countries make frequent appearance in the *Monthly Labor Review.* A report by the Bureau of Labor Statistics of a survey of the administration of workmen's compensation laws in the United States and Canada, of which parts were published from time to time, will be published in full this year.

Studies of foreign labor by the Bureau of Labor Statistics are many. In 1929 it prepared an extensive study of *Wages in Foreign Countries* (71st Congress, 1st Session, Senate Document No. 9) which was a compilation of the basic available data regarding wages in industrial and agricultural employment. Since then surveys of wages in foreign countries have been made every few years. These are based on detailed reports from foreign service officers, supplemented by data from the I.L.O. and other sources. A foreign wage survey was made in 1939 covering most of the industrial countries of Europe and of Latin America. The results have been published in the *Monthly Labor Review.* In addition to wage data, material was presented on hours of work, social charges, overtime provisions and related factors. Articles on the work of the I.L.O. appear frequently.

A series of studies of industrial relations in foreign countries was begun in 1938. These have been published from

[65] Compare Woytinsky, *Labor in the United States* (Washington: Committee on Social Security; Social Science Research Council, 1938).

time to time in the *Monthly Labor Review*. A general study of industrial relations machinery in a number of democratic countries is to appear shortly.[66] A brief sketch of "European Labor on a War Footing" appeared in the December, 1939, issue of the *Monthly Labor Review* and will be followed by several studies of the effect on European labor of wartime controls.

A subject of continuing research by the Bureau of Labor Statistics has been labor conditions in Latin America. Full-length studies in bulletin form were published between 1929 and 1932 of the labor legislation of Argentina, Ecuador, Mexico, Paraguay, Uruguay, and Venezuela. Since the creation of the Interdepartmental Committee on Coöperation with the American Republics, the Bureau of Labor Statistics has set up a special pamphlet series, "Labor Conditions in Latin America," containing reprints of all articles in the *Monthly Labor Review* dealing with Latin America. An interesting series of articles deals with legal restrictions on employment of aliens in Latin America. Commissioner Lubin notes in his report to the Secretary of Labor for 1939 that the Bureau has published one hundred and twenty-nine articles on Latin American labor topics between 1929 and 1939.

In connection with its consideration of the "relation of sustained-yield forestry to employment and the support of permanent communities," the Department of Agriculture made a study of *Forests and Employment in Germany* (Circular No. 471, July, 1938).

[66] A summary was published in *Monthly Labor Review*, November, 1939.

4. DISTRIBUTION FACTORS IN THE NATIONAL ECONOMY

Marketing and transportation

This field is one of the principal areas of government services to industry. The major roles are played by the Bureau of Agricultural Economics and the Agricultural Marketing Service of the Department of Agriculture, the Bureau of Foreign and Domestic Commerce, and the Federal Trade Commission. Other agencies, such as the Bureau of Mines, render important services but in narrower fields.[67] The material is voluminous and only a sample of the more important studies can be given.[68] Much of the material consists of practical aids to marketing and as such has no place here.

One of the principal means used by the Bureau of Foreign and Domestic Commerce to carry out its program to provide marketing and other aids to small business, which was described in Part I, is the improvement of current reporting services. An important experimental innovation is the reporting on a monthly basis of commodity activity in three industries at every stage from production to consumption. It is believed that such reporting may be of use in efforts to

[67] On the whole subject see "Marketing in Our American Economy," *Annals of the American Academy of Political and Social Science*, CCIX (May, 1940).

[68] As it happens, the bibliographical guides to publications in this field provided by government agencies are excellent. See Bureau of Foreign and Domestic Commerce, *Market Research Sources, 1940* (1940). This is a guide to sources of information on all aspects of domestic marketing. See also *Reports issued by Agricultural Marketing Service* (January, 1940), *Printed Publications—Agricultural Marketing Service* (1940), and the cumulative lists of publications in the *Annual Reports of the Federal Trade Commission*.

moderate short-run fluctuations in production. A *Monthly Industry Survey of Manufacturers* was inaugurated in November, 1939. It measures the month-to-month fluctuations in the value of manufacturers' inventories, new and unfilled orders, and shipments. It is thought that the changes in the relationships between these four factors may throw light on reasons for current changes in business activity. The sample includes companies which account for more than one-third of the total manufacturing activity in the United States.

A major research contribution in aid of the small business man was the *Industrial Market Data Handbook of the United States* (Domestic Commerce Series No. 107, 1939), prepared by the Industrial Marketing Unit of the Marketing Research Division, and issued in coöperation with the Bureau of the Census and the Bureau of Mines. It is described as "an effort to assemble for each of the 3,071 counties of the United States the basic statistical facts upon which manufacturers of industrial goods and supplies may build their individual market studies, and thereby measure the possibility of economical and profitable distribution of their merchandise in every section and every industry of the country." A parallel study is the new edition of the *Consumer Market Data Handbook* (Domestic Commerce Series No. 102, 1939) which offers consumption statistics for each county and each city in the United States with a population of 2,500 or more. Another study of importance is *Distribution Cost Accounting for Wholesaling* (Domestic Commerce Series No. 106, 1939).

In the Temporary National Economic Committee hearings on savings and investment, much attention was given to the problems of small business, the short-time credit needs of which were extensively explored. In his message to Congress of April 29, 1938 (75th Congress, 3d Session, Senate Document No. 173), urging the investigation of the concentration of economic power now being conducted by the Temporary National Economic Committee, President Roosevelt suggested the establishment of a Bureau of Industrial Economics

. . . which should be endowed with adequate powers to supplement and supervise the collection of industrial statistics by trade associations [and] perform for businessmen functions similar to those performed for farmers by the Bureau of Agricultural Economics.

It should disseminate current statistics and other information regarding market conditions and be in a position to warn against the dangers of shortages and bottleneck conditions and to encourage maintenance of orderly markets. It should study trade fluctuations, credit facilities, and other conditions which affect the welfare of the average businessman. *It should be able to help small businessmen to keep themselves as well informed about trade conditions as their big competitors.* (Italics added.)

By Senate Resolution No. 224, Seventieth Congress, 1st Session, the Federal Trade Commission was directed to make an exhaustive investigation of chain stores. The importance of the subject is evidenced by the fact that nearly twenty cents of each dollar spent in retail stores by the consumer went to chain stores and that chains with 1,000 stores or over, comprising less than one percent of the chains, accounted for approximately one-half of the stores and about 40 percent of the total sales. Altogether the Commission made thirty-four reports on the subject.[69]

[69] *Final Report on the Chain-Store Investigation* (74th Cong., 1st Sess., Sen. Doc. No. 4, 1935) contains a full list of the titles and document numbers of the 33 previous reports.

The *Agricultural Income Inquiry* made by the Federal Trade Commission and the studies of price spreads made by the Bureau of Agricultural Economics, both of which were described earlier, contain much data and have an important bearing on problems of distribution in agriculture. The Bureau of Agricultural Economics is studying the relative efficiency of different systems of marketing and their bearing on the bargaining power of farmers.

By Section 201(a) of the Agricultural Adjustment Act of 1938, as amended, the Secretary of Agriculture is authorized to make complaint to the Interstate Commerce Commission with respect to rates, charges, tariffs, and practices relating to the transportation of farm products. For the necessary economic analysis the Secretary relies on the Division of Marketing and Transportation Research of the Bureau of Agricultural Economics. That Division has under way several major studies in this field.[70] They include a study of

. . . aspects of interterritorial freight rate differentials of concern to agriculture; a study of the administration of freight rates by transportation agencies and government regulatory bodies in relation to achieving the social and economic ideal of high levels of employment, production, and consumption; a study and critical analysis of the salient features of motor-carrier rate policy adopted by the Interstate Commerce Commission under the Motor Carrier Act of 1935 and the probable economic implications of that policy to agriculture and to the general public; analysis of the economic implications to agriculture and the general public of current legislation relating to the promotion and regulation of transportation; a study to revise the present series of index numbers of freight rates for cotton, livestock, and wheat,

---

[70] See *BAE Handbook* (December, 1939), pp. 21-24.

and to prepare a new series of index numbers for other farm products, particularly fruits and vegetables.

In November, 1939, the Liberty of the Bureau of Agricultural Economics issued a valuable bibliography in three parts entitled *Transportation of Agricultural Products in the United States 1920–June 1939* (Agricultural Economics Bibliography No. 81, processed).

The Bureau of Agricultural Economics and the Agricultural Marketing Service have collaborated in a series of important economic surveys of city markets and shipping point markets for perishable farm products. These make recommendations for changes in the marketing systems of the areas concerned and thus reveal again the interplay of research and action program which is so conspicuous a feature of the work of the Department of Agriculture. The studies made so far relate to New York City, Philadelphia, the Kansas City area, Atlanta, and various concentration markets in the southeastern states. Studies are being made of the marketing of dairy products in the New England states. Problems of surplus diversion are also being studied, particularly in connection with the food stamp plan which originated in a suggestion made by F. V. Waugh, the present head of the Division of Marketing and Transportation Research. This device, variously spoken of as "domestic dumping" and the "two-price system" is now being considerably enlarged and will soon be in operation in more than one hundred cities.[71] The Division of Marketing and Transporta-

[71] Mr. Milo Perkins, head of the Surplus Marketing Administration, testified at great length concerning the food stamp plan and other methods of surplus diversion at the *Hearings before the Subcommittee of the Committee on Appropriations, United States Senate, Seventy-Sixth Congress, Third Session, on H. R. 8202* (1940), pp. 349–403. See, particu-

tion Research and the Surplus Marketing Administration collaborated in the preparation of an *Economic Analysis of the Food Stamp Plan,* issued in October, 1940, as an inter-bureau report.

Of interest in this context are the numerous studies of interstate trade barriers published or in progress. In March, 1939, the Bureau of Agricultural Economics made a special report to the Secretary of Agriculture on *Barriers to Internal Trade in Farm Products.* The report describes the internal restraints on trade in dairy products, margarine, and alco-holic beverages, and deals also with railroad and motor-vehicle regulation, merchant truckers, grades, standards and labelling, and quarantines. The Division of Commercial Laws of the Bureau of Foreign and Domestic Commerce has published several articles dealing with the problem in *Com-parative Law Series.* An elaborate investigation of interstate trade barriers is that now in progress as part of the Market-ing Laws Survey (A. H. Martin, Jr., Director) of WPA. The survey is being conducted in consultation with an ad-visory council consisting of law professors who are specialists in the field of trade regulation. The primary purpose of the Marketing Laws Survey is the

. . . compilation, review and analysis of the text of all the State laws directly affecting the marketing of goods from the place of production to the point of consumption. Interrelations with Federal marketing laws will be suggested.

The scope of the survey includes the following subject matter: Entry into business or market; sales promotion devices; trans-portation, storage and warehousing; financing and security;

---

larly, the charts and other statistical materials introduced by the witness, pp. 379 ff.

marketing organization and commodity exchanges; coöperatives; regulation of price policies and practices; regulation of monopolies and practices in restraint of trade; barriers to trade between the States; governmental purchasing and distribution; taxes directly affecting the marketing of goods.

In May, 1939, the Marketing Laws Survey published a preliminary study, *Comparative Charts of State Statutes Illustrating Barriers to Trade between States*. As a practical aid in combatting interstate trade barriers the Marketing Laws Survey also issued a *Digest of State Laws Relating to the Problem of Interstate Trade Barriers for States Whose Legislatures Convene in 1940* (1940, processed).

In October, 1939, an Interdepartmental Committee on Interstate Trade Barriers (Paul T. Truitt, Chairman) was set up at the suggestion of Secretary of Commerce Hopkins. The Committee is composed of representatives of the Departments of Agriculture, Commerce, Labor, and State, the Interstate Commerce Commission, the United States Tariff Commission, the Federal Alcohol Administration, and WPA. The Committee completed hearings on the subject of interstate trade barriers in March, 1940, before the Temporary National Economic Committee which explored the matter extensively. On March 31, 1940, the Interdepartmental Committee announced the initiation of a program for the promotion of research in American universities and colleges in the social and economic ramifications of interstate and municipal trade barriers. The outline of suggested study covers (1) social and political origins of barrier laws; (2) operation and administration of trade-barrier enactments, including methods and degree of enforcement; and (3) analysis of the social and economic consequences of particular barrier laws, including effects on employment, production, costs, and consumption.

The Council of State Governments has been the leader in the movement against interstate trade barriers and the various agencies mentioned above have coöperated with the Council in its work along these lines.

The impediments to commerce inherent in our present transportation system are also the subject of several lines of study. The vast mine of data in the decisions and the statistical products of the Interstate Commerce Commission must be passed by with this mere mention. The Federal Coördinator of Transportation has issued many important reports on the situation of the railroads. Of related interest is the voluminous series of reports issued by the Senate Interstate Commerce Committee in the course of its investigation of the financing, reorganization, and mergers of railroads (Senate Resolution 71, 74th Congress).

In 1937 the President transmitted to Congress a significant survey entitled *The Interterritorial Freight Rate Problem of the United States* (75th Congress, 1st Session, House Document No. 264) which had been prepared at his direction by the Tennessee Valley Authority. The report discusses the "existence of and the reasons and remedies for the barrier to interstate commerce in the form of the present interterritorial freight rate structure." The problem is stated as follows in the report:

A serious national problem has grown out of the fact that our transportation system as represented by the railroads, the dominant transport agency, has never developed into a complete unity, functioning for national purposes in an economic sense. Regionalization is a striking characteristic of the system. . . .

The effect of this regionalization of freight-rate structures is to localize commerce by hampering a national flow of goods across the territorial boundary lines. It is natural, however, for commerce to expand as civilization progresses, and as long as these barriers against a national flow of commerce remain economic progress of the Nation will be retarded.[72]

The National Resources Planning Board is reviewing the problem of transportation in the United States in order to advise on a national transportation policy. Examination will be made of the role of each type of carrier in the transportation system as a whole. Rate structures will be studied with reference to their influence on the economic development of geographic areas and the problem of government regulation, subsidy, and ownership will be explored.

Income and expenditures

Important over-all estimates of national income have been made regularly by the Bureau of Foreign and Domestic Commerce since 1934: *National Income, 1929–1932* [73] (73d Congress, 2d Session, Senate Document 124), *National Income in the United States, 1929–1935* (1936), *National Income, 1929–1936* (1937), *Income in the United States, 1929–1937* (November, 1938, processed), and "National Income in 1938 at 64 Billion Dollars" (*Survey of Current Business*, June, 1939). Revised estimates of national income for the period 1929–1939 were to be published in bulletin form toward the end of 1940. In 1939 the first estimates of income by states were issued in *State Income Payments,*

[72] Note may be made again of the Bureau of Agricultural Economics' study of interregional competition.
[73] Prepared in collaboration with the National Bureau of Economic Research.

1929–1937 (May, 1939, processed). The National Income Division of the Bureau of Foreign and Domestic Commerce, which makes all the foregoing studies, also compiles a monthly index of income which is published in the *Survey of Current Business*. A study now in progress relates to income distribution by size. A bulletin on monthly income payments in the United States, 1929–1940, was issued in December, 1940 (Economic Series No. 6).

In the national estimates income is broken down for each of the twelve major industries into which the economic activities of the nation have been classified. The breakdown is by number of persons employed, income produced, income paid out, types of income payments, and per capita incomes. National income produced is defined as the gross value of all the commodities produced and services rendered in the nation in a given year, minus the value of all raw materials and capital equipment consumed in the productive process. National income paid out is defined as the aggregate of wages, salaries, interest, dividends, entrepreneurial withdrawals, net rents, and royalties.

On July 22, 1940, it was announced by the Department of Commerce that the National Income Division of the Bureau of Foreign and Domestic Commerce had taken over and would carry forward the work of the National Bureau of Economic Research in the field of capital formation and final product analysis. The National Bureau of Economic Research has turned over all its data in this field to the National Income Division. This expansion of the national income studies is designed to provide an analysis of the composition of income in terms of the actual output of goods and services and will describe in detail the products of industry in a given year. In the announcement of the expansion of the national income studies it is stated that

From this study the National Income Division will be able to supply data measuring the amount of food, clothing, household appliances, automobiles, etc., produced in any year since 1929. These data will be broken down so as to show separately the changes in business inventories and the amounts that consumers actually spend for such commodities. Special attention will also be given to the output of items, such as machinery, new factory buildings, etc., which are eventually added to the sum total of our national wealth and which may be classified as capital formation. The amount of capital formation will be measured by estimating the total production of machinery, the volume of construction, etc., and then subtracting the estimated yearly depreciation. This phase of the study is particularly important at this time since its results will add considerably to knowledge of the output of durable goods industries. Such information is of great use in the preparation of the national defense program. It is anticipated that once the study is well under way, data can be made public at more frequent intervals than annually.

In the course of the study the National Income Division will summarize the output of hundreds of commodities, which in turn will be classified into 70 or 80 commodity groups. The National Bureau of Economic Research, whose studies of commodity flow and capital formation pioneered in this field, analyzed commodities only. The National Income Division will estimate consumers' expenditures on services as well as commodities so as to give a more complete understanding of the composition of our national income.

Other sections of the study that will be of special interest to business men include analyses of changes in distributive margins and in the volume of business inventories. Among the principal uses of this new data on the production of commodities and services, aside from its provision of background information for national defense are the following:

1. It will complement the present national income estimates by showing what goods and services make up the national income.

2. It will provide an analysis on a national scale of matters essential to every business man by providing him with detailed information as to total consumer expenditures for specific groups of products.

3. It will correlate prices with dollar values so as to provide an estimate of physical volumes of commodities.

Using WPA funds, the National Income Division and New York University are collaborating in comparative studies of the national income and public finances of various countries including the United States. They will examine, for the period 1928–1937, the technical methods of making income estimates in approximately twenty-three countries, the composition of national income estimates in about nineteen countries, the amounts and sources of tax revenues in about sixty-four countries, government expenditures in thirty-one countries, and national debt and debt charges for twenty-eight countries.

A study entitled *Allocation of Federal, State and Local Taxes to Consumer Income Brackets* was completed by the Department of Commerce in July, 1940. The purpose of the study is "to show the taxes borne by various income brackets in relation to their income level." The study seeks to show the burdens borne by consumers in the selected income tax brackets by estimating (1) the proportions of personal taxes and taxes on specific items paid by them and (2) the proportions of all other taxes probably paid indirectly by the same consumer income brackets, under various assumptions of shifting, but with the emphasis on tax shifting to consumers. "These tentative allocations are an attempt to present figures required for a realistic analysis both of the justice of a tax system and of its economic effects. The development of a rational tax system depends on knowledge of the incidence of all taxes, classified by types, on various income levels. As an experiment, the method developed was applied to calculating the probable incidence of the defense taxes of June, 1940." [74]

The most complete picture yet presented of the division of the national income among the American people and of the way they spend it is contained in two studies made by the National Resources Committee: *Consumer Incomes in the United States—Their Distribution in 1935-1936* (1938), and *Consumer Expenditures in the United States* (1939).[75] A third report, still to be published, will offer a more detailed breakdown of "family spending" into a greater number of kinds of commodities than does the consumer expenditure study. The reports are part of a larger study now being made by the same agency of the relation of the nation's consumption demands to its productive capacities. The data on which the reports are based were collected in a coöperative sampling-method study of consumer purchases undertaken by WPA, the Bureau of Labor Statistics, and the Bureau of Home Economics, with which the National Resources Committee and the Central Statistical Board collaborated. Two metropolitan communities, six

---

[74] *Domestic Commerce* (July 30, 1940), p. 52. This study has since been published by the Temporary National Economic Committee in its monograph series under the title, *Who Pays the Taxes?*

[75] A digest of both reports was published in June, 1939: *The Consumer Spends His Income* (1939).

large cities averaging 300,000 inhabitants, fourteen middle-sized cities of 30,000 to 75,000, twenty-nine smaller cities of from 10,000 to 20,000, one hundred and forty villages, and sixty-four farm counties were covered in the study. Its object and uses were described by Commissioner Lubin in the foreword to the Chicago study, as follows: [76]

The Study of Consumer Purchases has been directed toward two related objectives. The first is to ascertain the distribution of families according to income, occupation, and family composition. The second is to learn how families of different incomes, occupations and family types apportion their expenditures among specific goods and services in different parts of the country.

In selecting the data to be secured and the analyses to be made, consideration has been given to the different interests which may be served by a study of consumer purchases. . . .

Simultaneous studies of rural and urban family incomes, and the manner of their disbursement, can shed light on the relative abilities of farm and city to absorb each other's products, and on the manner in which that capacity changes as rural and urban incomes change. Welfare agencies are concerned with data bearing on the budgetary requirements of families in the maintenance of minimum standards of subsistence. Manufacturers and distributors will utilize the information on income distribution and consumer preferences in the planning of their production and sales programs. Finally, there is general interest in knowing how actual levels of living differ from commonly accepted standards of living.

---

[76] Bureau of Labor Statistics: *Family Income in Chicago* (Bulletin No. 642, 1939), I, vii–viii. In Appendix A of that Bulletin will be found a description of the scope and character of samples taken in the study of consumer purchases. See also "Plans for a Study of the Consumption of Goods and Services by American Families." *Journal of the American Statistical Association*, March, 1936; and Appendix A, Section 2, of the National Resources Committee's *Consumer Incomes* study.

Obviously, any economic program must have as one fundamental prerequisite, a definite knowledge of the distribution of families by incomes and of the choices made by families in the disbursement of their incomes. Heretofore we have not lacked impressive statistics of national production, bank clearings, and factory pay rolls. But with respect to the individual choices of the consumer—whose willingness and ability to absorb the offerings of the market go far to determine the smoothness with which the economic order functions—we have had to content ourselves with theories which changed with the current fashion in psychology, with guesses derived from data on population, total sales, and general price movements. We have not known at what income level a family of a given type is likely to enter the market for recreational equipment, electrical appliances, or other luxury goods. Even with respect to staple articles we are in doubt as to what proportion of the population must find them beyond economic reach. Moreover, the variation in purchasing habits of the population in different regions of the country, or of families living in cities of different size, has yet to be shown in terms which would measure the influence of these factors upon actual quantities purchased and prices paid.

The results of the Study of Consumer Purchases are being issued in parts by the participating agencies. The Bureau of Home Economics of the Department of Agriculture has issued two bulletins, one on family income in the Pacific Region, the other on family income in the Plains and Mountains region. The Bureau of Labor Statistics has issued four bulletins on family income. These relate to Chicago, five New England cities, the southeastern region, and four urban communities in the Pacific Northwest. Two bulletins on family expenditure contain data for New York City and Chicago. Several bulletins are yet to appear. Bulletin No.

648 (8 vols.) will present the data on family expenditure by the following items of expenditure: housing, food, clothing and personal care, furnishings and equipment, medical care, transportation, miscellaneous, and will also show changes in assets and liabilities.

For the purpose of bringing up to date the weights for the cost of living indexes currently published by the Bureau of Labor Statistics and based on the independent surveys of family income and expenditure made by it periodically since 1888, that agency undertook in 1934–1936 a nation-wide study of money disbursements of wage earners and clerical workers in forty-two cities with more than 50,000 population. Those parts of the study published thus far relate to New York City, five cities in the Pacific region, and five cities in the West North Central Mountain region. The final report which will appear as Bulletin No. 638 will present summary averages for all cities combined.[77]

The Division of Economic Studies of the Bureau of Research and Statistics of the Social Security Board is making a study of the effects on purchasing power of the old-age, employment, and public assistance programs, particularly as they affect the flow of money values and goods.

The *Agricultural Income* inquiry made by the Federal Trade Commission has already been described.

One of the principal sources of data concerning income is the compilation *Statistics of Income* issued annually by the Bureau of Internal Revenue of the Treasury Department since 1916. That publication is issued in two parts,

[77] Summary accounts will be found in the *Monthly Labor Review*, December, 1939, and January, 1940. The new cost of living index was presented in the August, 1940, issue.

of which the first is compiled from individual income tax returns, estate tax returns, and gift tax returns, while the second part is compiled from corporation income and excess-profits tax returns and personal holding company returns.

On the basis of the data obtained in the consumer purchases study, the Bureau of Home Economics proposes to make a study of ways of budgeting family resources. It will prepare food budgets and other material on planning adequate diets for families at different income levels and at different degrees of urbanization. It will also study the relationships between income in kind and money expenditures for living of farm families. Comparison will be made of the expenditures of families making larger than usual outlays for living with those of a "normal" group. The Bureau of Home Economics of the Department of Agriculture has issued a study of *Diets of Families of Employed Wage Earners and Clerical Workers in Cities* (U.S.D.A. Circular No. 507, January, 1939) based on 4,000 records of a week's food consumption collected by the Bureau of Labor Statistics in various cities of the country. The Yearbook of Agriculture for 1939, *Food and Life,* issued by the Department of Agriculture, is devoted to a comprehensive presentation of what has been called the newer knowledge of nutrition as it affects both animals and human beings. The Library of the Bureau of Agricultural Economics has issued an extensive annotated bibliography on *Rural Standards of Living* (Miscellaneous Publication No. 116, July, 1931). See also the critical bibliography by Faith M. Williams and Carle C. Zimmerman, *Studies of Family Living in the United States and Other Countries* (U.S.D.A. Miscellaneous Publication No. 223,

1935).[78] The Consumers' Counsel Division of AAA has, with the aid of WPA funds, made detailed studies of consumer goods standards both here and abroad.

The Division of Research of WPA and the Retail Price Division of the Bureau of Labor Statistics have made a study of *Inter-City Differences in Costs of Living, March, 1935, 59 Cities* (WPA Research Monograph XII, July, 1937).

A constantly increasing stream of research flows from the rehabilitation efforts which form an integral part of the adjustment, conservation, and land-use planning programs of the Department of Agriculture. These studies in rural sociology have been conducted by the Farm Security Administration (formerly the Resettlement Administration) and the Bureau of Agricultural Economics. In many of the studies the Division of Research of WPA has coöperated.[79]

Of these studies, *Social Status and Farm Tenure—Attitudes and Social Conditions of Corn Belt and Cotton Belt Farmers* (Social Research Report XII, April, 1938, processed), and *Disadvantaged Classes in American Agriculture* (Social Research Report VIII, April, 1938, processed) may be mentioned here as of most general interest. Altogether seventeen such studies have been issued to date. All of them throw much light on rural standards of living.

An important investigation of related interest is the *Farm-Housing Survey* (United States Department of Agriculture Miscellaneous Publication No. 323, March, 1939), based on

[78] Compare International Labour Office, *Methods of Family Living Studies*, Studies and Reports Series N (Statistics) No. 23 (Geneva, 1940); and Zimmerman's *Consumption and Standards of Living* (1936).

[79] Woofter and Winston's *Seven Lean Years* (1939), which is based on these studies, gives an excellent insight into the problems dealt with in some of them.

data obtained in a house-to-house canvass of 595,855 farm houses in 308 counties of 46 states, which was directed by the Bureau of Home Economics of the Department of Agriculture.[80]

From 1934 to 1938 real property inventories in more than two hundred urban areas were made by Federal work relief agencies. The inventories covered more than eight million dwelling units, that is, about 45 percent of the number of urban families in the United States in 1930. The surveys covered type, age, condition, value, and mortgage status of residential structure; the number of rooms, number of persons per room, sanitary facilities, and monthly rental of dwelling units.[81] There was assembled "the most detailed body of statistical information now available on the physical characteristics of housing in the United States." A summary of the data obtained through the survey was issued by WPA: *Urban Housing* (1938).

Mention was made earlier of the *National Health Survey* conducted by the Public Health Service. The results of this investigation are being issued in parts from time to time.

Many of the investigations conducted by the Tennessee Valley Authority and the Rural Electrification Administration bear on the problem of the standards of living of various sectors of the population.

The Temporary National Economic Committee has also been making studies of consumer problems and has devoted to that subject Part 8 of its published hearings (May 10–12, 1939).

[80] See also Department of Agriculture, *Housing Requirements of Farm Families in the United States* (Miscellaneous Publication 322, February 1939).

[81] A similar survey forms part of the 1940 census.

B. Structure of International Economic Organization

I. ORGANIZATION OF NATIONAL ENTERPRISE FOR EXTERNAL OPERATIONS

Among the studies made by the Department of Commerce for the Temporary National Economic Committee is an investigation of international industrial decentralization. That study brings up to date and expands earlier studies of branch factories by the Bureau of Foreign and Domestic Commerce.

American trade associations are the subject of another study made by the Bureau of Foreign and Domestic Commerce for the Temporary National Economic Committee. As part of the study it has made an extensive analysis of the experience of Webb-Pomerene groups and of their export price policies, which will help to fill the need for a critical account and analysis of experience under the Export Trade Act.[82] The Federal Trade Commission, which is charged with the administration of the Export-Trade (Webb-Pomerene) Act, has never made a comprehensive economic inquiry into the activities of the numerous export associations formed under the law. The Commission, two years before the passage of the Act, published a *Report on Coöperation in American Export Trade*, 2 volumes (1916). Its only subsequent publication has been a short brochure covering practice and procedure under the Act. Some figures on the operations of the associations are given in the Commission's

[82] See Barnes's *Government Promotion of Foreign Trade in the United States* (1933), pp. 20 ff.; and Notz and Harvey's *American Foreign Trade* (1921). The Bureau's study is T.N.E.C. Monograph No. 6 (1940).

annual reports. Another rather meager account was published by the Division of Commercial Laws of the Bureau of Foreign and Domestic Commerce in November, 1935, a revision of which appeared in *Comparative Law Series*, June, 1939.

The cartel hearings of the Temporary National Economic Committee will be published as Part 25 of the record. Their main purpose has been to explore the influence of the new international economic environment upon American economic problems. A study made for the Temporary National Economic Committee by the Division of Regional Information of the Bureau of Foreign and Domestic Commerce relates to British industrial reorganization in the coal and cotton industries. An investigation of the effect of the tariff on industrial concentration has also been made for the Temporary National Economic Committee by Clifford L. James of Ohio State University (Monograph 10, 1940).

2. INTERNATIONAL BUSINESS ORGANIZATION

The Division of Regional Information of the Bureau of Foreign and Domestic Commerce has long been concerned with this subject. Among its publications on the subject are: *Origin and Development of the Continental Steel Entente* (Trade Information Bulletin No. 484, 1927), *International Cartel Movement* (Trade Information Bulletin No. 556, 1928), and *Representative International Cartels, Combines and Trusts* (Trade Promotion Series No. 81, 1929). These studies have been kept somewhat up to date by brief resumés of developments which are published from time to time in *Commerce Reports*.

Important analyses of the position of international and

national cartels are presented in the industrial surveys of the Tariff Commission described earlier.

The Finance Division of the Bureau of Foreign and Domestic Commerce has lately completed a study for the Temporary National Economic Committee of the international affiliations of American enterprise in which the effort is made to determine the extent of the control of American industry by foreign capital, and of foreign industry by American capital. Related in interest is the study of *American Direct Investments in Foreign Countries, 1936* (Economic Series No. 1, 1938), issued by the Finance Division.[83]

The Federal Trade Commission notes in its annual reports foreign legislation of importance in this connection.

3. MONETARY AND FINANCIAL ORGANIZATION

The Bureau of Foreign and Domestic Commerce has made numerous studies in this field: *The Bombay Bullion Market* (Trade Information Bulletin No. 457, 1927), *Italy's Monetary Policy* (Trade Information Bulletin No. 512, 1927), *Silver Market in 1930* (Trade Information Bulletin No. 742, 1931), *Silver Market* (Trade Promotion Series No. 139, 1932), *The Monetary Use of Silver in 1933* (Trade Promotion Series No. 149, 1933), and *Handbook of Foreign Currencies* (Trade Promotion Series No. 164, 1936).

The research department of the Federal Reserve Bank of New York has made an investigation of international monetary organization and policy which consists of a series

[83] An earlier study, *American Direct Investments in Foreign Countries* (Trade Information Bulletin No. 731, 1930) described the situation as of 1929.

of closely related studies independently prepared by individual members. The studies cover

. . . (a) the adequacy of existing currency mechanisms under diverse circumstances; (b) the present monetary mechanism and position of the United States; (c) operations of the exchange stabilization fund and the gold transactions of the Treasury; (d) the British Exchange Equalization Account; (e) stabilization funds, general applicability; (f) trade areas; (g) monetary standards for young countries; (h) some general implications of recent currency developments. An appendix is devoted to a theoretical analysis of trade adjustments under fixed and free exchanges.[84]

The project was directed by J. H. Williams and was undertaken to meet internal needs for information. Publication is apparently not contemplated.

The Division of Research and Statistics of the Federal Reserve Board is continuously engaged in the analysis of current international capital movements, and results are published at intervals in the *Federal Reserve Bulletin*. With the adoption this year of the policy of publishing signed articles by members of the staff in the Bulletin, more latitude of interpretation has been obtained. The policy was inaugurated in the January, 1940, issue with an article by the Director of the Division, E. A. Goldenweiser, on "The Gold Problem Today." The March issue contained an article by Woodlief Thomas, "The Banks and Idle Money"; the April issue contains a study by Arthur Hersey, "Historical Review of Objectives of Federal Reserve Policy"; and the May issue an article by Mr. Goldenweiser on "Cheap Money and the Federal Reserve System." A new edition of the *Fed-*

[84] *A Program of Financial Research* (1937), II, 21–22.

eral Reserve Chart Book was issued in 1940. It contains about thirty charts on bank credit, money rates, security markets, and business conditions. A base book of banking statistics is also being compiled by the Board.

The Finance Division of the Bureau of Foreign and Domestic Commerce has issued numerous studies of foreign budgetary practices, and public and private finance. Among the countries whose public finances have been analyzed are Australia, Colombia, the Far Eastern countries, France, and Peru. The budgetary studies covered all of South America. Unfortunately, all these are now quite out of date. Of some interest is an account of the *Paris Bourse* (Trade Information Bulletin No. 719, 1930) by H. Merle Cochran.

On May 15, 1940, the Senate Committee on Banking and Currency began the investigation of the monetary and banking system of the United States which had been authorized by the Senate the previous August in order "to consider and recommend a national monetary and banking policy by which the monetary and banking authorities of the Federal Government shall be guided and governed, and to consider and recommend the character of governmental machinery best calculated to carry out such policy." According to the *New York Times* of May 15, 1940:

The questionnaire directed to the Treasury called for a comprehensive explanation of the silver and gold policies, the effect of additions to Social Security reserves on monetary and banking conditions and steps to promote foreign-exchange stability of Latin-American countries. The Treasury was asked also if it could suggest "any criteria for determining the appropriate size of the deficit (or surplus)."

The Federal Reserve Board was asked, among other questions, whether the Treasury's authority to issue $3,000,000,000 in greenbacks should be continued permanently or temporarily.

The Department of Commerce was asked about movements of foreign capital and American investments abroad.

State banking supervisors were asked: "are there too many banks or banking offices in your State?"

Members of the American Bankers Association and the Association of Reserve City Bankers were asked what factors have been mainly responsible for low interest rates in recent years; what is likely to be the course in the near future, and whether there was any considerable chance of a serious decline in prices of bonds and necessity for banks to sell bonds, "resulting in enormous losses to the banks and bank failures."

4. INTERNATIONAL ECONOMIC ACCESS

The problems subsumed under this head have been of much interest since the World War, particularly as to raw materials and the treatment of aliens and alien enterprises.

The Bureau of Mines has for many years been publishing digests of foreign legislation relating to alien ownership of raw material deposits of which eighty-two have appeared since 1929. The Division of Commercial Laws of the Bureau of Foreign and Domestic Commerce likewise publishes translations and analyses of foreign legislation and judicial decisions relating to this subject in *Comparative Law Series.* The Division of Commercial Laws has also issued a number of lengthy accounts of the problems confronting aliens trading under the laws of foreign countries. The latest study deals with Brazil. Earlier ones cover Argentina, Canada, Germany, Great Britain, Mexico, Venezuela, and others. These publications are practical handbooks designed to give the business-man an insight into the problems likely to confront him when he attempts to do business abroad. Numerous handbooks dealing with legal problems encountered in collecting accounts and extending credit in foreign countries have also been issued.

Another subject of interest in this connection is the taxation of foreign enterprises, and in this field, also, the Department of Commerce has issued many publications. New developments were reported by the Division of Commercial Laws in its *Comparative Law Series*, now discontinued.

The Office of the General Counsel for the Treasury Department has in preparation a series of compilations of the tax laws of foreign countries. Compilations of the *French Income Tax Laws* (1938) and the *Inheritance and Gift Tax Laws of Sweden* (1938) have been issued. These were prepared for the use of the congressional Joint Committee on Internal Revenue Taxation.

5. INTERDEPENDENCE OF NATIONAL ECONOMIES FOR RAW MATERIALS

The Bureau of Mines of the Department of Interior has published a series of thirty-four world flow charts showing for the year 1932 world production, consumption, and trade relations in so-called strategic minerals. Lack of funds has prevented the preparation of a final group of charts needed for purposes of comparison. Another set of fourteen flow charts prepared by the Bureau of Foreign and Domestic Commerce and the Bureau of Mines covers non-mineral strategic raw materials as of 1932.

Mention has already been made of the volume on *Mineral Raw Materials* (1937), prepared by the Bureau of Mines. In a volume to appear in the future, the Bureau will deal with the international aspects of mineral economics. Mention was also made earlier of the studies of the deficiency minerals requirements of the United States, which have been made by the Bureau of Mines and by the Mineral Advisory Committee to the Army and Navy Munitions Board (Dr. C. K. Leith, Chairman).[85]

Likewise of importance in this connection are the Tariff Commission's studies of nitrogen, sodium sulphate, iron and steel, mica, phosphate and superphosphates, which were cited earlier.[86] In December, 1939, the Library of the Tariff Commission issued an exceedingly helpful *Raw Materials Bibliography* (processed).

The Leather and Rubber Division of the Bureau of Foreign and Domestic Commerce has been continuously concerned with rubber since American interest in that commodity was aroused by the Stevenson restriction scheme. The following are among the more noteworthy rubber studies issued by the Division: *The Plantation Rubber Industry in the Middle East* (Trade Promotion Series No. 2, 1925), *Possibilities for Para Rubber Production in Philippine Islands* (Trade Promotion Series No. 17, 1925), *Rubber Production in Amazon Valley* (Trade Promotion Series No. 23, 1925), *Rubber Production in Africa* (Trade Promotion Series No. 34, 1926), *Possibilities for Para Rubber Production in Northern Tropical America* (Trade Promotion Series No. 40, 1926), *Marketing of Crude Rubber* (Trade Promotion Series No. 55, 1927), *Rubber Regulation and the Malayan Plantation Industry* (Trade Promotion Series No. 159, 1935), and *Rubber Statistics 1900–1937, Production, Absorption, Stocks and Prices* (Trade Promotion Series No. 181, 1938). The Division also issued semi-monthly a *Rubber News Letter* containing statistics of world rubber shipments, absorption, and stocks. It also carried news on the admin-

[85] See p. 160.
[86] See p. 162.

istration of the international rubber control agreement.[87]

Of the numerous studies of leather made by the Leather and Rubber Division only one, *Leather: World Production and International Trade* (Trade Promotion Series No. 157, 1935), need be cited here.

As part of the survey of essential raw materials authorized by the 67th Congress, the Chemical Division of the Bureau of Foreign and Domestic Commerce made a study of *Potash, The Significance of Foreign Control and the Economic Need of Domestic Development* (Trade Promotion Series No. 33, 1926). Before that date the Division had made a study of the *German Dyestuffs Industry* (Miscellaneous Series No. 126, 1924). While there have been few special studies since the date of those first cited, the Division has issued annual studies of the chemical industry as a whole. The earlier ones related to the more important countries of Europe, and since 1935 there has been an annual survey of *World Chemical Developments* (Trade Information Bulletin No. 832, 1936; Trade Promotion Series No. 169, 1937; No. 177, 1938; No. 195, 1939; and No. 211, 1940). The first world survey of *Synthetic Organic Chemicals* (Trade Promotion Series No. 189) was issued by the Division in 1938. Since 1917 the Tariff Commission has issued an annual report on the production and sales of synthetic organic chemicals in the United States. The 23rd report covering the year 1939 was issued in 1940 (2d Series, Report 140).

Fuel and power in Canada, Latin-America, Manchuria, Japan, and Great Britain are studied in a trade promotion series by the Bureau of Foreign and Domestic Commerce.

---

[87] See also *Crude Rubber* (processed, November 21, 1939), a brief summary by the Tariff Commission of the present situation respecting crude rubber with special reference to the effect of war conditions on United States imports.

C. INTERNATIONAL ECONOMIC RELATIONS

I. RATIONALE OF INTERNATIONAL TRADE

In 1933 in response to Senate Resolution 325 (72d Congress), the Tariff Commission prepared a comprehensive *Analysis of the Foreign Trade of the United States in Relation to the Tariff*, covering the trend of imports in relation to production and height of duties, and the factors favoring exportation of American commodities. In 1934 the Commission issued a *Graphic Analysis of the Foreign Analysis of the Foreign Trade of the United States*, consisting of twenty-four flow charts and twelve bar charts, illustrating exports and imports broken down by commodity groups and subgroups. An interesting collection of memoranda is contained in *Factors Affecting Foreign Trade Policy* (processed), prepared by members of the Bureau of Foreign and Domestic Commerce and issued by the Department of Commerce as a contribution to Foreign Trade Week in May, 1936.

Mention has already been made of the research in interregional competition of the Department of Agriculture. That research bears directly on the theoretical problems of international trade, as does the previously mentioned study, *Agricultural Exports in Relation to Land Policy*, which forms part of the Supplementary Report of the Land Planning Committee of the National Resources Committee.

The Departments of Commerce and State and the Tariff Commission issue a vast amount of explanatory material analyzing the results of the trade agreements program.[88]

[88] The hearings before the House Ways and Means Committee and

While some of the State Department's material is readily available in the speeches of its officers published in the weekly *Bulletin* (formerly *Press Releases*) and in the leaflets comprising the *Commercial Policy Series,* much of it is issued in fugitive mimeographed form. A list will be found in the Tariff Commission's bibliography of *Reciprocal Trade* (1937) and *Supplement* (1940), under the heading, "United States Department of State." The Bureau of Foreign and Domestic Commerce issues annually a brief results analysis of the trade agreements program which is published in *Commerce Reports.* The Tariff Commission has lately undertaken the job of results analysis in connection with trade agreements concluded by the government. In April, 1940, it issued a first series of statistical reports concerning the following industries affected by trade agreements: tobacco and tobacco products; sugar; fats, oils, waxes, and oil-bearing materials; glass and glassware; lace and lace articles; dairy products; and pottery. A second series was issued in June, 1940, covering cement and concrete products; fishery products; fruit and fruit products; grain and grain products; vegetables and vegetable products; alcoholic beverages; and leather and leather footwear. Eventually about sixty industries will be covered. In 1939 the Tariff Commission issued statistical compilations covering 1937 and 1938 imports of items in trade agreements with Belgium, Brazil, Finland, France, The Netherlands, Sweden, and Switzerland, and a volume covering those of Colombia, Guatemala, Haiti, and Honduras.

Many of the commercial policy studies of the Tariff Com-

the Senate Finance Committee are replete with material of this kind prepared by the agencies named as part of their sponsorship of the program or in response to specific requests by committee members.

mission described hereafter have a bearing on the theoretical problems of international trade, for example, the merits of triangular trade as against bilateral trade balancing. The Commission's cost of production studies are expressive of a theory, rather than an aid in establishing it.

2. THE PROCESS OF INTERNATIONAL EXCHANGE

Transportation

The Maritime Commission has made several extensive studies in this field: *Economic Survey of the American Merchant Marine* (1937), *Report on Tramp Shipping Service* (75th Congress, 3d Session, House Document No. 520, 1938), which was a study of the advisability of participation in such service by American citizens with vessels under United States registry; *Economic Survey of Coastwise and Intercoastal Shipping* (March 15, 1939, processed); *Aircraft and Merchant Marine* (November 13, 1937, processed); and *Training Merchant Marine Personnel* (1939). There has been some study of the scrapping of old or obsolete merchant tonnage owned by the United States or in use in the Merchant Marine. The Commission is also studying the relative cost of construction or reconditioning of vessels in the shipyards of the several coastal districts with a view to recommending how the respective yards may "compete on an equalized basis."

The Commission also makes many significant economic investigations in connection with the exercise of its regulatory powers over water carriers. The results of these are published in its opinions and decisions. One of particular importance is the *Intercoastal Investigation, 1935*. The studies of ship design and propulsion made by the Technical Division, of rates and services by the Legal Division and the Division of Regulation, of the operating phases of American maritime services by the Division of Operations and Traffic, and of marine insurance in the United States by the Division of Insurance—all have important economic bearings.

The present war has greatly influenced the Commission's current research program. Consideration is being given to the problems raised by the war's impact on American and foreign flag shipping services in our foreign trade, by changes in the flow of direction of American exports and imports, by changes in the movement and sources of origin of strategic and critical materials, and by merchant marine losses due to destruction. The current program of coöperation with the Latin American republics is the occasion for intensive study of the position of American flag services in the trade with them.

The Bureau of Agricultural Economics has made a study of the impact of war on ocean shipping with special reference to its effects on the agricultural exports of the United States. The problems dealt with relate to the factors affecting the tonnage supply available for the carriage of dry cargoes, the influence of our merchant fleet on the supply of shipping, the effect of modern war strategy on belligerent economic organization, practices, and policies, and their effect upon shipping. The study was issued in processed form in November, 1940. In May, 1940, the Tariff Commission issued a report on wartime increases in the transportation costs of the principal commodities imported into the United States (processed).

In 1938 the Transportation Division of the Bureau of Foreign and Domestic Commerce completed a study of the *Control of Ocean Freight Rates in Foreign Trade* (Trade Promotion Series No. 185), which is an important world survey of shipping conferences and pools, their rate practices, and their regulation by governments. The Transportation Division has published several supplements to an earlier study of *Shipping and Shipbuilding Subsidies* (Trade Promotion Series No. 129, 1932), and has issued a supplement to its study of *Railway and Highway Transportation Abroad* (Trade Promotion Series No. 155, 1935), under the title *Transport Control Abroad* (Trade Promotion Series No. 196, 1939). The ocean freight rate study was brought up to date in *Wartime Control of Ocean Freight Rates in Foreign Trade* (Trade Promotion Series No. 212), published in September, 1940.

The Tariff Commission has utilized WPA workers to correlate and summarize published information relative to the density and stowage factors of commodities in a study of *Commodity Packaging Data* (1937, processed), a compilation of information on typical containers and packing materials currently in use for domestic, import, and export shipments. The Bureau of Foreign and Domestic Commerce, in July, 1940, issued a practical handbook on *Modern Export Packing* (Trade Promotion Series No. 207) to serve as a guide to American manufacturers and shippers.

The annual compilation, *Report on the Volume of Waterborne Foreign Commerce of the United States by Ports of Origin and Destination*, is issued by the Maritime Commission. Other statistical reports cover intercoastal trade, trade with the insular possessions and territories, and foreign trade by commodities and ports. The annual compilation of *Merchant Marine Statistics* and the annual *Merchant Vessels of the United States* are both issued by the Bureau of Navigation and Steamboat Inspection of the Department of Commerce.

The Bureau of Foreign and Domestic Commerce issues studies of foreign ports from time to time, for example, *Port of Hamburg* (Foreign Port Series No. 1, 1930), *Port of Liverpool* (Foreign Port Series No. 2, 1929), and *Foreign Bunkering Stations and Charges against Vessels* (Foreign Port Series No. 3, 1932).

The course of trade

Statistical compilations relating to the foreign trade of the United States, both omnibus and special, regular and occasional, are many. The principal source for up-to-date information in this field is the *Monthly Summary of Foreign Commerce of the United States*, compiled by the Division of Foreign Trade Statistics of the Bureau of Foreign and Domestic Commerce. That compilation contains a summary of exports and imports by months; it presents exports and imports of merchandise by countries; exports of domestic merchandise by articles; imports of merchandise for consumption by articles; exports of foreign merchandise by articles; exports and imports of gold and silver by countries and by customs districts; a summary statement of commerce with noncontiguous territories; domestic exports and imports by economic classes; indexes of changes in quantity, unit value (price), and total value of exports and imports by economic classes; totals of exports and imports of merchandise by customs districts; domestic exports of cotton by countries; and imports of cotton by countries of production. There is also an index of commodities.

About March of each year the Bureau of Foreign and Domestic Commerce issues a *Summary of United States Trade with the World,* which contains a brief analysis and summary tables covering the trade in the preceding year. About August a more comprehensive bulletin, *United States Foreign Trade,* is issued. This contains, in addition to an analytical summary, statistics of principal commodities in the trade with leading foreign countries, index numbers, charts, graphs, and other information.

The definitive compilation is the annual *Foreign Commerce and Navigation of the United States,* which covers merchandise imports and exports of the United States by articles, countries, customs districts, rates of duty, tariff paragraph, and duty collected. It also covers exports and imports of gold and silver, re-exports, drawbacks paid, number and tonnage of vessels entered and cleared, and transit and transshipment trade. As a definitive compilation it is necessarily not current. The volume for 1938 was published in 1940.

The Bureau of Foreign and Domestic Commerce also issues five monthly mimeographed foreign trade statements: *Exports and Imports of Merchandise by Economic Groups* (Foreign Trade Statement 1701), *Exports and Imports of Merchandise, Gold and Silver* (Foreign Trade Statement 1702), *Exports and Imports of Merchandise by Grand Divisions and Principal Countries* (Foreign Trade Statement 1703), *Exports and Imports of Merchandise by Customs Divisions and Districts* (Foreign Trade Statement 1704), and *Trends of United States Foreign Trade* (Foreign Trade Statement 1705). The analytical text which accompanies these statements is prepared by the Foreign Trade Research Section of the Division of Foreign Trade Statistics of the Bureau. Analytical statements are also published at frequent intervals in the *Survey of Current Business* and *Commerce Reports*. In addition to the foregoing general statements, the Bureau issues more than two hundred mimeographed foreign trade statements each month giving statistical data on special commodities. A list of those issued in 1937 runs to thirty-nine pages. The special commodity statements have now been consolidated in the new reference services instituted in October, 1940, which were described on page eighteen.

Analyses of the trade of the United States with particular foreign countries are made by the Division of Regional Information of the Bureau of Foreign and Domestic Commerce at frequent intervals. Annual reviews prepared in coöperation with the Division of Business Review were issued for a number of countries in 1937 and 1938 (processed). Monthly statistical analyses of United States trade with Japan, China, Hongkong, and Kwantung are issued (processed). A comprehensive study was made of *The United States in India's Trade* (Trade Promotion Series No. 200, 1939).

The Bureau of Agricultural Economics and the Office of Foreign Agricultural Relations likewise compile statistical series relating to foreign trade in agricultural products. *Agricultural Statistics* is the yearly omnibus volume of the Department. Current figures appear in the weekly *Foreign Crops and Markets*, and annually a supplement is issued covering United States foreign trade in agricultural products in the period just ended. *Agricultural Situation* and the annual volume of *Agricultural Outlook* also contain important statistical tables. Various special statements are issued.

While the Tariff Commission issues no periodical statistical compilations, nevertheless, it has published many important statistical studies at frequent, if irregular, intervals. In this work it has been aided by three continuing WPA projects, one in Richmond, one in New York City, and one in Washington. The studies made in these projects are: *Imports for Consumption by Countries, 1931–1935*, 11 volumes (1936–1937, processed), *Imports for Consumption by Countries, 1936*, 4 volumes (1937, processed), *Imports for Consumption by Countries, 1929*, 4 volumes (1937, processed), *Statistical Classification of Imports into the United States, 1937, Arranged by Tariff Schedules and Tariff Paragraphs of the Act of 1930* (1937, processed), *Computed Duties and Equivalent ad Valorem Rates on Imports into the United States from Principal Countries, 1929, 1931, and 1935* (1937, processed), *United States Free and Dutiable Imports for Consumption from Selected Countries by Economic Classes by Months, 1932 and 1933* (1937, processed), *United States Imports and Duties, 1937, Arranged according to the Tariff Act of 1930 by Schedules, Paragraphs and Commodities* (1938, processed), *Current Trend of Imports, 1936 and 1937* (1938, processed), *United States Imports under the Reciprocal Trade Agreements Program, 1937 and 1938*, 8 volumes, covering Belgium, Brazil, Finland, France, The Netherlands, Sweden, Switzerland, Colombia, Guatemala, Haiti, and Honduras (1939 processed), and *Analysis of Imports by Parcel Post, 1937* (1939, processed). In March, 1940, the Tariff Commission issued an eight-volume report on *United States Imports and Trade Agreement Concessions* (processed), which gives

. . . statistics of United States imports in selected years from 1931 to 1939 for each product upon which the United States had granted tariff reductions or bindings of the present tariff status . . . Comments following the principal import classes indicate the nature of imports in relation to domestic production and give the available statistics of the domestic production and exports in recent years.

Soon to be published is an analysis of imports of miscellaneous chemicals, and of flower seeds. Projects under way include an analysis of imports entered under "basket" clauses of the Tariff Act of 1930, in which special attention is being given to classes covering strategic and critical materials essential to national defense, a tabulation of imports by customs districts (for staff use and not to be published), and others. The trade agreement digests and the results analyses issued by the Tariff Commission, which were mentioned earlier, are also important in this context.

A striking feature of the publications program of the Tariff Commission is the speed with which it is able to issue comprehensive statistical analyses of matters of current interest. Thus, within a month after the decision of the Treasury Department of March 18, 1939, with respect to the application of the countervailing duty provision (Section 303) of the Tariff Act of 1930 to imports from Germany, the Tariff Commission issued an elaborate *Compilation of Data on United States Trade with Germany* (1939, processed). Within two months after the outbreak of war, the Commission issued a comprehensive statistical survey, *The*

European War and United States Imports (1939, processed). The latter contains summary tables covering United
States import and export trade with principal countries in
1914–1918 and 1936–1938; individual analyses of principal
commodities imported into the United States in 1936, 1937,
and 1938; and leading imports in the 1914–1918 period and
principal sources of supply. Imports for consumption and
United States production are given: and the importance of
the commodity to the economy of the United States and the
possibilities of increase in domestic production, or of the use
of substitutes, are shown. A revision of this compilation has
been made which also contains supplementary analyses of
additional commodities which have been designated by the
Army and Navy Munitions Board as strategic or critical. The
Commission has compiled data on production and imports
of these commodities and also on the capacity to produce
them in the United States and in foreign countries.

Statistical compilations and analyses of the trade of countries other than the United States are made by the Division
of Regional Information of the Bureau of Foreign and Domestic Commerce, by the Tariff Commission, and by the
Office of Foreign Agricultural Relations. Among more recent studies by the Division of Regional Information are
those on *Russian-German Trade Relations, Recent Trends
in Japan's Trade with Latin-America, Trade Relationships
between the American Republics, Manchuria's Foreign
Trade, Twenty Years of Soviet Trade.*[89] Analyses of exports
of foreign countries by commodities and destination, and of

[89] Processed and available at five cents each from the Division of
Regional Information.

their imports by commodities and origin, of which some fifteen have been issued and others are in progress, have been made by the Division of Regional Information.[90] Of particular interest among such studies are those for the Latin American republics. Emphasis is placed on the changing character of international trade and the possible diversion of trade to the United States, and the studies have a bearing on the possibility of the adoption of regional policies and the formation of regional blocs after the war. The *Foreign Commerce Yearbook*, the *Economic Review of Foreign Countries*, and the various monthly economic and trade reports issued by the Division were described earlier. Mention was also made of the "Economic Situation" reports issued at frequent intervals. Among the more recent are studies of Finland, Japan, Iceland, Greenland, Brazil, the Netherlands Indies, France, and Germany.

A full-length study of the *Expansion of Japan's Foreign Trade and Industry* (Trade Information Bulletin No. 836, 1937) made by the Division of Regional Information has been supplemented by briefer special circulars issued at yearly intervals. The latest of these is Miscellaneous No. 398, 1939 (processed). The Tariff Commission has made a study of the same subject, particularly with relation to the trade of the United States: *Recent Developments in the Foreign Trade of Japan* (2d Series, Report No. 105, 1936).

Important studies in this field by the Office of Foreign Agricultural Relations were enumerated earlier. In 1940, that agency completed the preparation of an index of the quantity of imports of agricultural products into the United

[90] *Ibid.*

States, the first index of its kind. At the same time, its index of the quantity of exports was revised. Both series will be published in a forthcoming report.

Trade opportunities abroad

Passing from general statistical and analytical studies of the trade of the United States and other countries, we encounter a veritable morass of "promotion" studies. The primary aim of these is to aid in the marketing abroad of American goods. They range all the way from background studies to trade opportunity leads. It is not impertinent to point out here that while the agencies of government have always been alert to opportunities for profitable sales abroad by American producers, they have seldom regarded it as their duty to scan the field for opportunities of profitable purchase by American consumers. To such an extent are we producer-minded.

The "promotion" studies of the Bureau of Foreign and Domestic Commerce appear in two series: Trade Promotion Series and Trade Information Bulletins. In the former are published studies of relatively permanent interest,[91] many of which have been cited elsewhere in these pages, while in the latter are published the more ephemeral marketing aid studies, such as *Market for Canned Foods in British Malaya* (No. 534, 1928), *Market for Hosiery in South America* (No. 567, 1928); and *Small Island Markets for American Motion Pictures* (No. 756, 1931). The number

[91] The distinction does not always hold, however; e. g., *Markets for American Toilet Preparations* (Trade Promotion Series No. 86, 1929) and *Foreign Markets for American Medicinal Products* (Trade Promotion Series No. 193, 1939), and *Balance of International Payments of the United States in 1935* (Trade Information Bulletin No. 833, 1936).

of these studies has fallen off abruptly since 1933, although new ones occasionally appear, as, for example, *Advertising in Sweden* (No. 840, 1938), one of a series of numerous advertising brochures. For other titles see *List of Publications of the Department of Commerce* (June, 1940).

All this "promotion" work culminates in the "notification of specific opportunities for American firms to buy or sell abroad," which is one of the functions of the Commercial Intelligence Division of the Bureau of Foreign and Domestic Commerce.[92] Notice of "foreign trade opportunities" is published in *Commerce Reports,* and interested American firms may obtain full reports thereon from the Bureau for twenty-five cents each.

In the work of appraising and making available trade opportunities, the Industrial Divisions of the Bureau of Foreign and Domestic Commerce play an important part. The tendency is growing, however, to enlarge the Industrial Divisions' duties of economic analysis and to restrict their functions of commercial promotion. Even in the past the proportion of each kind of work done has varied from Division to Division. In raw materials, for example, economic analysis has bulked large and such Divisions as Leather and Rubber, Chemicals and, in part, Foodstuffs have been research rather than promotion agencies.

Businessmen stand in need of some kinds of information concerning foreign marketing requirements and practices which the government is best equipped to supply. A very useful handbook prepared by the former chief of the Commercial Intelligence Division and members of other Divi-

<hr/>

[92] See above, under Bureau of Foreign and Domestic Commerce, the description of this Division's duties.

sions of the Bureau of Foreign and Domestic Commerce is
Export and Import Practice (Trade Promotion Series No.
175, 1938). Similarly helpful are the numerous handbooks
prepared in the Foreign Tariffs Division concerning the
documentary requirements and custom regulations to be considered in preparing shipments to foreign countries. The
latest of these is *Preparing Shipments to British Countries*
(Trade Promotion Series No. 154, revised, 1939). The
texts of *Foreign Marks of Origin Regulations* (Trade Promotion Series No. 199, 1939) have been compiled and issued
in one volume by the Foreign Tariffs Division which keeps
the compilation up to date by the issuance of occasional supplements.

A new service to businessmen, inaugurated on April 1,
1940, is the circulation of "Trade-o-graphs" through the
daily newspapers. There will be twelve of these each month
—four pictographs showing domestic business developments,
five showing United States exports abroad, and three showing imports into the United States.

Finance and Investment

The research program of the Finance Division of the
Bureau of Foreign and Domestic Commerce has its point of
departure in the need to improve the estimates contained in
the *Balance of International Payments of the United States,*
prepared by it annually. In 1936 a study was made of *Insurance Transactions in the Balance of International Payments of the United States, 1919–1935* (Trade Information
Bulletin No. 834). A study of *American Direct Investments
in Foreign Countries as of the End of 1929,* made in 1931

(Trade Information Bulletin No. 731), was revised in 1938 (Economic Series No. 1) to show the situation as of the end of 1936. An analysis of *Foreign Investments in the United States* (Miscellaneous Series) was published in 1937. The latest study, apart from the balance of payments study for 1939, now in press, is *Oversea Travel and Travel Expenditures in the Balance of Payments of the United States, 1919–1938* (Economic Series No. 4, 1939). Studies now in progress or projected include: an examination of import invoices in the New York port to determine the difference between invoice value and entry value; [92a] a detailed estimate by countries of the debtor-creditor position of the United States (with breakdown by types of investment); a study of currency movements in order to determine how American currency gets abroad; and a study of the value of parcel post shipments. A statistical analysis is being made of foreign dollar bond repatriations. Analyses of royalty payments and receipts may also be made. Another projected study would examine the balance of payments in the light of the relations between American and foreign industry. The study of foreign investments in the United States is now being brought up to date.

Mention should also be made here of the Tariff Commission's report on *Depreciated Exchange* (2d Series, Report 44, 1932) prepared in response to a Senate resolution. The Bureau of Agricultural Economics has made a study of the effects of currency depreciation in the United States and in

---

[92a] The results of this study were published by the Bureau of Foreign and Domestic Commerce in September, 1940: *Merchandise Import Statistics in the Balance of International Payments* (mimeographed).

foreign countries on cotton prices and on acreage in these countries. The study has not been made public.[93]

The Research and Statistics Division of the Treasury Department publishes monthly in the *Treasury Bulletin* statistics of capital movements between the United States and foreign countries. The data published include short-term foreign assets and liabilities, security transactions and brokerage balances, transactions in United States domestic securities, and foreign exchange transactions. Figures concerning gold and silver stocks, silver production, movements, seigniorage, and foreign exchange and price data are also published monthly in the *Treasury Bulletin*. The balance sheets of the Exchange Stabilization Fund are also published at intervals. Monetary data and analysis are also contained in the Federal Reserve Board's *Annual Report*, *Monthly Bulletin*, and its mimeographed *Weekly Review of Periodicals*. Dr. Goldenweiser's article on "The Gold Problem" has been mentioned.

In addition to the studies made in connection with the balance of payments estimates, the Finance Division has made numerous studies of investments in various parts of the world; has issued several studies of experience with defaulted loans as, for example, *French Experience with Defaulted Foreign Bonds* (Trade Information Bulletin No. 656, 1929), and *Default and Adjustment of Argentine Foreign Debts, 1890–1907* (Trade Promotion Series No. 145, 1933); and has prepared a standard *Handbook of American Underwriting of Foreign Securities* (Trade Promotion Series No. 104, 1930). Supplements to this Handbook were

[93] A statement of the conclusions of the study will be found in *Report of the Chief of the Bureau of Agricultural Economics, 1939,* p. 28.

issued in 1931 and 1932. Important investigations in related fields have been made by the Securities and Exchange Commission and by various Senate Committees. The former published in 1937 the first comprehensive study of the activities of *Protective Committees and Agencies for Holders of Defaulted Foreign Governmental Bonds* (1937).[94] The Senate Finance Committee has made investigations of foreign investments in its hearings on the *Sale of Foreign Bonds* (71st and 72d Congress, 1931 and 1932) as has the Banking and Currency Committee in probing *Stock Exchange Practices* (72d and 73d Congresses, 1932 and 1933).

3. GOVERNMENTAL CONTROLS

Tariffs, subsidies, and trade regulations

The principal government agency engaged in study in this field is, of course, the Tariff Commission. Its industrial surveys and trade agreement digests contain important analyses of the effects of tariffs and other trade barriers. The Commission is now revising the valuable *Dictionary of Tariff Information*, first issued in 1924 and long out of print.

A study of the executive control of imports, which is a revision of *Regulation of Tariffs in Foreign Countries by Administrative Action* (Miscellaneous Series, 1934), has now been combined with a study of non-tariff trade barriers, and the two may be issued together as a general survey of commercial policies and methods of trade regulation. In addition, detailed separate studies of the trade, trade policies, and trade regulations of the following are now being made:

[94] See also the Finance Division's study, "Foreign Bondholders Protective Organizations," Department of Commerce Special Circular, No. 425, July 1, 1938.

Germany, Italy, Japan, and Latin America. Concerning the studies of the two countries first named, the Commission observes that integrated analysis has been difficult because of "the lack of official information regarding what has actually been done under the wide discretion left to the administrative officials as set forth in the published decrees." Concerning the Latin-American study the Commission states that

Special attention is being given to the potentialities of the area in supplying United States imports, to the experience of the Latin American countries during the depression when the prices of their principal export commodities declined materially, and to the effect of the decreased demand for some Latin American products as a result of the economic policies of certain other nations. Attention is being given also to the problems of competition faced in the Latin American area by United States exports as a result of the trade practices of other countries, and to those problems which may arise as a result of the present European war.[95]

The first part of the report on the *Foreign Trade of Latin America*, entitled "Trade of Latin America with the World and with the United States" (processed), was issued in May, 1940. It deals with the trade of Latin America as a whole. The second part of the report is a survey of the commercial policy and the foreign trade of each of the twenty Latin American Republics, with special emphasis on the trend, composition, and destination of exports and of imports. A separate section is issued for each country. Eleven sections have appeared: Argentina, Bolivia, Brazil, Chile, Colombia, Ecuador, Paraguay, Peru, Uruguay, Venezuela, and Cuba.

[95] *Twenty-third Annual Report* (1939), p. 34.

Part III, which deals individually with approximately thirty selected Latin American export commodities, for each of which there is a discussion of production, exports, trade barriers, competitive conditions, and the effects of the European war, was issued in two volumes in August, 1940 (processed). A useful aid in grasping this exhaustive work is the Tariff Commission's *Graphic Analysis of the Trade of Latin America* (processed, 1940). It is of interest to note in this connection that the Bureau of Foreign and Domestic Commerce is exploring the possibilities of increased trade with the Latin American countries, and especially the possibility of increased imports into the United States of non-competitive products. The Tariff Commission has issued a *Reference Manual of Latin American Commercial Treaties* (processed, 1940), in which the principal provisions of Latin American commercial agreements with all countries are summarized in convenient form.

The last of the Tariff Commission's projects in this general field is a report on Tariff Boards or Commissions in Foreign Countries. That study will probably be published in 1941. For the study of tariff boards the Commission has collected all the available laws relating thereto and proposes to publish the texts together with a comparative analysis and summary of their functions, organization, and procedure.

Since 1930, reviews of the salient developments and trends in foreign tariffs and commercial policies have been prepared annually by the Chief of the Foreign Tariff Division of the Bureau of Foreign and Domestic Commerce, and are available in reprint form.[96]

[96] Earlier pamphlets by the same author are: *European Tariff Policies Since the War* (1924) and *Export Duties of the World*, the latter issued in 1927 in connection with the World Economic Conference at Geneva.

The most extensive governmental study of hindrances to American exports was that made by the Department of Agriculture in 1933 in response to Senate resolution: *World Trade Barriers in Relation to American Agriculture* (73d Congress, 1st Session, Senate Doc. No. 70). That study is based in part upon information furnished by the Division of Foreign Tariffs of the Department of Commerce. It describes the restrictions upon international trade in major agricultural products throughout the world, measures undertaken in several countries to protect the position of their farm producers, and the effects of these restrictions and measures upon prices of farm products and the welfare of American farmers. Trade barriers have increased in complexity and altered in nature so much since the study was issued, that it is now out of date. A revision is much to be desired. Much supplementary material is, of course, available in *Foreign Agriculture* and in *Commerce Reports* as well as in various special circulars of the Foreign Tariffs and Finance Divisions of the Department of Commerce. The trade policy studies of the Tariff Commission mentioned above will also throw much light on developments in this field. Handbooks on foreign tariffs and other import restrictions affecting several groups of agricultural products have been issued by the Foreign Tariffs Division and have economic as well as commercial interest. The most recent of these concerns *Fresh Fruits and Vegetables* (Trade Promotion Series No. 206, 1940). The compilation of *Foreign Marks of Origin Regulations* issued by the Foreign Tariffs Division has already been cited.

The Federal Trade Commission in June, 1938, transmitted to Congress a report on *Antidumping Legislation in the United States and Foreign Countries,* which supplements a report of the same title printed in 1934 as Senate Document No. 112, 73d Congress, 2d Session. The later report is available in lithographed form. The measures adopted by the United States and thirty-nine foreign countries are reviewed in this study.[97]

Investigations arising out of the adoption of various devices for the marketing of agricultural surpluses, such as subsidies and the food stamp plan, have been made by the Department of Agriculture, the Department of Commerce, and the Tariff Commission. Those concerned with agricultural subsidies are of particular interest here. One such study was contained in a report on *Export Trade in and Byproducts Uses of Tobacco* (76th Congress, 1st Session, Senate Doc. No. 39), prepared by the Department of Agriculture at the beginning of 1939. It gave consideration to "the favorable and unfavorable effects which might result from recourse to artificial stimulants to export trade in tobacco."

The chief of the Bureau of Agricultural Economics stated in his Annual Report for 1939 that

Analyses were made of various export-dumping plans, and of the effect of the wheat-export subsidy, and probable effects of the cotton-export subsidy upon prices and incomes received by producers of these commodities and upon world prices. It was found that the wheat-export subsidy has operated mainly to increase domestic prices rather than to lower world prices.[98]

------

[97] A brief special report on antidumping legislation, countervailing duties, import and foreign exchange control, and tariff treatment in selected foreign countries was prepared by the Bureau of Agricultural Economics in June, 1937.

[98] The disparity in domestic and world prices made necessary the adoption of measures to discourage cotton imports. See the Tariff Commission report under Section 22 of the Agricultural Adjustment Act on *Cotton*

These studies have not been made public. The annual reports of the Division of Marketing and Marketing Agreements and of the Federal Surplus Commodities Corporation, now consolidated as the Surplus Marketing Administration of the Department of Agriculture, also throw light on the agricultural export programs of the government. Of interest in connection with the subsidy studies is an analysis by the Bureau of Agricultural Economics

. . . of the activities of the Federal Government in aid of agriculture bordering on price fixing during the period 1933–1938. It was found that only a few such measures might be termed price fixing, as clearly defined, but that several had features bearing an outward resemblance to it, or in actual operation have had effects similar in some respects to those of outright price-fixing measures. Such measures in aid of agriculture were found in connection with tobacco, dairy products, peanuts, rice, sugar, and other commodities.

The study has not been made public.

In 1936 the Tariff Commission made a report to the Senate on *Subsidies and Bounties to Fisheries Enterprises by Foreign Governments* (2d Series, Report No. 116).

Among studies of so-called "surplus commodities" the following made by the Bureau of Foreign and Domestic Commerce are of interest here: *International Marketing of Surplus Wheat* (Trade Promotion Series No. 130, 1932) and *International Trade in Coffee* (Trade Promotion Series No. 37, 1926), the latter being one of a series of noteworthy studies of coffee made by the Foodstuffs Division.

---

and Cotton Waste (2nd Series, Report No. 137, 1939). A similar investigation by the Tariff Commission of wheat and wheat products is under way.

A comprehensive annotated *Tariff Bibliography* (Miscellaneous Series) was issued in 1933 by the Tariff Commission. Among technical tariff studies issued by the Tariff Commission are the following: *Bases of Value for Assessment of ad Valorem Duties in Foreign Countries* (Miscellaneous Series, 1932) and *Methods of Valuation* (2d Series, Report No. 70, 1933).

There have been several studies of the effects of specific tariffs. In response to a request of the State Department, the Tariff Commission made a study of the *Tariff on Long-Staple Cotton* (2d Series, Report No. 85, 1935). The Bureau of Agricultural Economics has also made such a study: *The Tariff on Long-Staple Cotton and Its Effects* (July, 1938, processed). In response to Senate Resolution No. 167 (75th Congress), the Bureau of Agricultural Economics prepared an analysis of *Flaxseed Prices and the Tariff* (76th Congress, 1st Session, Senate Doc. No. 62, April 13, 1939).[99]

Since the passage of the Reciprocal Trade Agreements Act excise taxes have acquired a new interest from the point of view of the tariff. The Tariff Commission has made several comprehensive statistical studies of them: *Imports, Exports, Domestic Production, and Prices of Petroleum, Coal, Lumber, Copper, Certain Oils and Fats together with Excise Taxes Collected Thereon* (May, 1937, processed), *Imports, Exports, Domestic Production, and Prices of Petroleum, Coal, Lumber and Copper together with Excise Taxes Collected Thereon* (June, 1939, processed), and *Excise*

[99] Appendix C of the Flaxseed study contains a theoretical discussion of the method of determining tariff incidence.

Taxes on Fats and Oils and Oil-Bearing Materials (March, 1939, processed).[100]

The Finance Division of the Department of Commerce is continuously concerned with exchange control. It has issued three special circulars in the last two years dealing with this subject: "Restriction and Foreign Exchange Control of Imports into Germany" (Special Circular No. 424), "Regulations Governing German Trade with the United States under 'Inland Accounts' or Cotton Barter System" (Special Circular No. 426), and "Exchange Restrictions in Foreign Countries" (Special Circular No. 427). The changes in the use of this instrument for the governmental control of trade are so frequent that the Finance Division has rather sought to keep pace with developments by noting in *Commerce Reports* changes as they occur, instead of issuing elaborate accounts which would soon be out of date.

The report on *Reciprocity and Commercial Treaties*, published by the Tariff Commission in 1919, has become one of the classics of economic analysis on the topic treated. Since that time the Tariff Commission has explored intensively various segments of the area covered in the report: *Tariff Bargaining Under Most-Favored Nation Treaties* (2d Series, Report No. 65, 1933), and *The Extent of Equal Tariff Treatment in Foreign Countries* (2d Series, Report No. 119, 1937). A third edition of a current bibliography on *Reciprocal Trade* (processed) was issued in 1937 and a *Supplement* (processed) to that bibliography was issued in 1940. A useful feature of the principal volume of the bibliography is its topical indexing of material in the various

[100] See also *Taxes on Fats and Oils*, Hearings before the Senate Finance Committee, 76th Cong., 1st Sess., on H.R. 3790 (March 6–9, 1939).

congressional hearings on the trade agreements program. The Ways and Means Committee of the House has issued an index (prepared by the Tariff Commission) to its 1940 Hearings on the trade agreements bill.

Mention may be made here of a series of mimeographed analyses issued by the State Department in which the attempt is made to determine the benefits accruing to the several states and regions of the country from the trade agreements program.

4. RELATIONS WITH DEPENDENCIES

An Interdepartmental Committee on Philippine Affairs, composed of representatives of the Departments of State, War, Navy, Treasury, Agriculture, and Commerce, and of the Tariff Commission, was organized at the end of 1934 to coördinate the activities of the various agencies of government concerned with Philippine affairs. At the request of this Committee, the Tariff Commission revised an earlier study of *United States–Philippine Tariff and Trade Relations* (2d Series, Report No. 18, 1931) and brought it up to date with special reference to the Philippine Independence Act and other recent legislation. The revision, which was issued under the title, *United States–Philippine Trade* (2d Series, Report No. 118, 1937), provides basic data on United States–Philippine trade relations, and analyzes the probable economic effects on the United States and on the Islands of the execution of the Philippine Independence Act and related legislation.

The Interdepartmental Committee suggested the creation of a Joint Preparatory Committee to study the "imperfection and inequalities" in the Philippine Independence Act and to recommend changes and a program for the adjustment of the Philippine economy to eventual independence. Pursuant to an arrangement between the President of the United States and the President of the Philippines, such a Joint Preparatory Committee, composed of a chairman and twelve members,[101] six of whom were Filipinos and six Americans, was appointed on April 14, 1937. Mr. Francis B. Sayre, then Assistant Secretary of State, served as Chairman, and was later succeeded by Ambassador J. V. A. MacMurray. On May 20, 1938, the Joint Preparatory Committee on Philippine Affairs submitted its report. The transcript of the hearings, the briefs filed with the Committee, and the report itself were all published at the same time (Department of State Publication 1216–1219, Conference Series 36). The Office of Foreign Agricultural Relations has published a long study of "Philippine Agriculture, A Problem of Adjustment" (*Foreign Agriculture*, July, 1940).

In view of the special relations between the United States and Cuba, it will not be amiss to cite here the Tariff Commission's study of the *Effects of the Cuban Reciprocity Treaty* (Miscellaneous Series, 1929). The Tariff Commission's sugar and cigar industry reports, cited earlier, are also of importance in this connection. See also the study by the Bureau of Foreign and Domestic Commerce on *Cuban Readjustment to Current Economic Forces* (Trade Information Bulletin No. 725, 1930). The Sugar Division of the Department of Agriculture is also actively engaged in studies in this field.

The Tariff Commission has announced that it proposes to issue studies of the colonial tariff policies of the leading

[101] The members were the only ones who voted.

colonial empires which will bring up to date its standard monograph on *Colonial Tariff Policies* (Miscellaneous Series, 1922). A revision of the introductory chapter of that work was issued in 1938 as *Dominion and Colonial Statistics* (2d Series, Report No. 127). The revisions of the remaining parts will be issued in installments from time to time. In view of the current world situation this work will, however, probably not be done for some time.

WAR PROBLEMS

Defense economics

It is not possible to write a detailed account of the researches being conducted in connection with defense. Of the investigations made by the staff of the Advisory Commission there is little information available and that little is not precise. The attempt has been made in the earlier description of the organization of the Commission to indicate some of the problems with which it is known to be dealing. Of the related researches made by the permanent research agencies of the government more is known, but here too, much work is of a confidential character. That fact and the recent date of these studies account for the meagreness of publication. The investigations mentioned in the following pages are cited rather for the sake of giving some indication of the increase in research burdens and of the direction in which interest is turning because of defense than as a complete account of the work being done.

Data of use in gearing industry to defense production have been contributed by many agencies. The Census Bureau has made special tabulations of census data relating to seventy-five strategic industries for the Advisory Commission. The antitrust division of the Department of Justice has made available to the Commission detailed statistical data on finances, costs, prices, production, and sales for the rubber tire, plate and window glass, potash and sulphur, and aluminum industries. This unit has also made available elaborate analyses of eighteen tonnage steel products. The Securities and Exchange Commission has enlarged its Survey of American Corporations to include data on the defense industries.

Mention was made earlier of the joint analysis of the location and migration of industry developed by the Census of Manufactures and the Bureau of Agricultural Economics. The National Resources Planning Board has also lately begun a study of aspects of this problem.

Related in interest are the studies of the financing of plant expansion made by the Treasury Department; these resulted in the Emergency Plant Facilities Contract framed in collaboration with the Army, Navy, and Advisory Commission. In that connection the Federal Reserve Board has polled most of the country's banks to determine the amount of credit available on the security of such contracts.

Problems of labor supply constitute another field of intensive inquiry. The Bureau of Employment Security of the Social Security Board has made a nation-wide inventory of 5,100,000 active job-seekers registered in April, 1940, with Federal-state employment service offices. Systems of monthly reporting designed to locate and measure shortages in lines of work closely affected by national defense have been instituted. The Central Statistical Board has made efforts to bring about improvement in the comparability of occupational classifications. The Bureau of Labor Statistics is making studies of the occupational composition of certain industries and of their need for additional workers in an effort to discover existing or potential bottlenecks. It has made analyses of the relation between the number of workers possessing certain skills and the number of jobs requiring them, the trend of new work opportunities in particular occupations as compared with the number of persons who are being trained for them, the types of training and experience needed for particular jobs and how such training can be obtained. Trends in employment by industries and states are being analyzed and changes in the Bureau's employment and pay roll series are being made to increase coverage of establishments in seventy industries of interest to the Advisory Commission. The Women's Bureau is preparing handbooks for each major defense industry listing occupations best suited to women workers, the training required, and the standards to be maintained. The Office of Education has made a study of the training facilities for workers and has instituted a system of monthly reports from vocational schools on the numbers trained and placed in jobs. The Federal Home Loan Bank Board is making an investigation of the concentration of industrial workers in which the Bureau of Labor Statistics and the Bureau of Foreign and Domestic Commerce are coöperating. The problem of providing housing for workers has been the occasion for a WPA survey of dwelling units in certain shipbuilding and arsenal towns.

The problems of mineral raw materials have enlarged the burdens of inquiry resting on the Bureau of Mines. Surveys and periodical canvasses of production, consumption, and stocks of manganese, tungsten, tin, chromite, mercury, antimony, mica, graphite, toluol, naphthalene, aviation gasoline, scrap iron and steel, magnesium and magnesium alloys, and zinc are being conducted.

In the field of prices the Bureau of Labor Statistics has, since January, 1940, maintained a daily index of wholesale prices for twenty-eight basic commodities. New and revised price information is being obtained for certain products important to national defense, such as machine tools, certain chemicals, oils and drugs, and other materials. A weekly price index for strategic materials and another one for critical materials is being prepared. Indexes of commodities for which imports and exports are important are being developed. Finally, a new and more prompt weekly index of one hundred to one hundred and fifty commodities is being maintained. At the same time more accurate retail price reporting is being developed in coöperation with the Consumers' Counsel of the Department of Agriculture. The quarterly cost of living index of the Bureau of Labor Statistics is now supplemented by a monthly index.

The Price Stabilization Division of the Defense Commission has under way a number of price and financial studies. It is examining the Industrial Mobilization Plan's price-fixing proposals in terms of their economic implications, in the light of alternative proposals, and in respect to administrative procedures and forms of legislation. It is making a study of priorities in relation to prices and price administration. Price studies of strategic and critical materials are being made. In coöperation with the Securities and Exchange Commission it is making a study of capital markets and their place in emergency and wartime financing. Specialists have joined the staff of the Division to make studies of Japanese, German, Canadian, and British war finance. A survey of economic organization within the belligerent countries has been undertaken.

The requirements and capacities studies of the Defense Commission's Bureau of Research and Statistics are a contribution to the study of the effects of the defense program on the national economy. Another contribution in that area is a special study undertaken by the Division of Research and Statistics of the Federal Reserve Board under the supervision of Professor Alvin H. Hansen of Harvard University. That is an examination of the combined effects upon our economy of an enlarged defense program and of changes in American external trade. Various assumptions regarding the dimensions of our defense program and the changes in the character and volume of American foreign trade are being examined, and the effect of these factors upon the intensity of utilization of productive resources and the adaptation of available resources to altered patterns of demand are being analyzed and their implications for monetary policy developed.

Economic defense

Some of the studies bearing on economic defense have already been cited in other connections. Such are the report on *Wartime Control of Ocean Freight Rates* by the Bureau of Foreign and Domestic Commerce; the study of the impact of war on ocean shipping with special reference to its effects on the agricultural exports of the United States which has been made by the Bureau of Agricultural Economics; the statistical analyses of the shifts in trade caused by the war which the Division of Regional Information of the Bureau of Foreign and Domestic Commerce has issued; the investigation of the *Foreign Trade of Latin America* made by the Tariff Commission; and the Bureau of Mines' investigation of the mineral resources of the Latin American republics. In connection with the last-mentioned study it is worth noting that the Foreign Mineral Specialist of the Bureau of Mines has recently been recalled to assist in planning an investigation of mineral resources in South America in connection with the national defense program.

The Tariff Commission has issued a revision of its earlier *European War and United States Imports* under the title of *War and Its Effect on United States Imports* (December, 1940). The Department of Agriculture has prepared a report on *The Impact of War and the Defense Program on Agriculture* (October, 1940, processed), for the use of the annual agricultural outlook conference.

The Tariff Commission is making an analysis of the principal imports of the United States from Latin America, in which special attention is given to the problem of supplying our needs of strategic and critical commodities, such as mercury, tin, and coffee. Important research products may be expected from the Office of Foreign Agricultural Relations of the Department of Agriculture, where a new Division of Special Latin American Investigations has been established to handle the program of encouraging the production of complementary and non-competitive products in Latin America. The Bureau of Foreign and Domestic Commerce has had a specialist at work full time for nearly a year on the commercial and industrial phases of that program.

FINDING LIST OF GOVERNMENT
PUBLICATIONS

NLESS otherwise indicated, all the publications cited in this list are printed. Processed publications are indicated by the abbreviation "pr." Printed publications, with certain exceptions, are published by, and may be purchased from, the Superintendent of Documents, Washington, D.C. Prices are not included in the list below because such "advertising" (even of government documents) would make this volume ineligible for mailing at book rates under an unfortunate ruling of the Post Office Department. The inconvenience to readers and to the office of the Superintendent of Documents is regretted. Prices may be had on application to the Superintendent of Documents or may be found in the Monthly Catalog of United States Public Documents. Publications of the Federal Power Commission, the Federal Reserve Board, and the Work Projects Administration are obtainable only from those agencies. The publications of the last-named agency are, with one exception, free.

All government agencies are quite generous in supplying copies of their printed publications free. Periodicals and annuals are not generally so available. Note should be made, however, that editions are limited and unless there is serious need for a publication, good conscience would seem to require foregoing the mere addition of a pamphlet to the shelf.

Processed publications may generally be had free from the issuing office. The principal exceptions are the processed periodical services of the Bureau of Foreign and Domestic Commerce, for which there is a charge. Processed publications cannot be obtained from the Superintendent of Documents.

Printed publications can usually be consulted in depository libraries, but the completeness of library collections of processed publications varies with the assiduity, inventiveness, and good luck of the librarian. The District Offices of the Bureau of Foreign and Domestic Commerce carry files not only of Bureau publications but of some publications of other agencies. Bureau publications can often be purchased directly from the District Offices.

An effort has been made in the text to indicate ways of keeping abreast of the flood of government publications. The *Monthly Catalog* of the Superintendent of Documents lists not only all printed publications but many processed ones. The Superintendent also issues a free weekly selected list of publications. The free subject price lists, of which there are some seventy or more, show whether the Superintendent has a stock of the publication sought. Each government agency issues a list of its publications. These vary in completeness; most of them do not list publications out of print; and they are not revised at regular intervals. It would serve no useful purpose to list them here.

The National Economic and Social Planning Association, Washington, D.C., began, early in 1940, publication of the

Nespa Guide, a monthly (except July and August) which lists and describes current government and other reports on economic and social problems. For subscribers the service of obtaining listed materials is performed at cost.

There is no ready way to keep abreast of research plans other than by continual consultation of annual reports and by personal contact with the agencies involved, and even this is unsatisfactory. Budget officers usually have lists of agency projects, but these are rarely available. The hearings before appropriations committees contain nuggets of information but the labor of mining it is excessive.

The method of citation used is: title, date, and serial number. Where necessary, the periodical character of the publication is indicated and, if processed, that fact also. Except for the National Research Project studies published in Philadelphia, the place of publication is Washington in every case.

In this list the following abbreviations have been used:

DCS—Domestic Commerce Series
ES —Economic Series
FPS—Foreign Port Series
MP —Miscellaneous Publications
m.s. —Miscellaneous Series
o.p. —out of print
pr. —processed
TB —Technical Bulletin
TIB—Trade Information Bulletin
TPS—Trade Promotion Series

Executive Office of the President

CENTRAL STATISTICAL BOARD

Directory of Federal Statistical Agencies. 1940. pr.

Federal Chart Book. January, 1938. o.p.

Reports on the Returns Made by the Public to the Federal Government. 1939. 76th Cong., 1st Sess., House Doc. 27.

Statistical Services and Activities of the United States. May, 1940. pr.

NATIONAL RESOURCES PLANNING BOARD

Capital Requirements. 1940.

Consumer Expenditures in the United States. 1939.

Consumer Incomes in the United States—Their Distribution in 1935–1936. August, 1938.

Consumer Spends His Income. 1939.

Criteria and Planning for Public Works. June, 1934. pr.

Economics of Planning Public Works. 1935.

Energy Resources and National Policy. January, 1939.

Farm Tenancy, Report of President's Committee on. 1937.

Forest Resources of the Pacific Northwest. March, 1938.

Future of the Great Plains. December, 1936.

Inventory of the Water Resources of the United States. June, 1935. pr.

Little Waters. 1936.

Mineral Reserves of the United States and Its Capacity for Production. 1936. pr.

National Planning Board Report, 1933–34. November 16, 1934.

National Resources Board Report. December 1, 1934.

Our Energy Resources. 1939.

Our Cities. June, 1937.

2. Agricultural Exports in Relation to Land Policy.
3. Agricultural Land Requirements and Resources.
4. Land Available for Agriculture through Reclamation.
5. Soil Erosion: a Critical Problem in American Agriculture.
6. Maladjustments in Land Use in the United States.
7. Certain Aspects of Land Problems and Government Land Policies.
8. Forest Land Resources, Requirements, Problems, and Policy.
9. Planning for Wildlife in the United States.
10. Indian Land Tenure, Economic Status, and Population Trends.
11. Recreational Use of Land in the United States.

Technological Trends and National Policy. June, 1937.
The Loan of Expert Personnel among Federal Agencies. 1935. pr.
Urban Government. February, 1939.

OFFICE OF GOVERNMENT REPORTS

Report on Economic Conditions of the South. 1938. free.
United States Government Manual, July, 1940. Issued three times a year.

DEPARTMENT OF AGRICULTURE

Achieving a Balanced Agriculture. Revised. April, 1940.
Agricultural Statistics. Annual since 1936, previously (1898–1935) included in Yearbook of Agriculture.
Atlas of American Agriculture: Physical Basis. 1936.
Crop and Livestock Reporting Service of the United States. 1933. MP 171.
Directory of Organization and Field Activities of the Department of Agriculture, 1939. 1940. MP 376.
Economic Analysis of the Food Stamp Plan. October, 1940.

Economic Basis for the Agricultural Adjustment Act. December, 1933.

Experiment Station Record. Monthly since September, 1889.

Extension Service Review. Monthly since May, 1930.

Farmers in a Changing World. Yearbook of Agriculture, 1940.

Food and Life. Yearbook of Agriculture, 1939.

Forests and Employment in Germany. July, 1938. Circular 471.

History of Agricultural Education in the United States, 1785–1925. 1929. MP 36.

History of Agricultural Experimentation and Research in the United States, 1607–1925. 1937. MP 251.

History of Agricultural Extension Work in the United States, 1785–1923. 1928. MP 15.

Index to Publications, 1901–1925. 1932.

    1925–1930. 1935.

    1931–1935. 1937.

Planning for a Permanent Agriculture. 1939. MP 351.

Soils and Men. Yearbook of Agriculture, 1938.

Technology on the Farm. August, 1940.

United States Department of Agriculture, Its Structure and Functions. Revised 1940. MP 88.

AGRICULTURAL ADJUSTMENT ADMINISTRATION

Agricultural Adjustment, May, 1933, to February, 1934. 1934.

Agricultural Adjustment in 1934. 1935.

Agricultural Adjustment, 1933 to 1935. 1936.

Agricultural Conservation, 1936. 1937.

Agricultural Adjustment, 1937–38. 1939.

Agricultural Adjustment, 1938–39. 1939.

BUREAU OF AGRICULTURAL ECONOMICS

Agricultural Economics Literature. Monthly since 1927. pr.

Agricultural Finance Review. Semi-annual since 1938. pr.

Agricultural Outlook. Annual since 1923. pr.

Agricultural Situation, Monthly since December, 1921.

Analysis of Interregional Competition in Agriculture. April, 1939. pr.

An Analysis of the Effects of the Processing Taxes Levied under the Agricultural Adjustment Act, 1937 (published by Treasury Dept., Bureau of Internal Revenue).

BAE Handbook. December, 1939. pr.

Barriers to Internal Trade in Farm Products. 1939.

Cash Farm Income and Government Payments. Annual. pr.

Changes on Wheat Farms in Southwestern Kansas, 1931–37. June, 1940. pr.

Changing Trends of Farm Production, Farm Prices, and Gross Farm Income since the Civil War. In progress.

Cotton Crop Insurance. May, 1939. 76th Cong., 1st Sess., House Doc. 277.

Crop Insurance in Foreign Countries. October, 1937. pr.

Crops and Markets. Monthly since 1922 (formerly Crop reporter, 1867–1920, and Weather, Crops and Markets, 1920–1922).

Demand and Price Situation. Monthly. pr.

Determining Input Output Relationships in Milk Production. January, 1940. Farm Management Reports No. 5. pr.

Dollar Sales, Capitalization and Earnings of Leading Food and Tobacco Corporations. February, 1938. pr.

Economic and Social Problems and Conditions of the Southern Appalachians. January, 1935. MP 205.

Economic Situation of Hog Producers. February, 1933. 72d Cong., 2d Sess., Sen. Doc. 184.

Evolution of the Land Program of the United States Department of Agriculture. 1939. pr.

Export Credit Insurance in Europe Today. 1934. 73d Cong., 2d Sess., Sen. Doc. 225.

Export Trade in and Byproducts Uses of Tobacco. March, 1939. 76th Cong., 1st Sess., Sen. Doc. 39.

Factors Affecting Exports of United States Hog Products. November, 1932. pr.

Farm Population Estimates. Annually since 1923. pr.

Farm Population and Rural Life Activities. Quarterly since 1927. pr.

Farm Tenancy in the United States, 1918–1936. June, 1937. Agric. Ec. Bibliography 70. pr.

Fats, Oils, and Oleaginous Raw Materials. May, 1937. Statistical Bulletin 59.

Flaxseed Prices and the Tariff. April, 1939. 76th Cong., 1st Sess., Sen. Doc. 62.

Food, Feed, and Southern Farms. November, 1939. Farm Management Reports No. 1. pr.

Graphic Summary of American Agriculture:

  1. Physical Features and Land Utilization. May, 1937. MP 260.
  2. Farm Tenure. December, 1936. MP 261.
  3. Farm Taxation. February, 1937. MP 262.
  4. Value of Farm Property. July, 1937. MP 263.
  5. Farm Machinery, Facilities, Roads and Expenditures. July, 1937. MP 264.
  6. Farm Labor and Population. November, 1937. MP 265.
  7. Number, Size, and Type of Farm and Value of Products. October, 1937. MP 266.
  8. Farm Crops. March, 1938. MP 267.
  9. Agricultural Credit. September, 1938. MP 268.
  10. Farm Animals and Animal Products. February, 1934. MP 269.

Gross Farm Income and Government Payments. Annual beginning 1938. pr.

Gross Farm Income. Indexes of Farm Production and of Farm Prices in the United States, 1869–1937. TB.

Guide to Collecting, Describing and Summarizing Price Data. August, 1940. pr.

Impact of the Present War on Ocean Shipping with Special Reference to the Effects of War Shipping Conditions on United States Agriculture. November, 1940. pr.

Income. May, 1938. Agr. Ec. Bibliography 73. pr.

Income Parity for Agriculture. 5 parts (21 sections published). pr. In progress.

Industrial Prices and Their Relative Inflexibility. 1935. 74th Cong., 1st Sess., Sen. Doc. 13.

Inventory of Reports and Research Studies Completed and in Progress, Relating to Adjustments of Population to Resources in the Northern Great Plains States. January, 1940. pr.

Land Policy Review. Monthly since September, 1940. Previously (1938–July–August, 1940) bimonthly.

Land Settlement. Bibliography. August, 1934. MP 172.

Land Utilization, 1918–1936. Bibliography. January, 1938. MP 284.

Large Scale and Corporation Farming. April, 1937. Agric. Ec. Bibliography 69. pr.

Large Scale Farming in the United States. April, 1938. pr.

Large Scale Organization in the Dairy Industry. July, 1939. Circular 527.

Operation of Agricultural Conservation Programs in Illinois. January, 1940. Farm Management Reports No. 4. pr.

Orchard Farming in Pennsylvania, Virginia, and West Virginia. March, 1938. pr.

Organization and Crop Production Practices on Grain Farms in Selected Areas of the Pacific Northwest. October, 1939. pr.

Plantation Organization and Operation in the Yazoo-Mississippi Delta Area. May, 1939. TB. 682.

Power and Machinery in Agriculture. 1933. MP 157.

Price Fixing by Government in the United States, 1926–1939. July, 1939. Agric. Ec. Bibliography 79. pr.

Price Fixing by Government in Foreign Countries, 1926–1939. July, 1940. Agric. Ec. Bibliography 86. pr.

Price Spreads between the Farmer and the Consumer. February, 1939. pr.

Probable Effects of the Agricultural Conservation Program of Livestock Production in the Midwest Dairy Region. Part I: A Summary of the Studies of Selected Areas. January, 1940. pr.

The Problems of Submarginal Areas and Desirable Adjustments with Particular Reference to Public Acquisition of Land. 1933. National Land Planning Problems 6.

Production and Consumption of Manufactured Dairy Products. April, 1940. TB. 722.

Production Costs and Returns. June, 1939. pr.

Regional Adjustments to Meet War Impacts. 1940. pr.

Regional Variations in Prices Received by Farmers, 1925–1934, for Ten Selected Commodities. May, 1939. pr.

Rural Population Density in the Southern Appalachians. March, 1940. MP 367.

Rural Standards of Living: A Selected Bibliography. July, 1931. MP 116.

Size of Farm in Relation to Family Requirements in the Northern Plains. June, 1939. pr.

Some Effects of the World War on Cotton. June, 1937. pr.

Soybeans in the United States. June, 1938. TB 619.

Statistics on Cotton and Related Data. December, 1939. pr.

Tariff on Long-Staple Cotton and Its Effects. July, 1938. pr.

Tariff Rates on Principal Agricultural Products. May 10, 1939. pr.

Tenure Status and Land Use Patterns in the Corn Belt. August, 1939. Land Economics Report No. 5. pr.

Transportation of Agricultural Products in the United States,

1920–June, 1939. November, 1939. Agric. Ec. Bibliography
81. pr.

Wholesale Fruit and Vegetable Markets of New York City.
Special Report. April, 1940.

Wholesale Markets for Fruits and Vegetables in 40 Cities. 1938.
Circular 463.

World Acreage and Production of Tobacco by Countries.
August, 1938. pr.

World Production and International Trade in Butter and
Cheese. May, 1939. pr.

World Trade Barriers in Relation to American Agriculture.
1933. 73d Cong., 1st Sess., Sen. Doc. 70. o.p.

FARM CREDIT ADMINISTRATION

Agricultural Credit in Germany. 1940.

FARM SECURITY ADMINISTRATION

Disadvantaged Classes in American Agriculture. April, 1938.
Social Research Report No. VIII. pr.

Farm Mechanization and Farm Labor Changes, 1938. (In
progress.)

Land Settlement Technique Abroad

    I. Organization. July, 1935. Land Policy Circular Supple-
ment. pr.

    II. Financing. October, 1935. Land Policy Circular Sup-
plement. pr.

    III. Selection of Settlers. July, 1936. Land-Use Planning
Publication No. 5. pr.

North of 66. 1940. pr.

Social Status and Farm Tenure: Attitudes and Social Conditions of Corn Belt Farmers. April, 1938. Social Research
Report No. IV. pr.

Tenure of New Agricultural Holdings in Several European

Countries. September, 1937. Social Research Report No.
II. pr.

FOREIGN AGRICULTURAL RELATIONS, OFFICE OF

Agriculture in Southern Africa. 1935. TB 466.

Citrus Industry of Palestine. December, 1938. pr.

Consumption and Production of Tobacco in Europe. 1937.
TB 587.

Consumption of American and Other Growths of Cotton in
Japan. June, 1935. pr.

Cotton Production in Egypt. October, 1934. TB 451.

Cotton Production in Northeastern Brazil. December, 1939.
pr.

Cotton Production in Southern Brazil. September, 1939. pr.

Edible Fat Problem in Germany. June, 1934. pr.

Foreign Agriculture. Monthly since January, 1937. pr.

Foreign Crops and Markets. Weekly. pr.

Tobacco Market in the British Isles. pr.

Tobacco Production and Consumption in China. pr.

Tobacco Production and Consumption in Manchuria. 1940. pr.

Wheat Requirements in Europe. 1936. TB 535.

BUREAU OF HOME ECONOMICS

Diets of Families of Employed Wage Earners and Clerical
Workers in Cities. January, 1939. Circular 507.

Family Income and Expenditure:

    Pacific Region (Urban and Village Series), Part One, Family
Income. 1939. MP 339.

    Pacific Region Plains and Mountain Region (Urban and
Village Series), Part One, Family Income. 1939. MP 345.

    Pacific Region Plains and Mountain Region (Farm Series),
Part One, Family Income. 1939. MP 356.

Southeast Region (Urban and Village Series), Part One,
  Family Income. 1940. MP 375.
Farm-Housing Survey. March, 1939. MP 323.
Housing Requirements of Farm Families in the United States.
  1939. MP 322.
Studies of Family Living in the United States and Other Coun-
  tries. 1935. MP 223.

SOIL CONSERVATION SERVICE

Land in Flood Control. 1938. MP 331.
Soil Conservation. Monthly.
Soil Erosion and Soil and Water Conservation Bibliography.
  1938. MP 312.
To Hold This Soil. 1938. MP 321.

DEPARTMENT OF COMMERCE

BUREAU OF THE CENSUS

Earnings of Factory Workers, 1899 to 1927. 1929.
Estimated National Wealth, 1922. 1924.
Farm Population of the United States, 1920. 1926.
Financial Statistics of States, 1937. 1940.
Growth of Manufactures, 1899–1923. 1928.
Immigrants and Their Children, 1920. 1927.
Increase of Population in the United States, 1910–1920. 1922.
Integration of Industrial Operation. 1924. o.p.
Introduction to the Vital Statistics of the United States. 1933.
Social-Economic Grouping of the Gainful Workers of the
  United States. 1938.
Statistical Abstract of the United States. Annual since 1878.
  Issued by Bureau of the Census since 1939.
Women in Gainful Occupations, 1870 to 1920. 1929.

BUREAU OF FOREIGN AND DOMESTIC COMMERCE *

Advertising in Sweden. 1938. TIB 840.

American Direct Investments in Foreign Countries as of the End of 1929. 1930. TIB 731.

American Direct Investments in Foreign Countries, 1936. 1938. ES 1.

Balance of International Payments of the United States. Annually since 1922. Current issue for 1939.

Bombay Bullion Market. 1927. TIB 457.

Changing Character of International Trade (Statistical Analyses by Division of Regional Information) pr.

1. German Exports to Latin America in 1938. September 6, 1939.

2. United Kingdom Exports to Latin America in 1937. September 7, 1939.

3. Italian Exports to Latin America in 1938. September 8, 1939.

4. French Exports to Latin America in 1938. September 12, 1939.

5. Belgian Exports to Latin America in 1938. September 14, 1939.

6. German Exports to British Dominions and Possessions in 1938. September 16, 1939.

7. Latin American Imports and Exports (totals) for 1938 to Leading Countries. (See No. 23.) September 19, 1939.

8. German Exports to Greece and Turkey in 1938. September 21, 1939.

* The entries marked "discontinued" have been consolidated since October, 1940, in condensed form in Foreign Commerce Weekly. Note should be made that many processed statistical statements of the Bureau have now been consolidated into three loose-leaf subscription services: International (printed), Economic (printed), and Industrial (processed), the last-named divided into twelve parts which may be subscribed for separately.

24. Exports and Imports of Twenty Latin American Republics, Totals and to the United States, Germany, the United Kingdom, Japan, France and Italy, 1939. (See No. 28.) July 1940.

25. Principal Imports and Exports of European Countries, 1938. July 1940.

26. European Foreign Trade in, and Production of, Principal Commodities, 1938. September 1940.

27. Principal Imports and Exports of Africa, 1938. September 1940.

28. Exports of Twenty Latin American Republics, Totals and to the United States, Germany, the United Kingdom, Japan, France and Italy, 1939. (Supersedes Nos. 18 & 24.) September 1940.

29. Inter-Latin American Export-Import Trade of the Latin American Republics—1938. November 1940.

30. United States Trade with Europe by Commodity Groups, 1938-1939. November 1940.

31. Exports and Imports of the Twenty Republics of Latin America by years, 1930–1939. November 1940.

32. Latin American Import-Export Trade with Europe— 1938. November 1940.

Charts of World Production, Imports, and Exports of Major Minerals of Industry, 1929. 1933. MP.

Chemical Developments Abroad, 1939. 1940. TPS 211.

Commerce Reports. Weekly since September, 1921. Previously (1910–1921) daily. Became Foreign Commerce Weekly with October 5, 1940, issue.

Company Law and Business Taxes in Great Britain. 1933. TPS 147.

Comparative Law Series. Monthly (April 1925-1929, 1932-1940). Discontinued.

Construction Activity in the United States, 1915–1937. 1938. DCS 99.

Foreign Import Duties and Regulations on Fresh Fruits and Vegetables. 1940. TPS 206.

Foreign Investments in the United States. 1937. MP.

Foreign Long-Term Investments in the United States, 1937–39. 1940. ES 11.

Foreign Markets for American Medicinal Products. 1939. TPS 193.

Foreign Marks of Origin Regulations. 1939. TPS 199.

Foreign Tariffs and Commercial Policies. Annual statement by Chief of Division of Foreign Tariffs. pr.

Foreign Trade of the United States. Annual since 1922.

French Experience with Defaulted Foreign Bonds. 1929. TIB 656.

Fuel and Power in the British Empire. 1935. TPS 161.

German Dyestuffs Industry. 1924. Miscellaneous Series 126.

Handbook of American Underwriting of Foreign Securities. 1930. TPS 104. Supplement. 1931. TIB 802.

Handbook of Foreign Currencies. 1936. TPS 164.

Income in the United States, 1929–1937. 1938.

Industrial Market Data Handbook of the United States. 1939. DCS 107.

Insurance Transactions in the Balance of International Payments of the United States, 1919–1935. 1936. TIB 834.

International Cartel Movement. 1928. TIB 556. o.p.

International Marketing of Surplus Wheat. 1932. TPS 130.

International Trade in Coffee. 1926. TPS 37. o.p.

International Trade in Wheat and Wheat Flour. 1925. TPS 10.

Japan Monthly Trade Report. pr. Discontinued.

Latin-American Financial Notes. Semi-monthly. pr. Discontinued.

Leather: World Production and International Trade. 1935. TPS 157.

Potash: the Significance of Foreign Control and the Economic Need of Domestic Development. 1926. TPS 33.

Preparing Shipments to British Countries. Revised ed. 1939. TPS 154.

Promotion of American Commerce at Home and Abroad. 1938. free.

Railway and Highway Transportation Abroad. 1935. TPS 155.

Real Property Inventory. 1934. 65 vols.

Representative International Cartels Combines and Trusts. 1929. TPS 81. o.p.

Rubber: History, Production and Manufacture. 1940. TPS 209.

Rubber Industry of the United States. 1940. TPS 197.

Rubber News Letter. Bi-monthly. pr. Discontinued.

Rubber Production in Africa. 1926. TPS 34.

Rubber Production in Amazon Valley. 1926. TPS 23.

Rubber Regulation and the Malayan Plantation Industry. 1935. TPS 159.

Rubber Statistics, 1900–1937: Production, Absorption, Stocks, and Prices. 1938. TPS 181.

Russian Economic Notes. Semi-monthly. Discontinued.

Shipping and Shipbuilding Subsidies. 1932. TPS 129.

Silver Market. 1932. TPS 139.

Silver Market in 1930. 1931. TIB 742.

Small Island Markets for American Motion Pictures. 1931. TIB 756.

Source-book for the study of industrial profit. 1932.

Southeastern Asia Quarterly. pr. Discontinued.

State Income Payments, 1929–1937. 1939. pr.

Summary of United States Trade With the World. March of each year. Free.

Survey of Current Business. Monthly with Weekly Supplement. Since 1921. Biennial Supplement.

Synthetic Organic Chemicals. 1938. TPS 189.

Trade Review of Canada. Monthly. pr. Discontinued.
Trade Review of France. Monthly. pr. Discontinued.
Trading under the Laws of Argentina. 1935. TPS 160.
Trading under the Laws of Brazil. 1938. TPS 183.
Trading under the Laws of Canada. 1938. TPS 176.
Trading under the Laws of Colombia. 1932. TPS 142.
Trading under the Laws of Germany. 1933. TPS 150.
Trading under the Laws of Great Britain. 1935. TPS 153.
Trading under the Laws of Mexico. 1935. TPS 152.
Trading under the Laws of Venezuela. 1937. TPS 170.
Transport Control Abroad. 1939. TPS 196.
Tung Oil: Economic and Commercial Factors in Development of Domestic Tung Oil Industry. 1932. TPS 133.
Twenty Years of Soviet Trade. 1939. Special Circular No. 399. pr.
The United States in India's Trade. 1939. TPS 200.
United Kingdom: Industrial, Commercial, and Financial Handbook. 1930. TPS 94.
Wartime Control of Ocean Freight Rates in Foreign Trade. 1940. TPS 212.
World Chemical Developments in 1938. 1939. TPS 195.
World Economic Review. Annual. 1934. 1935. 1936: Pt. 1, Pt. 2. Continued by Economic Review of Foreign Countries.

BUREAU OF NAVIGATION AND STEAMSHIP INSPECTION

Merchant Marine Statistics. Annual since 1924.
Merchant Vessels of the United States. Annual.

DEPARTMENT OF INTERIOR

BUREAU OF MINES

Coal Mining in Europe. 1939.
Flow Charts Showing World Production, Consumption, and

Principal Trade Relations of Various Raw Materials, 1932. 1936.

Foreign Minerals Quarterly. pr.

International Coal Trade. Monthly. pr.

International Petroleum Trade. Monthly. pr.

Mineral Raw Materials. 1937. New York: McGraw-Hill.

Mineral Trade Notes. Monthly. pr.

Minerals Yearbook. Since 1932–1933, previously (1882–1931) Mineral Resources of the United States.

The Iron and Steel Industries of Europe. 1939.

World Retail Prices and Taxes on Gasoline, Kerosene and Motor Lubricating Oils. Quarterly. pr.

DEPARTMENT OF LABOR

BUREAU OF LABOR STATISTICS

Building Construction, 1921 to 1938. 1940. Bulletin 668.

Changes in Cost of Living. Quarterly since November, 1934.

Characteristics of Company Unions, 1935. 1938. Bulletin 634.

Consumers' Coöperation in the United States, 1936. 1939. Bulletin 659.

Employment and Payrolls. Monthly since July, 1923.

Family Expenditure in Chicago, 1935–1936. 1939. Bulletin 642.

Family Income in Chicago, 1935–1936. 1939. Bulletin 642.

Family Income in Five New England Cities, 1935–1936. 1939. Bulletin 645.

Family Income in Four Urban Communities in the Pacific Northwest Region, 1935–1936. 1939. Bulletin 649.

Family Expenditure in New York City. 1939. Bulletin 643.

Family Income in Nine Cities of the East Central Region, 1935–1936. 1939. Bulletin 644.

Family Expenditure in Six Urban Communities of the West

Central-Rocky Mountain Region, 1935–1936. 1940. Bulletin 646.

Family Expenditures in Selected Cities, 1935–1936. 1940. Bulletin 648, Vol. II (Food); Vol. V (Medical Care); Vol. VI (Travel and Transportation).

Family Income in the Southeastern Region, 1935–1936. 1939. Bulletin 647.

Family Expenditure in Three South-eastern Cities, 1935–1936. 1940. Bulletin 647.

Handbook of American Trade Unions. 1936. Bulletin 618.

Handbook of Labor Statistics. 1936. Bulletin 616.

History of Wages in the United States from Colonial Times to 1928; with Supplement, 1929–1933. 1934. Bulletin 604.

Labor Information Bulletin. Monthly since September, 1934. Free.

Labor Laws and Their Administration. Annual.

Labor Offices in the United States and Canada. 1938. Bulletin 632.

Mechanization and Productivity of Labor in the Cigar Manufacturing Industry. 1939. Bulletin 660.

Money Disbursements of Wage Earners and Clerical Workers

Five Cities in the Pacific Region, 1934–36. 1939. Bulletin 639.

North Atlantic Region, 1934–1936. 1939. Vol. 1: New York City. Vol. 2: Eleven Cities. Bulletin 637.

East North Central Region, 1934–36. 1940. Bulletin 636.

West North Central Mountain Region, 1930–36. 1939. Bulletin 641.

Monthly Labor Review. Since July, 1915.

Productivity of Labor in the Cotton-Garment Industry. 1939. Bulletin 662.

Retail Prices. Monthly since March, 1932.

State Labor Legislation, 1937. 1938. Bulletin 654.

Statistics of Building Construction, 1920–1937. 1938. Bulletin 650. 2 vols.

Strikes in the United States, 1880–1936. 1938. Bulletin 651.

Union Scales of Wages and Hours in the Building Trades in 70 Cities. 1938. Bulletin 657.

Union Scales of Wages and Hours in the Printing Trades. 1937. Bulletin 631.

Wages in Cotton Goods Manufacturing. 1938. Bulletin 663.

Wages in Foreign Countries. 1929. 71st Cong., 1st Sess., Sen. Doc. 9.

Wholesale Prices. Monthly since January, 1932.

WOMEN'S BUREAU

Conditions in the Millinery Industry in the United States. 1939. Bulletin 169.

Differences in Earnings of Women and Men. 1938. Bulletin 152.

Employed Women and Family Support. 1939. Bulletin 168.

The Woman Wage Earner—Her Situation Today. 1940. Bulletin 172.

The Woman Worker. Irregularly issued, 1921–30. Processed monthly, 1931–37. Bi-monthly since 1938.

Trends in the Employment of Women, 1928–1936. 1938. Bulletin 159.

Women at Work. 1939. Bulletin 161.

Women in the Economy of the United States. 1937. Bulletin 155.

STATE DEPARTMENT

Report of the Joint Preparatory Committee on Philippine Affairs. 1938. Conference Series 36. Vol. 1: Report; Vol. 2: Hearings; Vol. 3, Pt. 1: Printed Briefs; Pt. 2: Typewritten Briefs.

Sayre, Francis B. How Trade Agreements Are Made. State Department, Commercial Policy Series 47.

The Assistance Rendered by Government in the Promotion and
    Protection of American Foreign Trade. 1939. State Depart-
    ment, Commercial Policy Series 62.

TREASURY DEPARTMENT

Bulletin of the Treasury Department. Monthly since January,
    1939. pr.
German Income Tax Laws. 1938.
Income Tax Laws of France. 1938.
Inheritance and Gift Tax Laws of Sweden. 1938.
Statistics of Income. Annual, beginning 1916. 2 parts.

WAR DEPARTMENT

Industrial Mobilization Plan, Revision of 1939. 1939. 76th
    Cong., 2d Sess., Sen. Doc. 134.
Outline for Commodity Committee Procedure. June 1, 1940.
    Army and Navy Munitions Board Circular No. 1. pr.
The Strategic and Critical Materials. March, 1940. pr.
War Department Procurement Planning. 1940. pr.

FEDERAL COMMUNICATIONS
COMMISSION

Proposed Report on Telephone Investigation. 1938.
Report of the Federal Communications Commission on the In-
    vestigation of the Telephone Industry in the United States.
    1939. 76th Cong., 1st Sess., House Doc. 340.
Supplemental Report on the Telephone Industry. International
    Telegraph Service. February, 1940. pr.
Report on Social and Economic Data Pursuant to the Informal
    Hearing on Broadcasting. 1938.

Federal Loan Agency

FEDERAL HOUSING ADMINISTRATION

Structure and Growth of Residential Neighborhoods in American Cities. 1939.

Federal Power Commission

National Power Survey:
  Interim Report. 1935. P-1.
  Power Requirements in Electrochemical, Electrometallurgical, and Allied Industries. 1938. P-5.
  Principal Electric Utility Systems in the United States. 1936. P-2.
  The Cost of Distribution of Electricity. 1936. P-3.
  The Use of Electric Power in Transportation. 1936. P-4.
Rate Series:
  National Electric Rate Book. Annual. R-16.
  Comparative Rates of Publicly and Privately Owned Electric Utilities. 1936. R-5.
  Rates for Electric Service to Commercial and Industrial Customers. 1936. R-4.
  (Numerous other reports have also been published in this series)
Statistical Series:
  Statistics of Electric Utilities in the United States. Annual. Current issue for the year ended 1938. 1940.

Federal Reserve Board

Federal Reserve Bulletin. Monthly beginning 1915.
Federal Reserve Chart Book. 1940.
Federal Reserve System: Its Purposes and Functions. 1939.
Weekly Review of Periodicals. pr.

FEDERAL SECURITY AGENCY

SOCIAL SECURITY BOARD

A Dictionary of Occupational Titles. 3 vols. June, 1939.
Job Descriptions:
    Automobile Manufacturing Industry. June, 1935. o.p.
    Bakery Products Industry. 1939.
    Cleaning, Dyeing and Pressing Industry. October, 1938.
    Construction Industry. July, 1936.
    Cotton Textile Industry. 1935. o.p.
    Hotels and Restaurants. April, 1938.
    Job Foundries. April, 1938.
    Job Machine Shops. April, 1938.
    Laundry Industry. June, 1937.
    Retail Trade. April, 1938. 3 vols.
Final Report of the Advisory Council on Social Security. 1938.
    76th Cong., 1st Sess., Sen. Doc. 4.
Old Age in Sweden. 1940.
Seasonal Workers and Unemployment Insurance in Great Britain, Germany and Austria. 1939.
Social Security in America. 1937. Publication 20.
Social Security Bulletin. Monthly since January, 1938.
Unemployment and Health Insurance in Great Britain, 1911–1937. 1938.

FEDERAL TRADE COMMISSION

Agricultural Implement and Machinery Industry. 1938. 75th Cong., 3d Sess., House Doc. 702.
Agricultural Income Inquiry:
    1935. 74th Cong., 2d Sess., House Doc. 380.
    1937. 75th Cong., 1st Sess., Sen. Doc. 17; Sen. Doc. 54.

1938: Part 1, Principal Farm Products. Part 2, Fruits, Vegetables and Grapes. Part 3, Supplementary Report.

Antidumping Legislation in the United States and Foreign Countries. 1934. 73d Cong., 2d Sess., Sen. Doc. 112; Supplement. 1938. pr.

Cement Industry. 1933. 73d Cong., 1st Sess., Sen. Doc. 71.

Cottonseed Industry. 1930–33. 71st Cong., 2d Sess., Sen. Doc. 209. 13 parts.

Iron and Steel Industry, Report on Basing-Point System in. 1935.

Milk and Dairy Products.

    1935. 74th Cong., 1st Sess., House Doc. 152.

    1936. 74th Cong., 2d Sess., House Doc. 387; Doc. 451; Doc. 501; Doc. 506.

    1937. 75th Cong., 1st Sess., House Doc. 95; Summary, Doc. 94.

Motor Vehicle Industry. 1938. 76th Cong., 1st Sess., House Doc. 468.

Practices of the Steel Industry under the Code. 1934. 73d Cong., 2d Sess., Sen. Doc. 159. o.p.

Prices Bases Inquiry: the Basing Point Formula and Cement Prices. 1932.

Report on Coöperation in American Export Trade. 1916. o.p.

Textile Industry. 1935–37. Numerous parts. Inquire of commission.

Utility Corporations. 70th Cong., 1st Sess., Sen. Doc. 92. 84 parts in 95 vols. A price list may be obtained from the Federal Trade Commission.

Federal Works Agency: Work Projects Administration *

Subject Index of Research Bulletins and Monographs issued by Federal Emergency Relief Administration and WPA, Division of Social Research. September, 1937. pr.

Catalog of Research Bulletins issued by WPA. October, 1938. pr.

Index of Research Projects. Vol. 1. 1938; Vol. 2. 1939; Vol. 3. 1940. Supplements have been issued.

MARKETING LAWS SURVEY

Comparative Charts of State Statutes illustrating Barriers to Trade Between States. May, 1939.

Problems of Interstate Trade Barriers for States Whose Legislatures Convene in 1940. pr.

NATIONAL RESEARCH PROJECT †

General

Effects of Technological Developments upon Capital Formation. March, 1939. G-4.

Industrial Change and Employment Opportunity; a Selected Bibliography. July, 1939. G-5.

Research Program of the National Research Project. August, 1937. G-2.

Selected References on Practices and Use of Labor on Farms. October, 1937. A-3.

Summary of Findings to Date. March, 1938. G-3.

Survey of Economic Theory on Technological Change and Employment. May, 1940. G-6.

* Until July, 1939, the Works Progress Administration.

† All National Research Project publications are processed, except those issued as Bureau of Labor Statistics Bulletins.

Unemployment and Increasing Productivity. March, 1937.
    G-1. o.p.
Unemployment and Technological Change. April, 1940. G-7.

Types and Rates of Technological Change: Manufacture.

Industrial Instruments and Changing Technology. October,
    1938. M-1.
Industrial Research and Changing Technology. January, 1940.
    M-4.
Mechanical Changes in the Cotton-Textile Industry, 1910–
    1936. October, 1937. B-2.
Mechanical Changes in the Woolen and Worsted Industries,
    1910–1936. January, 1936. B-3.
Mechanization in the Brick Industry. June, 1939. M-2.
Mechanization in the Cement Industry. December, 1939. M-3.
Mechanization in the Lumber Industry. March, 1940. M-5.
Systems of Shop Management in the Cotton-Garment Industry.
    August, 1938. B-5.

Types and Rates of Technological Change: Mining.

Fuel Efficiency in Cement Manufacture, 1909–1935. April,
    1938. E-5.
Mechanization Trends in Metal and Nonmetal Mining. June,
    1937. E-3.
Mineral Technology and Output per Man Studies:
    Grade Ore. August, 1938. E-6. o.p.
    Rock Drilling. February, 1940. E-11.
Technology and the Mineral Industries. April, 1937. E-1. o.p.

Types and Rates of Technological Change: Agriculture.

Field Implements. August, 1939. A-11.
Mechanical Cotton Picker. August, 1937. A-2.
Tractors, Trucks and Automobiles. December, 1938. A-9. o.p.

Production, Productivity, and Employment: Manufacture.

Production, Employment, and Productivity in 59 Manufacturing Industries, 1919–1936. May, 1939. 3 parts. S-1.
Productivity and Employment in Selected Industries:
   Beet Sugar Industry. October, 1938. N-1.
   Brick and Tile. February, 1939. N-2.
Labor Productivity in the Boot and Shoe Industry. February, 1939. B-6.
Effects of Mechanization in Cigar Manufacture. May, 1938. B-4.
Labor Productivity in the Leather Industry. October, 1937. B-1.
Mechanization and Productivity of Labor in the Cigar Manufacturing Industry. September, 1938. Bureau of Labor Statistics Bull. 660.
Productivity of Labor in the Cotton-Garment Industry. November, 1938. Bureau of Labor Statistics Bull. 662.

Production, Productivity, and Employment: Mining.

Production, Employment and Productivity in the Mineral Extractive Industries, 1880–1938. June, 1940. S-2.
Small-Scale Placer Mines as a Source of Gold, Employment, and Livelihood in 1935. May, 1937. E-2. o.p.
Employment and Related Statistics of Mines and Quarries, 1935: Coal. July, 1937. E-4.
Technology, Employment and Output per Man in Phosphate-Rock Mining, 1880–1937. November, 1938. E-7.
Changes in Technology and Labor Requirements in the Crushed-Stone Industry. February, 1939. E-8.
Mechanization, Employment, and Output per Man in Bituminous Coal Mining. August, 1939. 2 vols. E-9.

Technology, Employment, and Output per Man in Petroleum and Natural Gas Production. July, 1939. E-10.

Technology, Employment, and Output per Man in Copper Mining. February, 1940. E-12.

Technology, Employment, and Output per Man in Iron Mining. June, 1940. E-13.

Employment and Income from Gold Placering by Hand Methods, 1936–37. E-14.

Production, Productivity, and Employment: Agriculture.

Changes in Technology and Labor Requirements in Crop Production:

Sugar Beets. August, 1937. A-1.

Potatoes. March, 1938. A-4.

Corn. June, 1938. A-5.

Cotton. September, 1938. A-7.

Wheat and Oats. April, 1939. A-10.

Vegetables. September, 1939. A-12.

Trends in Size and Production of the Aggregate Farm Enterprise, 1909–1936. July, 1938. A-6.

Trends in Employment in Agriculture, 1909–1936. November, 1938. A-8.

Effects of Industrial Change in Labor Markets.

Recent Trends in Employment and Unemployment in Philadelphia. December, 1937. P-1.

The Labor Force of the Philadelphia Radio Industry in 1936. April, 1938. P-2.

Employment and Unemployment in Philadelphia in 1936 and 1937. 1938. 2 parts. P-3. o.p.

Ten Years of Work Experience of Philadelphia Weavers and Loom Fixers. July, 1938. P-4.

Ten Years of Work Experience of Philadelphia Machinists. September, 1938. P-5.

Reëmployment of Philadelphia Hosiery Workers after Shut-Downs in 1933–1934. 1939. P-6.

The Search for Work in Philadelphia, 1932–1936. May, 1939. P-7. o.p.

The Long Term Unemployed in Philadelphia in 1936. August, 1939. P-8.

Cigar Makers—After the Lay-Off. December, 1937. L-1.

Decasualization of Longshore Work in San Francisco. April, 1939. L-2.

Employment Experience of Paterson Broad-Silk Workers, 1926–36. May, 1939. L-3.

Selective Factors in an Expanding Labor Market, Lancaster, Pa. June, 1939. L-4.

Labor and the Shut-Down of the Amoskeag Textile Mills. November, 1939. L-5.

Changes in Machinery and Job Requirements in Minnesota Manufacturing, 1931–1936. July, 1939. L-6.

Farm-City Migration and Industry's Labor Reserve. August, 1939. L-7.

Trade-Union Policy and Technological Change. April, 1940. L-8.

Research Monographs and Special Reports

Chronology of the Federal Emergency Relief Administration, May 12, 1933–December 31, 1935. 1937. Research Monograph VI.

Disadvantaged Youth in the Labor Market. 1940. pr.

Effects of the Works Program on Rural Relief. 1938. Research Monograph XIII.

Farmers on Relief and Rehabilitation. 1937. Research Monograph VIII.

Inter-City Differences in Costs of Living in March, 1935. 59 Cities. July, 1937. Research Monograph XII.

Landlord and Tenant on the Cotton Plantation. 1936. Research Monograph V.

Migrant Families. 1938. Research Monograph XVIII.

The Migratory-Casual Worker. 1937. Research Monograph VII.

Migratory Cotton Pickers in Arizona. 1939. Special Report.

Part-Time Farming in the Southeast. 1937. Research Monograph IX.

Rural Families on Relief. 1938. Research Monograph XVII.

Rural Households: Relief and Non-Relief. 1935. Research Monograph II.

Rural Migration in the United States. 1939. Research Monograph XIX.

Rural Regions of the United States. 1940. Special Report.

Rural Youth on Relief. 1937. Research Monograph XI.

Rural Youth: Their Situation and Prospects. 1938. Research Monograph XV.

Seasonal Employment in Agriculture. September, 1938.

Six Rural Problem Areas: Relief—Resources—Rehabilitation. 1935. Research Monograph I.

The Transient Unemployed. 1935. Research Monograph III.

Trends in Relief Expenditures, 1910–1935. 1937. Research Monograph X.

Urban Housing: a Summary of Real Property Inventories Conducted as Work Projects, 1934–1936. 1938. Special Report.

Urban Workers on Relief. 1936. Two parts. Research Monograph IV.

Urban Youth: Their Characteristics and Economic Problems. 1939. pr.

Workers on Relief in the United States, March, 1935. Vol. 1: A Census of Usual Occupations. April 27, 1939; Vol. 2: A

Study of Industrial and Educational Backgrounds. July 17, 1939.

Youth in Agricultural Villages. 1940. Research Monograph XXI.

Pamphlet Series

Facts about Unemployment. 1939. Social Problems No. 4.
Depression Pioneers. 1939. Social Problems No. 1.
Rural Relief and Recovery. 1939. Social Problems No. 3.
Rural Youth. 1939. Social Problems No. 2.

NATIONAL LABOR RELATIONS BOARD

Governmental Protection of Labor's Right to Organize. 1936. o.p.

Written Trade Agreements in Collective Bargaining, November, 1939. 1940.

NATIONAL RECOVERY ADMINISTRATION

See above, p. 196.

SECURITIES AND EXCHANGE COMMISSION

Investment Trusts and Investment Companies:
  Report:
    Part 1. Nature, Classification and Origins of Investment Trusts and Investment Companies. 1939. 75th Cong., 3d Sess., House Doc. 707.
    Part 2. Statistical Survey of Investment Trusts and Investment Companies. 1939. 76th Cong., 1st Sess., House Doc. 70.
    Part 3. Abuses and Deficiencies in the Organization and

Operation of Investment Trusts and Investment
Companies. Chapters I and II. 1940. 76th Cong.,
3d Sess., House Doc. 279.

Supplementary Reports:

Commingled or Common Trust Funds Administered by
Banks and Trust Companies. 1939. 76th Cong., 2d
Sess., House Doc. 476.

Fixed and Semi-Fixed Investment Trusts. 1940. 76th
Cong., 3d Sess., House Doc. 567.

Investment Counsel, Investment Management, Investment
Supervisory and Investment Advisory Services. 1939.
76th Cong., 2d Sess., House Doc. 477.

Investment Trusts in Great Britain. 1939. 76th Cong., 1st
Sess., House Doc. 380.

Companies Sponsoring Installment Investment Plans. 1940.
76th Cong., 1st Sess., House Doc. 482.

Companies Issuing Face Amount Installment Certificates.
1940. 76th Cong., 3d Sess., House Doc. 659.

Protective Committees and Agencies for Holders of Defaulted
Foreign Governmental Bonds. 1937.

Survey of American Listed Corporations. 1940. 3 vols. pr.

Temporary National Economic Committee

Investigation of Concentration of Economic Power:

Hearings

Part 1:   Economic Prologue. December 1–3, 1938.
Part 2:   Patents: Automobile Industry, Glass Container
            Industry. December 5–16, 1938.
Part 3:   Patents: Proposals for Changes in Law and Pro-
            cedure. January 16–20, 1939.
Part 4:   Life Insurance. February 6–17, 1939.

Part 5:   Monopolistic Practices in Industries; Development of the Beryllium Industry. February 28, March 1–8, 14, May 8–9, 1939.

Part 5A: Federal Trade Commission Report on Monopolistic Practices in Industries. March 2, 1939.

Part 6:   Liquor Industry. March 14–17, 1939.

Part 7:   Milk Industry; Poultry Industry. March 9–11, May 1–3, 1939.

Part 8:   Problems of the Consumer. May 10–12, 1939.

Part 9:   Savings and Investment. May 16–26, 1939.

Part 10:   Life Insurance. June 6–21, 1939.

Part 10A: Operating Results and Investments of the Twenty-six Largest Legal Reserve Life Insurance Companies in the United States, 1929–1938.

Part 11:   Construction Industry. June 27–July 14, 1939.

Part 12:   Industrial Insurance. August 23–September 7, 1939.

Part 13:   Life Insurance. September 11–December 22, 1939.

Part 14:   Petroleum Industry. September 25–30, 1939.

Part 14A: Economic Outline and Data relating to the Petroleum Industry. September 25, 1939.

Part 15:   Petroleum Industry. October 2–7, 1939.

Part 15A: Report on Marketing Practices in the Retail Distribution of Motor Fuel and Motor Lubricant Products. October 7, 1939.

Part 16:   Petroleum Industry. October 9–13, 16, 1939.

Part 17:   Petroleum Industry. October 17–20, 23–25, 1939.

Part 17A: Replies of Oil Companies to the Committee Questionnaire on Financial Data and Related Topics. October 20, 1939.

Part 18: Iron and Steel Industry: Iron Ore. November 1–3, 1939.

Part 19: Iron and Steel Industry: General Price Policies. November 6–7, 9–10, 1939.

Part 20: Iron and Steel Industry: Price Policies on Specific Products; Pacific Coast Problems; Steel Export Association. November 8, 13–15, 1939.

Monographs *

1. Price Behavior and Business Policy. 1940.
2. Families and Their Life Insurance. 1940.
3. Who Pays the Taxes? 1940.
4. Concentration and Composition of Individual Incomes. 1940.
5. Industrial Wage Rates, Labor Costs and Price Policies. 1940.
6. Export Prices and Export Cartels (Webb-Pomerene Associations). 1940.
7. Measurement of Social Performance of Business. 1940.
8. Toward More Housing. 1940.
9. Taxation of Corporate Enterprise.
10. Industrial Concentration and Tariffs. 1940.
11. Bureaucracy and Trusteeship in Large Corporations. 1940.
12. Profits, Productive Activities and New Investment. 1941.
13. Relative Efficiency of Large, Medium-sized and Small Business. 1941.
14. Hourly Earnings of Employees in Large and Small Enterprises. 1940.
15. Financial Characteristics of American Manufacturing Corporations. 1941.
16. Antitrust in Action. 1940.

* Not yet published unless publication date is given.

17. Some Problems of Small Business. 1941.
18. Trade Association Survey. 1941.
19. Government Purchasing: an Economic Commentary. 1941.
20. Taxation, Recovery, and Defense. 1940.
21. Competition and Monopoly in American Industry.
22. Technology and Economic Balance.
23. Agriculture and the National Economy. 1940.
24. Consumer Standards.
25. Recovery Plans. 1940.
26. Economic Pressures and Political Power.
27. The Structure of Industry.
28. Study of Legal Reserve Life Insurance Companies. 1940.
29. Distribution of Ownership in 200 Largest Non-financial Corporations.
30. Survey of Shareholdings in 1,710 Corporations with Securities Listed on a National Securities Exchange. 1941.
31. The Patent Laws and the State of Industrial Arts.
32. Economic Standards of Government Price Control.
33. Geographical Differentials in Prices of Building Materials.
34. Control of Unfair Competitive Practices through Trade Practice Conference Procedure of the Federal Trade Commission. 1941.
35. Large-Scale Organization in the Food Industries. 1940.
36. Reports of the Federal Trade Commission on Natural Gas and Natural Gas Pipelines in the U.S.A., Agricultural Implement and Machinery Inquiry and Motor Vehicle Inquiry. 1940.
37. Government Competition with Private Enterprise.
38. National Standards for National Corporations.
39. The Investment Consumption Problem.
40. Regulation of Economic Activities in Foreign Countries. 1941.
41. Price Discrimination in Steel. 1941.

42. Declaratory Rulings in Antitrust.
43. Substantive Law of Restraint of Trade, Monopoly and Unfair Competition.

TENNESSEE VALLEY AUTHORITY

A History of Navigation on the Tennessee River and Its Tributaries. 1937. 75th Cong., 1st Sess., House Doc. 254.
Interterritorial Freight Rate Problem. 1937. 75th Cong., 1st Sess., House Doc. 264.

UNITED STATES MARITIME COMMISSION

Aircraft and Merchant Marine. November, 1937. pr.
Economic Survey of the American Merchant Marine. November 10, 1937.
Economic Survey of Coastwise and Intercoastal Shipping. March 15, 1939. pr. Also printed as House Doc. 209, 76th Cong., 1st Sess.
Reorganization of American President Lines, Ltd. 1939.
Report on the Volume of Waterborne Foreign Commerce of the United States by Ports of Origin and Destination. Annual since 1921.
Report on Tramp Shipping Service. 1938. 75th Cong., 3d Sess., House Doc. 520.
Training Merchant Marine Personnel. 1939.
Waterborne Intercoastal (Freight) Traffic of the United States. Annual, 1923–1937.

UNITED STATES TARIFF COMMISSION

Analysis of Imports by Parcel Post, 1937. 1939. pr.
Analysis of the Foreign Trade of the United States in Relation to the Tariff. 1933. 72d Cong., 1st Sess., Sen. Doc. 180.

Part I. "Trade of Latin America with the World and with the United States."

Part II, Section 1: Argentina; Section 2: Bolivia; Section 3: Brazil; Section 4: Chile; Section 5: Colombia; Section 6: Ecuador; Section 7: Paraguay; Section 8: Peru; Section 9: Uruguay; Section 10: Venezuela; Section 18: Cuba.

Part III. "Thirty Selected Latin-American Export Commodities." 2 volumes.

Glues, Gelatines, and Related Products. 1940. 2d Ser., 135.

Grapes, Raisins, and Wines. 1939. 2d Ser., 134.

Graphic Analysis of the Foreign Trade of the United States. 1934. m.s.

Graphic Analysis of the Trade of Latin-America. 1940. pr.

Imports, Exports, Domestic Production, and Prices of Petroleum, Coal, Lumber, Copper, Certain Oils and Fats, Together with Excise Taxes Collected Thereon. 1937. pr.

Imports, Exports, Domestic Production, and Prices of Petroleum, Coal, Lumber, and Copper, Together with Excise Taxes Collected Thereon. 1939. pr.

Imports for Consumption by Countries, 1931–35. 1936. 11 vols. pr.

1936. 1937. 4 vols. pr.

1929. 1937. 4 vols. pr.

Imports under Trade Agreements, 1937 and 1938: Belgium, Brazil, Finland, France, Netherlands, Sweden, Switzerland, one vol. each. Colombia, Guatemala, Haiti, Honduras, 1 vol. 1939. pr.

Incandescent Electric Lamps. 1939. 2d Ser., 133.

Iron and Steel. 1938. 2d Ser., 128.

Italian Commercial Policy and Foreign Trade. 1941. 2d Ser., 142.

Laces and Lace Articles. 1934. 2d Ser., 83.

Long-Staple Cotton. 1935. 2d Ser., 85.

Methods of Valuation. 1933. 2d Ser., 70.

Mica Industry. 1938. 2d Ser., 130.

Nets and Netting and Other Fishing Gear. 1937. 2d Ser., 117.

Phosphates and Superphosphates. 1935. 2d Ser., 100.

Pocket Cutlery. 1939. pr.

Range and Variety of Costs of Production. Part III of Analysis of Foreign Trade of United States.

Raw Materials Bibliography. December, 1939. pr.

Recent Developments in the Foreign Trade of Japan. 1936. 2d Ser., 105.

Reciprocal Trade; a Current Bibliography. 1937. pr.; Supplement, 1940. pr.

Reciprocity and Commercial Treaties. 1919. m.s.

Reference Manual of Latin American Commercial Treaties. 1940. pr.

Regulation of Tariffs in Foreign Countries by Administrative Action. 1934. m.s.

Reports on Industries Affected by the Trade Agreements Program. 1940. 23 vols. pr. Others being prepared: See the Commission's Public Information Releases of June 7, 1940 and November 25, 1940.

Salmon and Other Fish. 1937. 2d Ser., 121.

Sodium Sulphate. 1937. 2d Ser., 124.

Statistical Classification of Imports into the United States, 1937, arranged by Tariff Schedules and Tariff Paragraphs of the Act of 1930. 1937. pr.

Statistics on Sugar. 1939. pr.

Starches and Dextrines. 1940. 2d Ser., 138.

Subsidies and Bounties to Fisheries Enterprises by Foreign Governments. 1936. 2d Ser., 116.

Sugar. 1934. 2d Ser., 73.

Summaries of Tariff Information. (No longer published; kept in ms form; the 1929 summary was published in 15 parts.)

Synthetic Organic Chemicals in the United States, 1939. 1940. 2d Ser., 140.

Synthetic Resins and Their Raw Materials. 1938. 2d Ser., 131.

Tariff Bargaining under Most-Favored-Nation Treaties. 1933. 2d Ser., 65.

Tariff Bibliography. 1934. m.s.

Transportation Costs and Value of Principal Imports. 1940. pr.

Tuna Fish. 1936. 2d Ser., 109.

United States Free and Dutiable Imports for Consumption from Selected Countries by Economic Classes; by Months, 1932 and 1933. 1937. pr.

United States Import and Duties 1937, Arranged According to the Tariff Act of 1930 by Schedules, Paragraphs, and Commodities. 1938. pr.

United States Imports and Trade Agreement Concessions. March, 1940. 8 vols. pr.

United States Philippine Tariff and Trade Relations. 1931. 2d Ser., 18.

United States–Philippine Trade. 1937. 2d Ser., 118.

War and Its Effect on United States Imports. December, 1940. pr. A revision of European War and United States Imports. 1939. pr.

War-Time Increases in Transportation Costs of Principal Imports. 1940. pr.

Wheat and Wheat Products. In progress.

Whiskey, Wine, Beer, etc. 1935. 2d Ser., 90.

Wood Pulp and Pulpwood. 1938. 2d Ser., 126.

Wool Prices. 1937. 2d Ser., 120.

INDEX